GW00546463

THE
GAME
OF
LIVES

BOOKS BY JAMES DASHNER

THE MORTALITY DOCTRINE SERIES

The Eye of Minds
The Rule of Thoughts
The Game of Lives

THE MAZE RUNNER SERIES

The Maze Runner
The Scorch Trials
The Death Cure
The Kill Order

THE 13TH REALITY SERIES

The Journal of Curious Letters
The Hunt for Dark Infinity
The Blade of Shattered Hope
The Void of Mist and Thunder

THE
GAME
OF
LIVES

JAMES DASHNER

DELACORTE PRESS

This is a work of fiction. Names, characters, places, and incidents either are the product of the author's imagination or are used fictitiously. Any resemblance to actual persons, living or dead, events, or locales is entirely coincidental.

Text copyright © 2015 by James Dashner
Jacket art copyright © 2015 by Richard Jones

All rights reserved. Published in the United States by Delacorte Press, an imprint of Random House Children's Books, a division of Penguin Random House LLC, New York.

Delacorte Press is a registered trademark and the colophon is a trademark of Penguin Random House LLC.

Visit us on the Web! randomhouseteens.com

Educators and librarians, for a variety of teaching tools, visit us at RHTeachersLibrarians.com

Library of Congress Cataloging-in-Publication Data is available upon request.
ISBN 978-0-385-74143-9 (hc) — ISBN 978-0-375-99003-8 (lib. bdg.)
ISBN 978-0-375-98465-5 (ebook) — ISBN 978-1-101-93433-3 (intl. tr. pbk.)

The text of this book is set in 12.5-point Adobe Garamond.
Book design by Stephanie Moss

Printed in the United States of America
10 9 8 7 6 5 4 3 2
First Edition

Random House Children's Books supports the First Amendment and celebrates the right to read.

For Lynette

PROLOGUE

Michael welcomed sleep. The small bumps of the road and the hum of tires on asphalt relaxed him for the first time in days, and his eyes grew heavy. He was an expert at dealing with reality—or *un*reality—but after what he'd been through lately, if he could pass a little time unconscious, he would be eternally grateful. There had been a lot to digest. Any chance to escape the world and its many ills—he'd take it. Though, fat chance he'd be slipping inside a Coffin anytime soon.

Michael's head bobbed. He caught himself and sank back into the seat. He knew it was a dream because he was no longer sitting in Sarah's dad's car. He was at his kitchen counter before it all began, where his nanny, Helga, had served him breakfast hundreds of times. If not thousands. He thought about the man who'd visited him in prison, his strange speech about dreams within dreams, how the looping logic applied to the VirtNet as well. Things that could drive you crazy if you thought about them too much.

"These are some great waffles," Michael said. He was surprised at how real they tasted. Warm, buttery goodness. He swallowed a bite and smiled.

And then Helga was there! Sweet, stern Helga. She gave him a look as she put some dishes away. It was a look Michael had seen many times over the years. A look that said he'd better not be trying to pull a fast one on her. A look he normally got when he faked a cough to miss school or lied about his homework.

"Don't worry," he said. "This is a dream. I can have as much as I want!" He smiled and took another bite, chewed and swallowed. "I guess Gabby's still missing, haven't heard anything from her. It sure is sweet to be back with Sarah and Bryson, though. The Terrible Trio, live and still kickin'. Even if we are crammed into a backseat. Anyway. Who would've thought my life could get so weird, huh? Crazy stuff."

Helga nodded, smiled, bent over the dishwasher; the room filled with the clank of glass and porcelain.

Michael frowned, feeling as if Helga didn't seem to care one whit. "Maybe you don't know everything, my little German. Oh, let's see. Somehow we got tricked into blowing up the VNS systems, pretty much shut the whole thing down. Sarah's parents—who'd been kidnapped, mind you—show up out of the blue to rescue us from jail, talking about *you* and a bunch of former Tangents behind it all. *You*, Helga. Care to enlighten me on that?"

His nanny gave him a guilty shrug, barely pausing from her work. Clinks and clanks rang out, the thumps of cabinet doors closing. Michael knew it was too good to be true—

that he could just sit there and enjoy his dream. There wasn't a place in the universe he could run to escape his thoughts—his own mind less than anywhere else. He stabbed a last few bites of waffle into his mouth, relishing the crisp outside and the soft interior, sensing that the dream was about to end anyway. And Helga had yet to say a single word to him.

"I guess you can't talk to me in my dreams, can you?" Michael said. "That's just plain weird. Kaine told me he'd killed you, killed my parents." Picturing his mom and dad sent a deep ache through his dreaming heart. "Maybe you escaped somehow? I don't know. Either way, can't you at least live on in my head? Maybe that's too much like talking to my—"

Helga turned sharply, her face afire. "The Hallowed Ravine, boy. You know that's where you've got to go. Back to the Hallowed Ravine. End it where it started!"

Michael started to reply, but wouldn't you know it, that was right when a pothole had the gall to disturb his slumber.

CHAPTER 1

A NICE PLACE IN THE COUNTRY

1

When Michael woke up, he had the not-so-pleasant sensation of bile rising in his throat. Not the happiest way to greet the conscious world.

He sucked in a slow breath. He wished he'd taken something for motion sickness. Sarah's dad seemed to think he was a NASCAR driver, and the road wasn't cooperating. Gerard the Gear Hound, the country's next great race-car superstar on the world's twistiest, most torn-up track.

As they wound their way around the tight curves of the north Georgia mountains, Michael leaned into each turn with his entire body, as if that would somehow keep the car on the road. Lush foliage and trees overgrown with kudzu formed a great tunnel through a cave of green, sparkles of sunlight winking between leaves as they drove.

"You're sure she said Helga?" Michael asked once again, his dream fresh in his mind. *Go to the Hallowed Ravine.*

4

That's what she'd said. Which meant, logically, that his own mind was telling him the same thing. They had to go back to the place where it all started if they wanted to end it. Seemed reasonable enough.

Gerard, clutching the steering wheel as if he feared it might try to spin away from him, sighed at the question. His wife, Nancy, shifted in the passenger seat to face Michael.

"Yes," she said with a kind smile, then turned to the front again. Her patience made it seem as if that were the first time Michael had asked the question, though, in fact, it was probably the fifth or sixth.

He sat in the middle of the backseat, Bryson to his left, Sarah to his right. No one had spoken much since their initial reunion. Between being chased down, imprisoned, and rescued, it had been a long several days, and everyone seemed as dazed as Michael. Michael himself didn't know what to think. Sarah's parents had been kidnapped, then rescued by a group of mystery people. Those same mystery people had then directed Gerard and Nancy to pick up their daughter and her friends and take them to an address in the Appalachian Mountains.

But there'd been something about Tangents. And a woman named Helga.

It couldn't possibly be his nanny, Michael thought for the hundredth time. Could it? His Helga was gone—wasn't she? As far as he knew, she was a Tangent that had been decommissioned by Kaine, just like his parents. At the very least he'd hastened their Decay. Real or not, their deaths had emptied his soul, and not much had filled it since.

Sarah nudged him with her elbow, then awkwardly fell into him, her whole body pressing against his as Gerard whipped around yet another curve. The tires squealed and a flock of birds exploded from the foliage at the side of the road, screeching as they flew away.

"You okay, there?" she asked, righting herself. "You don't seem very chipper for someone who just got broken out of jail."

Michael shrugged. "I guess I'm still trying to put it all together."

"Thanks for the message you sent me," she whispered. While separated, both Michael and Sarah had hacked through the prison firewall systems to send notes to each other. "It helped a lot."

Michael nodded, gave a half smile. A horrible image formed in his mind—Sarah dying beside the lava pits, her last struggle for breath before exiting Kaine's Path in the deepest folds of the VirtNet. Michael had dragged her into all this. And her parents. And Bryson. It had broken his heart to see her in so much pain, and he couldn't stop wondering—did worse fates await them than virtual molten rock?

Bryson leaned forward to look at them. "Hey, no one sent me a message. That's not cool."

"Sorry," Michael said. "I know how much you love your naps—I didn't want to interrupt."

As if to rub it in, Sarah clicked her EarCuff, illuminating her NetScreen. Michael's message, *We will win,* hovered before them. A thrill of happiness warmed his chest to see that she'd saved it there. He smiled, more than a little embarrassed.

"Real sweet." Bryson leaned back, eyeing Michael. "I'm pretty sure I haven't slept in, oh, about three weeks—which I blame you for, by the way."

"Blame accepted." Michael knew his friend was joking—mostly—but he still felt bad. Bryson might have never said something so simple and yet so perfectly true. The nausea from the roller-coaster driving suddenly shot up a few notches. "Oh, man," he groaned. "Sir? Uh . . . Gerard? Could we pull over a second? I'm not feeling so well."

"Turn toward Bryson," Sarah said, inching away from Michael. She rolled down the window. "Does that help?"

But her dad had already slowed—the sudden braking sending Michael's whirling stomach up another notch—and was pulling into a little patch of dirt on the side of the narrow road.

"There you go, son," the man announced. He seemed familiar enough with the maneuver that Michael was sure it wasn't the first time he'd driven someone to the brink of losing their lunch. "But hurry—we're already late."

Sarah's mom smacked her husband on the arm lightly. "Have a heart, honey. For heaven's sake. No one likes to throw up."

Michael was already climbing over Sarah. He opened the door and jumped out of the car before she could complain. His horrible prison breakfast was coming up, and there was no stopping it. He found the closest bush and gave it a very unpleasant surprise.

2

"Ah, man, I think there's something on your shirt," Bryson said a few minutes later. They were back on the road and Gerard had resumed practicing his racing skills.

Michael smiled—he didn't care. He felt so much better that the world had brightened and cleared.

"I'm glad that makes you so happy," Bryson muttered, then patted his friend on the shoulder. "Actually, thanks for not spewing all over me."

"You're very welcome," Michael replied.

"You feel better?" Sarah asked.

"Tons." Michael folded his arms and shifted his legs to get more comfortable. "I guess I'm feeling better about everything. I mean, I'm not sure what happened back in Atlanta— but it's something that we're all still alive, right? And now we're on our way to people who want to help."

And I have a plan, he thought. It was the first time in ages he'd had one, and it felt good. He would go to the Hallowed Ravine, back to where this had all started. He just had to find the right time to tell his friends about it.

"Dude," Bryson said, "you're a glass-half-full kind of guy. I like it."

Sarah smiled and covertly grabbed Michael's hand between them, slipping her fingers through his. The world brightened even more. *And we need to make sure Gabby's okay,* he thought. The last time he saw her she'd been unconscious— hit in the head—and it was Michael's fault for dragging her into the whole mess. He didn't want to pull her in any deeper, but he needed to make sure she was all right.

"We're almost there," Gerard called back to them, slowing. "Uh . . . I think."

Butterflies filled Michael's stomach. Still holding Sarah's hand, he leaned forward, peering through the front windshield as they continued tunneling through the leafy forest. He had absolutely no idea what to expect—where they were going or why—but his excitement built in leaps and bounds as he watched the road ahead. It made him think of the Path, and with a jolt of anxiety he wondered if he was truly in the real world, in the Wake, or somewhere in a box, connected to wires and uploaded to the VirtNet. He'd been fooled so many times and in so many ways, he'd never be certain again.

He thought back to the man, the one who had visited him at the prison right before Agent Weber. It had come back to him in his dream also. Something about waking up over and over again, within layers upon layers of VirtNet levels. What was it? Like a dream within a dream. That really creeped him out.

The road pitched steeply downward, and Michael shook the thought out of his head. He'd get dizzy again if he kept it up. He focused on the world around him—real or virtual—as it was.

Outside, the trees had thinned to reveal a wide valley nestled between two heavily forested mountains. Clouds covered the sun, casting the day back into gloom, as if to make up for the shade they'd lost.

"Is that where we're going?" Bryson asked. Releasing his seat belt, he scooted as close to Gerard as he could, gripping the headrest in front of him. "That place looks a thousand years old."

"That's gotta be it," Nancy answered. "It doesn't look like there's anything else around."

Michael stared. Down below them, scattered among the trees of the valley floor, were several long, low buildings that reminded him of battered shipping crates. They looked like military barracks, something you might see in one of those ancient war movies set in a jungle somewhere exotic. The roofs had holes torn in them—some were patched; most were gaping wide, though, and open to the elements. Kudzu and ivy crept everywhere, blanketing sections of the buildings so that certain parts resembled neglected topiaries in the garden of some forgotten giant.

"Man," Bryson moaned. "I was kind of hoping for something more along the lines of a Marriott. At least the prison had working toilets."

"Snakes," Sarah whispered, as if in a trance. "I bet that place is full of snakes."

Michael refused to let his newfound enthusiasm be dimmed. His curiosity more than made up for the dilapidated appearance of . . . whatever the place was. "So, you haven't been here before, right?" he asked Gerard, then tried a new tack. "Where'd you meet Helga and the others? How'd you know where to find us, how to get here?"

Nancy turned to face him. "Not a lot to tell, I'm afraid. My guess is you three probably know more than we do. These . . . Tangents—that's what they called themselves— barged into that horrible warehouse our kidnappers took us to, released us, gave us this car, gave us instructions. Everything happened in a whirlwind. We didn't have much choice but to trust them. I mean, look, it meant getting to you kids and getting out of there."

Michael could've responded in a lot of ways to that one. Trusting others was something he'd never find easy again. At the moment, it was just about staying alive, and he had to admit that this did seem to be their best option.

And there was Helga. He had to meet this Helga.

The road leveled out, cutting off their view, and suddenly they were pulling into the overgrown complex of barracks. What Michael had been unable to see earlier were the dozen or so cars parked under the shade of several big trees. The cars were beat up. They looked so old that, if it weren't for the complete lack of kudzu on their surface, one would think they'd been there as long as the buildings themselves.

Gerard had barely pulled to a stop when a tall woman appeared at a door of one of the buildings. She wore dusty jeans, boots, and a black sweatshirt, and her sandy blond hair was pulled back into a ponytail. She walked confidently toward them, her face twisted into a scowl.

"That's her," Gerard whispered as he rolled down the window.

Michael didn't recognize her, and his heart fell even though he'd have no reason to know what Helga looked like in the Wake.

She leaned in the driver's-side window, resting on her forearms, and peered inside at each of the occupants. She nodded back toward the building from which she'd come.

"Let's get you inside," she said, her accent far from the

German that Michael realized he'd been expecting, "before the world falls apart."

Then she turned and headed back toward the barracks.

3

"Today, dude, today." It was a bad time for Bryson to take a year and a half to get out of the car. Michael had never been so impatient in his life. He had to find out the truth about this Helga and the people she was with. They could help him get back to the Hallowed Ravine.

"I'm coming, man, chill!" Bryson responded. But he still hadn't moved. He gave Michael a hard look. "Are we sure about this?"

"Yes," Michael and Sarah answered at the same time. Sarah's parents were already out of the car, closing their doors.

"Would you go so far as to say . . . you're sure as heckfire?" Bryson pressed. "My grandma used to say that. If you say you're sure as heckfire, then I'm in."

Michael willed himself to calm down. "Yes. I'm sure as heckfire."

"Okay, then." Bryson climbed out of the backseat, Michael half pushing his friend to get him out faster. Sarah got out on the other side, and the group followed her father up a trampled path of weeds to the door, which stood ajar. Gerard didn't hesitate. He walked right in. Michael and his friends followed.

The tall woman who'd greeted them was waiting for them, but that wasn't what got Michael's attention.

When his eyes adjusted to the light, he was shocked by what he saw. It was as if he'd stepped into a completely different world. The beat-up, weathered building housed a technological wonderland. Low-glare LED lights lined the ceiling, illuminating the green haze of dozens of NetScreens. A row of blue Coffins lined one wall; a row of desks lined another, men and women working furiously at them. Fresh lumber had been used to reinforce the walls and ceiling, and Michael noticed that they'd used some sort of plastic to patch the various holes in the roof.

Their host's voice cut through Michael's daze, breaking the silence. "We had to find a location that was remote—"

"Mission accomplished," Bryson muttered.

"—and yet had a power source and access to the satellite VirtNet feeds. This is an old training facility for army tech warriors, abandoned a decade ago due to budget cuts. Turns out it worked perfectly for our needs. Took a couple of weeks to set up, but here we are. Already down to business."

Michael had a million questions, but one stood out above all others.

He faced the tall woman and took a step closer to her, looking into her eyes carefully. "Gerard said you told him your name was Helga. And that you're a Tangent. Does . . ." He had no idea how to phrase what he wanted to ask.

Michael was surprised to see tears glistening in her eyes, blurring the reflections of the lights in the room. "Yes," she said. Then she wrapped her arms around him, pulling him into a crushing hug. "So you must be Michael, then. My boy."

Michael's eyes widened and it took him a moment to

return the embrace. "You're . . . Helga? Really? But how?" She'd quickly come to accept him in his new body, but he didn't know if he could do the same.

She pulled back from him, her eyes fierce despite being wet. "There's a lot to tell. A lot to catch up on. In brief, we've been on Kaine's trail since even before you crossed paths with him. We stole the Mortality Doctrine program from him. Copied a version of it, anyway. We had to do it, Michael. We had to come here into the real world if we ever wanted to save the virtual one."

The carsick feeling washed over Michael again. "Wait . . . you . . . stole people's bodies?" He took a step backward. "You . . . How do I even know you're really Helga? How can I trust any of you? At all?"

The woman who claimed to be his old nanny smiled kindly. "Good questions, all," she said. "And I'll answer each and every one. I think it will be easy enough to prove who I am. I'll answer something only you know. . . ."

She paused, carefully looking over Michael's group. It was obvious they were as concerned as he was. They'd committed themselves to stopping this sort of thing. And yet their rescuers were no better than Kaine, apparently.

"We haven't . . . killed anyone," the tall woman finally clarified. Her stance had grown formal again, her expression no longer tender. But Michael could see a deep sadness in those eyes. "Not the true death, anyway."

"The true death?" Sarah repeated, shooting a wary look at Michael. He suddenly felt like the ground below him was shifting.

"Please," the woman said, clearly frustrated by her audience's turn. "Let's just sit down and talk through it all, okay? Please." She motioned toward a circle of chairs set up near the glowing Coffins.

Michael looked at Bryson and Sarah and shrugged, then started for the chairs, the words *true death* ringing in his ears.

4

"Let's start at the beginning," the tall woman said once they'd all taken a seat. "You need to know that I am who I say I am before you can trust me." Helga gave the group a moment to get settled, then turned to Michael directly, looking into his eyes as she spoke. "I was your nanny, Helga. I *am* Helga. A part of me suspected that we might be Tangents, but you were real to me, Michael. Apart from everything Kaine has done, I think there were many of us who'd taken the leap to sentience—which slows down the Decay process significantly. I know you and I had taken that leap." She'd begun to stare off into space, as if lost in a desert of old thoughts, then came back just as fast, waving it all away. "My point: you have been and always will be like a son to me. But let me prove it to you."

Michael furrowed his brow, looking long and hard at her, as he thought through his options. The woman sat forward, leaning toward him, arms resting on her knees, hands clasped. She seemed genuine, her gaze intense and full of pain. The rest of the room was quiet as he focused all his attention on this woman. Helga. His future hung in the balance.

"Okay," he said, trying to think clearly. "What was my favorite breakfast?"

"Wait a minute," Bryson said just as their host opened her mouth to speak. "This isn't going to prove a thing." He turned to face Michael. "If your nanny was a Tangent, then Kaine could easily know every single detail about your life. An instant download, boom. Or worse, he could've programmed her! This is pointless."

"You're not helping," Michael replied. His friend was right, and it was as frustrating as ever.

"No, he's right," the woman replied, standing up. "Not about Kaine—but about it being impossible for me to convince you beyond a doubt that I'm Helga. I could talk all day about how you love to eat waffles for breakfast and how when you were barely five years old you begged me to let you read that Stephen King novel and I made you stick to Judy Blume. Or about your broken leg when you were seven, or how many times I caught you trying to sneak into your dad's Coffin before you were legal. How many nights I brought you cheese and crackers while you studied the coding logs on your NetScreen in bed, or how we worked frantically to clean up after the infamous Sleepover Party Incident before your parents got home from that business trip."

She paused, a warm smile spread across her face, and Michael could do nothing but stare at her, slack-jawed.

"I could go on and on and on," she continued. "But you'd never fully be convinced. Neither would your friends. I'm a piece of code, Michael. Nothing more. No one understands the pain of that more than I do, trust me. I'm not sure I know how to completely gain your trust."

"Sheesh, I didn't mean to insult everybody," Bryson said sheepishly, looking down at the floor.

Michael realized that he himself was trembling, emotion welling up in his chest. Bryson had made an excellent point, and they couldn't afford to ignore its implications. But at some point, Michael had to let himself trust again. Something. Some*one*. And if he had a truth radar, it was pinging like never before.

"It's you," he whispered.

No one responded. Maybe they hadn't heard him.

"It's you," he said louder.

And then he ran to her and hugged her before anyone could see the tears spill from his eyes.

CHAPTER 2

A CIRCLE OF HANDS

1

"It *is* me," Helga whispered in his ear, patting him on the back. "I promise you. We're going to get through the madness together."

It had been a long time since Michael had felt anything like this—and it all crashed down on him at once. Happiness, sadness, nostalgia. He cried into his nanny's shoulder as he remembered the parents he'd lost, the home he'd lost, the life he'd lost. He had his two best friends, but Helga was the only link to the world he'd known without them. And he'd been sure she was gone forever.

There were questions, yes. Concerns. But in that moment all he could feel was the sweet, burning warmth in his chest.

Finally, Helga gently took him by his shoulders and held him away from her. He was relieved to see that she had shed a tear or two as well.

"I might've convinced you," she said through a weak smile, "but not them." She nodded toward the others.

Totally embarrassed, Michael composed himself, wiped the tears from his cheeks. Then he turned to face his friends. "It's her," he said with all the force he could muster after making such a scene. "I don't know how to explain it, but I know it's her."

Surprisingly, it was Sarah who showed the most doubt. "Well, you're going to have to figure out a way to explain it, Michael. We can't just hand our lives over to this lady. What she did . . . stealing a body . . . it's no better than what Kaine's doing."

The last word had barely come out of her mouth before the rest of the group erupted into chatter, talking on top of talking, until Michael shouted for them to shut up.

"Listen to me!" he said, looking straight at his friends and Sarah's parents. "You don't have a clue what it's like to be a Tangent. We might be a bunch of code to you guys, but I can't accept that. There's more to us. I know it. I'm a person, I have a mind, I can think for myself, and I don't care what anyone else says. I mean, I could just as easily be programmed as Helga. At some point you have to go with your heart! My parents were real, as far as I'm concerned, until Kaine wiped them out. And Helga . . . she's like a grandma to me. This is Helga. I know it."

"Grandma?" Helga asked. "Really?"

"Sorry. Best aunt ever."

Sarah walked up to stand right in front of Michael, and she stared at him for several seconds. "You're sure?"

He nodded firmly. "I'm positive." He looked over at Bryson. "Sure as heckfire."

Bryson shrugged. "I guess we just have to trust you," he said reluctantly.

"You don't need to worry about us being like Kaine," Helga interjected. "There's a difference. A huge difference." It was Gerard's turn to speak. "Yeah?" he pressed. "So enlighten us. What's this huge difference?"

Michael trusted Helga, but he was definitely interested.

"The difference," Helga said, "is that we're here to stop what Kaine's doing. The difference is that we triggered the Mortality Doctrine only because it was a last resort. And the biggest difference . . ." She paused for a moment. "The biggest difference is that we plan to give these bodies back. Hopefully very soon. I highly doubt Kaine plans to do the same."

"Give them back?" Bryson asked. "How?"

Helga sat down in her chair. "It's time I tell you about the Hive."

2

The Hive. The words jarred Michael, and his group quieted. He looked at Sarah and Bryson and nodded to the chairs. "Can we listen to what she has to say, guys?" he asked. The group didn't answer, but everyone sat down, ready to hear her out.

"The Hive," she repeated, once everyone was settled.

"Kaine created it—for what ultimate purpose we're not completely sure—and he protects it and maintains it, and we've figured out how to get there. To break in, I should say. The Hive is the key to everything, the key to restoring things to the way they were, before"—Helga gestured to herself sadly— "all this."

"But what *is* the Hive?" Sarah insisted. "We've never heard of it."

"Ah, yes," Helga said quietly, "of course. The Hive is where intelligence is stored. Intelligenc*es,* actually. Plural."

"You mean, like the brain of the VirtNet?" Bryson asked.

Helga shook her head. "No, nothing like that. It's a quantum storage facility. It has the capacity to store massive amounts of data, including backups of Tangent programs. We've discovered that it's also where a consciousness is sent when a Tangent takes over a body. Where the *mind* is stored." Helga turned to Michael. "What's the name of the person you replaced? Jackson Park?"

"Porter," Michael corrected her.

"Yes, Porter. Well, Kaine didn't destroy him when he enacted the Mortality Doctrine on you. It doesn't work that way. Again, for reasons we don't know, the intelligence, the . . . memories, the personality, the knowledge of Jackson Porter, must be preserved. We have theories—for instance, it might be a necessary part of the process. For the human body left behind to survive, the consciousness might need to be kept alive as well. If such a connection was completely severed, who knows if the physical body could handle it. What I'm saying is that your body still has a link to Jackson

Porter . . . to what makes him, him. We think it's similar to the technology used for the Core you need to Sink in a NerveBox."

Michael's heartbeat picked up uncomfortably. "Wh-what are you saying?" He could barely get the question out.

"I'm saying that the intelligence of the person you re-placed still exists, intact and whole. His consciousness is stored in a place called the Hive."

"That's . . ." Michael swallowed. "That's . . . confusing?"

Helga stood up. "I think the best way to do this is to show you."

Michael looked at Bryson and Sarah and her parents. Everyone appeared as stunned as he felt.

"Yes," Helga said. "I think that's what we'll do. Let's Sink."

3

There were fifteen Coffins total lined up against the long wall of the old barracks building, glowing blue, like phos-phorescent sea creatures. A few showed they were occupied, but most were empty, awaiting their next guest.

"I'm sure I haven't fully gained your trust yet," Helga said, standing next to the line of machines. "I'll leave it up to you to decide whether you'd like to Sink with me. Everyone can come, if they'd like, or just you, Michael. Whatever you feel most comfortable doing. I guarantee your safety." Helga ges-tured to the strangers busily working around the room.

"Everyone you see here has sworn to protect you. To protect all of you. We're all on the same team."

"You three go," Sarah's dad said. "Nancy and I will stay behind and . . . keep an eye on things." The message was clear. Gerard didn't trust these people. Not yet. He'd stay and guard his daughter's physical body—probably well aware he'd be no match for the forces that could attack her mind in the Sleep.

Michael looked at his friends, and he could see reflected in their eyes what he himself was feeling: curiosity. Though Michael wasn't so sure how he'd feel about what they learned at this place. This . . . Hive.

Michael hadn't yet opened his mouth to accept Helga's offer and Bryson was already taking off his shirt.

"Sounds good to me," he said, unzipping his pants. "Let's go."

"Can we please stick to a full-underwear policy?" Sarah pleaded, shielding her eyes. "Some things in life you can never unsee."

"You say that now," Bryson teased, batting his lashes.

Helga cleared her throat, reminding them she was there. She began to remove her shirt, though Michael noticed right away that she wore one of those fancy Sink suits underneath. Full-body spandex to cover yourself in mixed company.

"Enough chitchat," Helga announced. "Let's get in. Walter," she called to a man at a nearby NetScreen, "can you help us?"

The man gave Helga a slight nod and clicked his EarCuff,

turning off his screen. He was medium height, had dark hair, and wore a look of such intensity that Michael wondered if his face hurt.

"This is Walter Carlson," Helga announced as he approached, "temporary replacement for one Keith Sproles, whose intelligence lies in wait within the Hive, from which one day he will be returned." Her tone had a note of respect to it, as if she wanted them to know she didn't take lightly these borrowed bodies and stored intelligences.

"Hey, Walter," Bryson said.

Michael reached out and shook the man's hand; Sarah did likewise.

"We try our best to remember who we are and what we've done to those we replaced," Helga explained. "As for myself, I'm the temporary replacement of Brandi Hambrick, whose intelligence lies in wait within the Hive, from which one day she will be returned."

Michael nodded, hoping the sudden and unexpected fear he felt wasn't showing on his face. What did this all mean for him? Was Jackson Porter really out there somewhere, waiting to come back to his body? If he *was* stored, was he aware? Conscious? *Thinking?* Or was it more like cold storage? Meat in a freezer. He'd thought about Jackson a lot, but now the thought felt like a cold blade in his side. He was scared, plain and simple.

"Nice to meet you, ladies and gents," Walter said, snapping Michael back to the present. "We've heard a lot about you. Helga has a hard time shutting up about you, actually. She's right as rain, though, when she says we're on the same team. I can promise you that. No one despises Kaine quite as spectacularly as I do, that's for sure."

Sarah flashed the man a smile. "That's good to know," she said, then looked back at Helga. "I think we're ready now."

Michael breathed a sigh of relief that Sarah seemed to have decided to trust Helga. It made him feel better about his own decision.

Walter started getting busy on the Coffins. He worked down the line, moving from one to the next, tapping screens and pressing buttons. One by one the hinged doors swung open, and Michael felt that familiar rush of adrenaline. That excitement that came right before Sinking into the Sleep. It never got old. Even after everything he'd gone through.

Stripped to his boxers, he was the first to step inside a machine. Just as he sat down in his Box, Helga shot him a huge smile.

"Walter is going to work his magic with the settings," Helga said as she lowered herself into the Coffin right next to Michael. "He'll take us where we need to start, and then we'll have to do some serious code maneuvering once we're in."

Michael gave Helga a big smile back. He really liked the sound of that.

4

The Coffin door swung shut, clicked, and hissed as it sealed tight. Then came the NerveWires, snaking across Michael's body and nestling into the familiar places, pricking him as they broke his skin. The LiquiGels calibrated hot, then cold; then came the cool whoosh of the AirPuffs, and he let out a relaxing breath into the hum of machinery working around him. It seemed like an eternity since he'd done this.

He closed his eyes as the system initiated fully and plunged him into the VirtNet.

5

Michael stood next to Bryson, Sarah, and Helga on a huge expanse of hard white sand, stretching in all directions as far as the eye could see. The outline of a mountain range in the distance laid a hazy smudge against the horizon. Shimmering heat danced along the sand as the sun beat down from a brilliant blue sky. And it was hot—a dry heat that made Michael's throat feel layered in dust.

"Salt flats," Helga announced. "Patterned after the famous site on the western side of Utah. A lot of land speed records were broken there. You can imagine the ridiculous stunts that take place here in the virtual version. It's very popular with the VirtCar enthusiasts. Speeds over a thousand miles per hour, usually ending up in death and a heap of broken metal and glass. The things people do for kicks."

"That's cool and all," Bryson said, "but what does this have to do with the Hive?"

"We're admiring the landscape," Helga answered. "Try to stop and smell the roses every now and then."

Michael turned, taking in the hot, dusty scene. He reveled in this new perspective on the world and its virtual counterpart. He was still trying to understand the human body and its senses and what it meant to have a real body compared to a programmed one. On the surface, everything at the salt flats seemed real enough, but he could almost taste the fabrication, like that waxy texture of cheap cake.

"We're not in the Deep, are we?" he asked, interrupting Bryson muttering about roses and salt.

"No, we're not," Helga answered. "The Hive is actually nowhere near the Deep or any of the programs that have achieved that status. Very purposefully. It's separate in every way from most of the VirtNet—as quantum level as you get within the programming. We're not in the Hive yet, though. To get where we want to go, it's going to take some work, and it might not be what you'd call . . . pleasant."

"Why do we keep hearing that?" Sarah asked. "People are always telling us, 'What you're about to do is not going to be very pleasant.'"

Michael couldn't agree more. The Squeezing they'd gone through to get into *Lifeblood Deep*—or what they'd been told was *Lifeblood Deep*—had been one of the worst experiences of his life.

"I know you guys have heard of Squeezing, right?" Helga asked.

Michael almost laughed out loud. Bryson actually did.

Helga nodded. "I'll take that as a yes. Well, what we're about to do is worse."

"Worse?" Sarah repeated.

"Yes. Instead of being Squeezed, you're going to be . . . annihilated. Completely destroyed, then put back together again on the other side. Walter will turn your pain levels down all the way to minimum, but you're still going to feel it. And trust me, it *won't* be pleasant."

Michael sighed. "Do we really have to do this?"

"Yes," Helga replied gravely. "You need to see the Hive. It's very important to me that you see it and understand it. Everything we do to counter Kaine depends on the Hive. It grows each and every day. Ironically, we wouldn't have it if it weren't for Kaine himself."

Michael and his friends exchanged a look. No words needed for Michael to know they felt the same way he did—terrified and full of questions. The feeling was far too familiar.

"Now," Helga pronounced. "Join hands. We'll form a circle."

The friends all took a step toward each other and clasped hands. Michael stood across from Sarah, holding her gaze. Despite everything that was at stake, one thing sat like a pit in his stomach: He couldn't shake the feeling that whatever Helga was about to show them, it would mean that he and Sarah could never be what he had always wished they could be. Some possible future that he'd held far back in his consciousness since the day he'd met his friend was about to be taken away from him. A heavy sadness weighed on him as they stood there with the hot breeze rustling their clothes, the sun baking their virtual skin.

"Close your eyes," Helga instructed. "Access the code. Stay close. Then follow my lead."

She paused, then added:

"No matter how much it hurts."

CHAPTER 3

A KNOCK AT THE DOOR

1

They floated in a blackness like space, but instead of stars, fragments of code swirled around them, lit up in brilliant light, a whirlpool of information that never ceased revolving. Michael had never seen code like this—so congested, so . . . tight. Helga had to have figured out where one of the data hubs resided; that was the only explanation. No wonder she'd taken them to the salt flats. It was probably one of the only locations in the Net with enough space for a hub this size. This was how they'd get where they needed to go.

"It helps to translate everything to visual mode," Helga said. "Gather everything you see even remotely related to the quantum digits I'm about to uplink to you. When you collect it, put it all together, build it up around us. Envelop us. And then we're going to smash it to bits."

Bryson smiled his mischievous smile.

"Sounds like fun," Sarah said.

"It's not," Helga replied. Then she reached out with virtual hands and started manipulating the code. Numbers and letters transformed into building blocks, pipes, sheets of thick plastic-like matter, glass panes, cut lumber. They swirled and twisted and flipped, connecting to each other in perfect geometric fashion to create a device that fascinated the eye. Michael watched carefully as she did it. He uploaded the digits she'd just sent him, then began the same process, transforming the code into a visual manifestation of the quantum path she'd set up. It was all new to him, but he had enough experience to catch on quickly.

Bryson and Sarah mimicked Michael, and quickly they had objects orbiting them, growing and connecting, then expanding. Bigger and bigger and more and more complex the structures grew, until Helga suddenly stopped her construction and fused what she'd been building to Michael's, doubling its size, then to Sarah's and Bryson's.

The group worked together on the same structure until it was large enough that they floated within it. It resembled an enormous sphere, almost solid, so that it was smooth on the inside and they could no longer see its outer surface. Above their heads was an open space, and as they continued to work, they released new threads up and out. Michael imagined them completing the outside of the structure, making it larger by the minute. The whole thing was unlike anything he'd ever done, but he understood the theory. Kind of. They were creating a visual representation of quantum code that Helga said would transport them to a normally inaccessible place within the Sleep.

What Michael couldn't work out was how it was going to be so painful to make the journey.

They kept at it for what felt like another hour, transforming the code, following the odd path that Helga laid out, manifesting it in an ever-expanding, massive structure around them.

"We're almost there," Helga finally announced. She was concentrating so fiercely that it looked comical. "You have to stay with me now, and do exactly as I do. And don't stop working until I tell you."

Michael followed Helga's instructions, building and building, letting her take away his creations. Up the hole they flew, then disappeared in different directions. The curved shell surrounding them shone with a bluish glow.

"Okay," Helga said after a long period of silence and heavy work. "Stop. Now, here's the access code to what we just built." She blinked her eyes hard and sent it over. Michael caught it with a thought.

"Release yourself into the structure," Helga commanded. "I know you've never done anything like this before, but remember, right now you're nothing but a string of data; you're not your physical self. You have to let any concept of having a body go. Then use the access code and flow into the structure. I'll go first and you can follow me. Initiating. Now."

It wasn't easy. It was weird. Really weird. Every other interface Michael had ever used within the Sleep ignored the literal code of the user himself. You didn't have to think about it. In other words, within the VirtNet, you felt as real as it was possible to feel. But now Helga was essentially breaking herself down into a long series of numbers and letters, then transmitting it into the gigantic visual structure they'd just built. Not letting himself take the time to think it through, Michael did the same thing. It was so foreign, so *against* every instinct he'd ever had in the Net, it was like stepping into an alien world. But he did it before they left him behind.

He immediately lost all sense of direction or time or matter. There was nothing. He couldn't see, couldn't hear, couldn't feel. A pressure began to push on him from all sides, and suddenly up was down and down was up and the universe had turned inside out.

"We're in," Helga said. He couldn't see her, but he understood the message loud and clear.

"Where are we?" he heard Bryson ask.

"We're on the quantum path to the Hive," Helga explained. "Actually, we *are* the quantum path. But we can't access it this way. This is where we pull it all apart. We have to destroy *it* and *us*. Completely. And when it puts itself back together, we'll be truly inside. It'll take us along."

Michael tried to speak but realized he didn't know how to do it in this strange place. He was utterly lost. Yet his friends seemed to have no problem.

"How do we destroy it?" Sarah asked. "What do we do?"

"Just pull," Helga instructed. "Like this."

A sudden wind hit Michael with a fierce bite, and a horrendous roar ripped into his unstable mind. The odd world in which he floated shook violently. Space seemed to both shudder and expand, then contract, then expand again. Everything erupted around him.

And then there was pain. Pain so terrible that he would've thought it impossible if it weren't tearing him apart.

2

Michael didn't understand what was happening to him. He couldn't see shapes, but the pain that tore through him appeared as color—the deep ache of blue mixed with a sheer orange that was complete agony, then escalated to a bloody red that was almost unbearable. He screamed without screaming, spun within this world of madness, and reached out with arms he didn't have, utterly lost and confused.

"Michael!" someone yelled. The voice was unidentifiable, but it manifested as another stab of pain. He could barely form coherent thoughts, much less call out to someone. How were Sarah and Bryson faring well enough to form a word?

He focused on Helga. On what she'd said. Reach out and destroy. He would do anything to make this stop, but how? He tried. He focused on imagining his body again and pictured himself as a giant. He motioned with arms he couldn't feel, kicked with legs miles away.

Nothing.

Only pain.

He'd thought he was one of the best coders ever. But this made no sense to him.

He was lost.

Instead of fighting, he embraced the pain and tried to sweep himself away into the black oblivion. But he was still there, the agony stretching out before him, forever.

3

Suddenly Michael noticed that something felt different. There was still pain, but could it be . . . receding?

Then, in a flash, it ended. The agony stopped abruptly, like an anesthetic hitting his bloodstream. He was instantly pain-free, the bliss of it euphoric.

He opened his eyes. His virtual eyes. Then realized, with a shock, that he *had* eyes again.

His body—his Aura—was intact once more. He looked down at himself, touched his arms and legs, patted his chest. He was completely injury-free—it was crazy, but nothing even hurt. Finally, he looked to see where he was.

He still floated in darkness, but everything around him had changed. An endless purple sky filled with what looked like planets floating in the distance behind him. A bright, shining wall of orange light pulsed before him. Michael craned his neck and looked up, then down. The orange wall stretched in both directions as far as he could see. And as his eyes adjusted to the brilliant light, he could see that it wasn't just a flat wall. It was broken into a repeating pattern of thousands of pods. A figure flashed in one pod and he squinted to better make it out, then realized the pods were full of dark shapes. Like ghostly fish, they swam one to a pod.

This was the Hive? He stretched his arms out, maneuvering himself in a circle to confirm what he'd already suspected. He was alone.

He turned back toward the wall of orange pods. The pulsing light hummed rhythmically, he realized, almost like a heartbeat. It vibrated through his bones and filled his body. He wanted to get closer, to see what those shapes could be. He worked his arms and legs through space. In places like this in the Net, he'd always been able to maneuver from one location to another as if he were swimming, but no amount of flapping his arms or kicking his legs would move him more than what he'd already mastered—spinning in place. He stopped, intently studying the structure in front of him. There was a flash of movement, and suddenly his nose was almost touching the orange glow. He'd moved instantly—somehow he'd done it with his mind.

He looked back toward the vast purple sky, then sent out a quick thought and the world bent as he was catapulted miles away from the thrumming orange light. He turned back, shot to the next place his eyes met. For a moment the exhilaration of this instantaneous travel, this moving with his mind, made him forget the reason he was there. He focused more intently, concentrating on where he wanted to be, and with a snap, once again he was floating just outside the massive, never-ending wall of brilliant orange pods.

He thought himself closer, now in complete control. His body moved slowly forward until a pod was just a few inches from his face. Those same shadows he'd noticed before, starker now, slithered behind the filmy surface. He leaned in, following the forms, but the moment he caught one with his gaze it would move away, slipping just out of sight. He wondered what it was like on the other side of the wall.

The thought barely formed before he shifted once again, this time blinded for an instant by a moment of complete darkness. Then he was exactly where he wanted to be—on the other side of the wall. And things were different there.

From this vantage Michael saw that the Hive was actually an enormous sphere, and that he was now on the *inside* of it. Surrounded by countless pods, almost like a honeycomb, glowing, pulsing, humming.

From within the sphere, the individual pods were flat on this side. They almost looked like one of those old computers he'd heard about with a glassy screen called a monitor. The moment he thought it, he was there, nose to the surface of the "glass," gazing in. Printed digitally on it was a name.

EDGAR THOMAS FINCH

He reached out and touched the letters—the entire screen flashed red, once, and then the name reappeared. He did it again and the same thing happened. Silently he concentrated on sending a command to the screen to reveal more information, but nothing happened. There was just the name, the orange light of its pod broken up only by those shifty shadows swimming in the murkiness behind it.

He quickly moved from unit to unit. Each pod had a name, none of them familiar.

That was when he realized he wanted to see it for himself. He had to see it.

Jackson Porter, he thought. *Take me to the pod of Jackson Porter.*

4

His ears popped with the sudden movement and the Hive instantaneously shifted around him. With of a blur of orange, his mind tilted, his stomach pitched. Then all became still and there it was, just a few feet in front of him, the letters spelling out a name that made his chest tight.

JACKSON BLAYNE PORTER

Michael drifted closer, reached out, and lightly touched the surface of the screen that revealed the name. The name of the person from whom he'd taken everything. The screen flashed red just like the one before it, then went back to normal. It was probably some kind of signal showing that he didn't have authority to access information on whatever lay inside that pod.

What *did* lie inside the pod? Michael didn't understand just how real the Hive might be. Was it a literal place? Or something more symbolic? He moved himself to the right of the screen and leaned in as close to the bright orange surface as he dared. Shadows shifted inside, swirling, growing, and shrinking. Michael stared, mesmerized—it felt as if he was on the cusp of understanding the afterlife, the spirit world, some supernatural thing he could never truly fathom before. The shadows suddenly coalesced into one large spot, right in front of Michael, just inches from his face. The orange light pulsed around the spot—it was an oval and almost a foot in height, positioned vertically. Darker shadows formed within shadows. Michael gasped and almost hurtled himself away from it, terrified, shivering in virtual chills.

A face.

Two eyes. A nose. A thin mouth drawn in a line. Cheekbones. A chin. All vague, but there. A face of shadows looking out at Michael as the light of the pod pulsed and the thrum of a deep heartbeat vibrated around him.

Michael's chest hurt. His body felt like a block of ice. What was this? Was he confronting the essence of Jackson Porter, whose body—whose *life*—he'd stolen? He didn't understand. He didn't understand any of this. And yet he couldn't look away.

"I'm sorry," he whispered, as absurd as it seemed. The dark, blurry face dissolved back into indistinct shadows, scattering throughout the inside of the pod.

"I wanted you to see this," a voice said from behind him.

Michael yelped, so startled he spun around and swung his right arm out, hitting nothing but air. Helga—now in the form he'd known her his whole life, the Helga from home, his nanny who'd been like a second mother—floated a few feet away, with Bryson and Sarah behind her. Michael didn't know when or how she'd switched her Aura, but he had to admit it calmed him on sight and made him feel a little better.

"What's going on?" he asked, wanting to take all the frustration and angst that had built up inside him and throw it at someone else. "What's the point of all this? You're telling me that Jackson Porter is stored inside this pod? Like some kind of living, breathing data file? What, do I just tap in a password and he slides back into my brain? Is that why you brought me here?"

It came out in a rush, and the hurt look that crossed Helga's face made him wish he could take it all back.

Almost as quickly as it appeared, it was gone, though, and her no-nonsense, I'm-in-charge face returned.

Sarah flashed away from Helga and to Michael's side in a blur and wrapped her arm around his shoulder. "Sorry we lost you there for a while," she said softly. "I just tried to stay close to Helga and figured you'd be with her, too."

Michael took her hand but didn't take his eyes off Helga.

"It was really important to me that you come here, Michael," Helga said. "I know it took a lot of effort and more than a little risk. But this place is real, and it has to be seared inside your mind so you understand what we're up against and what our purpose is."

"What *are* we up against?" Michael said, ashamed that his voice came out a little angry. "What *is* our purpose?"

"Yeah," Bryson added, distancing himself from Helga so he could look at her straight on. "Those are some great questions."

Helga gestured with outstretched arms toward the massive Hive around them. "These pods are filling up at an exponential rate. And honestly, we can't even tell if it's all Kaine's doing at this point. There's still a lot we need to figure out. But these are people, Michael. *People.* Stolen from their bodies. And I know we agree on one thing—that's about the most sacred thing in the universe you can mess with. It's as bad as what Kaine did to you, playing with your life, your mind, your feelings, like it was all some kind of VirtNet game."

"I want to help, but how?" Michael snapped, feeling worse by the second. He didn't understand why, but it felt like his heart was breaking. "Or maybe I should just give up. Jackson can have his stupid body back. I don't care anymore. How do I do it?"

Helga sighed. "Michael, you're missing my point completely. I didn't bring you here to make you feel bad. I'm glad you want to do something about this. It's about saving these people and stopping it from happening to others. Righting the world—both the real one and the virtual one—before it falls apart beyond repair."

"Okay," Michael said. "So we already know we have to stop Kaine, and I want to go back to the Hallowed Ravine. I think we need to go back there to destroy the Mortality Doctrine program. But I don't see why you had to make me face the kid whose body I stole. If you wanted to make me feel worse, mission accomplished."

Helga didn't respond at first. She just looked at him for seconds that felt more like minutes. Finally, she broke the silence. "You disappoint me, Michael. Let's go back and Lift out."

She disappeared from the center of the orb before Michael could reply. Which was good, because he had no idea what to say.

5

The journey out of the Hive wasn't nearly as bad as the horror they'd experienced to get in. Helga explained that the difference had something to do with using the path that they'd already established. A path that was still painfully fresh to Michael. When Michael finally opened his eyes back in the Coffin, he wanted to cheer despite the embarrassment of how he'd acted at the Hive.

He climbed out of the NerveBox and started pulling his clothes back on, doing his best to avoid eye contact with anyone. Even Sarah, whom he needed but couldn't quite face yet. He felt stupid and miserable and just wanted to sleep for a few days—maybe weeks.

It took longer for Helga to exit her Coffin, and when she did, Walter practically dragged her away, whispering fiercely into her ear. Michael watched her cross the room to a group huddled around a desk with a NetScreen illuminated at its center. The discussion intensified between the group, and finally Helga looked up at Michael, her face pinched with concern. Something had happened. Something big.

Sarah and Bryson were at Michael's side.

"What's going on?" Bryson asked. "She doesn't look too happy."

"Were you serious about going back to the Hallowed Ravine?" Sarah added.

Michael shrugged, not in the mood to talk.

Sarah nudged him. "You okay?"

Another shrug.

"Don't worry, man, we'll figure all this stuff out," Bryson said. "Hallowed Ravine, whatever you want—but, dude, you look like someone just murdered your cat."

"That's how I feel," Michael managed to say. He knew he shouldn't take out his misery on his best friends, but he was in the rottenest mood ever.

Bryson opened his mouth to answer but was interrupted by a bang that sent Michael's heart into his throat. The noise came from the front door—the one through which they'd entered earlier. It was someone pounding on the wood with what sounded like an iron fist. After a dozen hammering bursts, it stopped as abruptly as it had started, and a deep silence settled across the barracks. Anxious glances were exchanged across the room.

The person outside hammered on the door again, harder and faster.

Michael saw Helga straighten up and smooth out the clothes she'd just put on.

"Everyone arm yourself," she ordered. "Walter, see who it is."

Walter didn't hesitate. He crossed the room swiftly as the others busied themselves seemingly conjuring weapons from thin air. Michael wished he had something other than Jackson Porter's fists.

Walter flipped open a small window in the old door and peered out, then glanced at Helga. "It's just one person. At least, that's all I can see. Short, with a . . . hood over his head. Or hers. Can't tell which from here, but it looks like a kid." He turned back toward the door. "Who are you?" he yelled.

"I'm alone!" a voice shouted back. A girl's voice. "Please let me in, sir."

Walter looked at Helga, eyebrows raised.

"You're sure she's alone?" Helga asked.

"As far as I can tell."

"Well, I highly doubt she's a local farm girl who's lost her way." Helga waved an arm in frustration. "I suppose we might as well find out what it's all about—if we have enemies outside waiting to kill us." She sighed. "Let her in, then bar the door behind her."

Walter nodded, released several locks that Michael hadn't noticed before, then quickly opened the door and motioned the girl inside. She stepped in and he slammed the door behind her, relocking everything. Another person patted her down to make sure she had no weapons; then they both stepped back and Walter repeated his question.

"Who are you?"

The girl couldn't have been more than twelve years old. She wore jeans and tennis shoes and had on a bright-red cape, with a hood draped over her head. She looked like she'd walked straight out of the old fairy tale. All that was missing was the basket full of cakes for Grandma. And a wolf.

The young stranger reached up and pulled her hood down, revealing dark hair and pale skin, and an odd half smile.

"Who are you?" Walter asked for a third time, his tone now charged with impatience.

The girl gave him a curtsy, then looked around the room until her eyes fell on Michael.

"My name is Janey," she said, in a voice so innocent it sounded cartoonish. "I was wondering if Michael could come out and play."

CHAPTER 4

INTO THE WOODS

1

She smiled after she said it, still staring straight at Michael with doe eyes. On the surface she seemed harmless, but Michael knew better. She was creepier than a zombie who'd just crawled out of a muddy grave.

Despite all the people in the room, it felt like it was only him and the strange girl. "How do you know my name?" Michael asked, fearing the answer.

A hurt look flashed across her face, only turning up the weirdness. "How can you be surprised?" she asked, and bit her lower lip in confusion. "You're the First; we all know who you are. We practically worship you. Won't you come out and play with us?"

"*Us?*" Helga repeated sharply, marching up to stand between Michael and their new visitor. "Who else is out there?"

The girl named Janey gave Helga a hard look. "I prefer to speak with the First only, please. We're grateful that . . . *other*

Tangents have chosen to protect him for us, but we'll take it from here, thank you."

"You don't sound much like a kid," Walter said, inching closer to Helga.

Janey glanced sharply at him, her odd smile suddenly gone. "Because I'm not. Why so many of you choose to take over bodies that are already so . . . *old* completely baffles me. If you're going to take over a human, why would you pick one that's already close to its deathbed?"

Michael was frozen, unable to move or even think properly. He still hadn't recovered from his trip to the Hive, and now he had to deal with this? Janey wasn't the only person who'd recognized him since he'd gained a body, or referred to him as the First, but he still had no idea what they wanted from him. He wished he could just go back to being Michael the Tangent, living in blissful ignorance with his parents and Helga in *Lifeblood Deep*. He didn't want this new life. He didn't want any of it.

"You didn't answer my question," Helga said calmly. "Who else is out there?"

Janey started to walk toward Michael, but Helga and Walter stepped in front of her, arms out. Janey glanced at each of them, annoyed, then rested her eyes on Michael.

"There are so many of us," she said. "We're waiting for you. Things have changed, you know. We don't work for Kaine anymore—we broke off. He's not right in the head. All we want is freedom to . . . live like humans were meant to live. Come with us. Bring your two friends if you like. We could use your help if Kaine retaliates. These other Tangents have to stay here, though. I'm sorry. It's clear they want to end the Mortality Doctrine, and we can't allow that."

Michael shivered. It was so eerie seeing this little girl speak like an adult. Bryson and Sarah were at his sides, one at each shoulder. Sarah had a reassuring hand on his arm.

"You can leave," he said, telling himself he didn't need to be scared of a twelve-year-old. "You get your buddies and waltz right on out of here. If you're against Kaine, then we've got no beef with you." He left out that little part about the Doctrine.

As he spoke, Janey's smile widened, and when he finally finished, she let out a high-pitched laugh. "You're as adorable as we were told. But the First needs to be educated, obviously. I'm not sure your friends here are the best people to entrust your life to."

"Cut the act," Sarah snapped. "Tell us what you want."

Janey glared at Sarah as she answered. "The Tangent you know as Kaine played a very important part in making the Mortality Doctrine come to life. But he was never the one in charge. There was someone far more important pulling the strings. There always is, isn't there?"

"Still talking in riddles," Sarah answered.

"Then let me spell it out for you," Janey shot back. Michael had never seen a little girl look so menacing. "Kaine has lost his relevance. If at one time he was in charge—and that's by no means certain—he no longer is. He lost his value with those who matter, and he's been . . . relieved, accordingly."

Michael didn't know what to think of that news. Was it good or bad?

"Then who is it?" he asked. "Who's in charge?"

"I'd rather not say," Janey replied, "but I believe she's a friend of yours."

Weber, Michael thought immediately. It had to be. What in the world was going on?

Helga had finally had enough. She grabbed Janey by the shoulders and forcefully turned her around, motioning for Walter to open the door. "Time for you to go now," she announced.

Janey wrenched free of Helga's grip and faced Michael.

"You're right," she said. "There's been more than enough talk for one day. No more. So here's the deal: we'll give you one hour to make your decision. It's your choice, Michael. Either you leave this place and join us, or you—all of you—will face the consequences. It's like the old saying—"

Helga grabbed Janey again, was pulling her away as she struggled to get out her last few words.

"—you're either with us or against us!" she yelled.

Helga pushed the girl outside and Walter slammed the door.

2

Michael and the others gathered again at the circle of chairs, a heavy mood hanging over them. No one had spoken much, and Michael felt as confused as he ever had. At least before this girl had shown up, they'd clearly known who they were up against: Kaine. Although Michael put Agent Weber right up there with the Tangent.

"Obviously, she could be lying," Bryson said. "For all we know, she's some crazy inbred chick from the backwoods."

"Oh, come on," Sarah countered. "How would she have known all that stuff about Kaine and the First? She knew Michael's name!"

Bryson nodded. "I know. Okay. A crazy inbred chick taken over by a Tangent, then."

Sarah groaned; Michael wished she wouldn't take out her frustration on Bryson all the time.

"Look," Bryson said, "I'm just saying there's absolutely no reason for us to trust a word that comes out of her mouth. Maybe she's really Kaine and he's messing with us, trying to make us chase our own tails."

"Or," Michael offered, "Weber's doing it."

Helga spoke up. "All that matters right now is figuring out the immediate threat. We might have a bunch of gun-toting children hiding in the woods out there, ready to make us their very own VirtGame."

"Okay, so what do we do?" Michael asked.

"We need to know exactly what we're up against," Walter replied. He turned to the three closest people. "Chris, Amy, Richard, grab your weapons and let's go have a look."

As they prepped themselves, Michael stepped closer to Helga.

"I want to go with them," he whispered to her.

She patted him on the head. Actually patted him on the head. "Nice try, Michael. No."

"I can't stay in here," he said, angrily brushing his hair as if she'd messed it up.

Helga pointed at him. "I didn't risk the true death and break every moral law in the universe by stealing someone else's body just to have you go out there and get killed by a demon child possessed by one of Kaine's programs. No way. End of discussion."

Michael changed tack and gently touched her arm, flashing big, sad eyes. "Helga, please."

It was something he'd learned to do as a young boy when he wanted something, and it worked—further proof she was really his beloved Helga. Her expression softened.

"Michael, why?" she asked quietly.

"I need to do something. I'll go crazy if I stay here waiting. And I really don't think they'll hurt me. Judging from how that Janey girl acted and how others have treated me, it's like I'm a god to them. It could give us an advantage until we know more." He paused, giving his nanny the saddest eyes he could muster. "Please let me go."

Helga let out a frustrated sigh. "You've been stubborn since the day you were born." They exchanged a look, and then they both laughed, a welcome change of pace. "I guess they programmed you that way!"

"Guess so." Michael shrugged.

"Do you have any idea how to use a gun?" He opened his mouth to answer, but Helga held up a hand to stop him. "Never mind. Dumbest question I could ask a boy who's conquered every game on the planet. Walter! Michael and I are heading out, too."

"You know you're not leaving us in here, right?" Sarah asked.

Michael looked at Helga, who rolled her eyes.

"Fine," she said. "Grab a weapon and let's get out of here. And no killing any children unless you absolutely have to! For a nanny, I sure am sick of kids."

Michael couldn't tell if she was joking.

3

Michael held a long, heavy rifle. It was the worst thing ever for slinking around in the woods. He figured Helga thought if she'd given him the semiautomatic handgun he had wanted, he'd just blast away at the first thing he saw. He was crouched behind the very car in which he'd driven to the abandoned barracks with Sarah's parents. It was because of them that Sarah wasn't there at his side. She'd argued relentlessly, but her mom finally quieted her by saying, "If you've ever loved me, then you will not go out there and risk your life again."

It was impossible to argue with, and Michael was glad Helga didn't use a similar line on him.

"All right," Walter whispered. He and Bryson were with Michael behind the car; the others had slipped around the back of the building to check things on that side. "We'll do a zigzag sweep, starting here and heading out that way"—he pointed toward the woods—"and see if we come across anyone hiding."

"Shouldn't we split up?" Bryson asked. "We could cover way more ground."

"Helga swore to give me the true death if I let you two boys out of my sight," he replied. "After she cut off all my special parts."

"Ouch," Bryson whispered. "She's one tough nanny."

"What is the true death?" Michael asked, ignoring his friend. "No one ever told us in there."

"Really?" Walter responded. "Right now?"

Michael shrugged.

Bryson sided with Walter. "How about he tells us when we're done dealing with Janey and her creepy friends?"

Michael sighed. "Fine."

Walter gave him a curt nod—he had a handgun similar to the one Michael had wanted—then crouched and inched up to the back of the car, peeking around the edge. Bryson was next, then Michael, who lifted his head enough to look through the window. On the other side of the vehicle, trees crowded the hillside, growing thicker and thicker until they formed a dark forest. Michael felt that familiar gaming itch—the curiosity of the unexplored, the certainty that there was something sinister hidden out there. He realized that it helped him feel braver to approach this like a game.

Walter turned back and motioned for Michael and Bryson to follow him, then made a break for the woods. Michael stayed close to Bryson, crouching as low as possible, with a tight grip on his rifle. He stopped at the first line of trees, holding his weapon as if it were a lance in a joust. Even though he was trying to think of this as a game, he couldn't fathom pulling the trigger any time soon. What he was really hoping for was a chance to talk to Janey or any other Tangent. He'd already thought it through. He'd decided that if the opportunity presented itself, he would accidentally "get lost" and take off on his own. He needed information, not dead children—no matter who lived in their heads.

It got darker as they crept deeper into the woods and the canopy of leaves grew thicker over their heads. Dry pine straw crackled under Michael's feet. Branches scratched his arms as he swept his gun left and right. Shadows passed, drawing his attention to the dark corners of the forest, and curling bark and thick branches of pine needles twisted into long arms and fingers reaching out to tug at his hair and clothes. No one spoke as they moved through the maze of the forest. Only their footsteps and the buzz of insects broke the silence.

They pressed forward for ten or fifteen minutes, like three hunters looking for a hapless deer. The fading sunlight barely illuminated the forest floor, creating a shadowy gloom that made Michael wonder if they might not be stepping right past the very Tangents they were searching for.

Suddenly he caught a glimpse of movement off to his right, a quick flash of something bright moving from one tree to another. Walter and Bryson were already moving on, so Michael slowed his steps until he stopped completely, and continued to crunch the pine straw underfoot. His companions were so lost in concentration that they didn't notice they'd left Michael, and soon they'd turned a corner, disappearing behind a huge oak. Michael took his opportunity.

He turned as slowly as possible toward the movement he'd seen in the forest.

He crept up to the tree where he'd seen the movement stop.

"I don't want any trouble," Michael whispered. "I'm . . . uh . . . the First. Please, just let me talk to whoever's leading you guys out here. Let me talk to Janey."

A couple of seconds went by before an answer came, a soft but harsh rasp. A man. "Janey's a child. What would make you think she leads us?"

Michael definitely hadn't been expecting that to be the response. "Um, okay. She said—"

"Yes," the voice interrupted. "Many of my friends have chosen to take the bodies of children. But the agreement is that they're too weak to lead."

It was already a weird conversation, and Michael didn't have much time. "Look, I'm a Tangent, just like you guys. They call me the First."

"We know who you are, Michael."

"Okay. Well, I just want to talk to someone who knows what's going on. That Janey girl threatened us, but I'm pretty sure we're on the same side. I don't get it."

Another long pause stretched on. Michael looked back, worried that Walter would come charging through those distant trees at any second. Finally, the man behind the tree responded.

"Wait here and I'll bring our leader to you. But give me your weapon first." A weathered but muscled arm appeared, the hand palm up and fingers outstretched.

A flurry of thoughts whirled through Michael's mind. How insane to even consider—

"Fine," he said, cutting it all off. He handed over the rifle and the man vanished into the woods, barely making a sound.

4

It was too good to be true that he'd lose his friends for long. Moments after he handed over his rifle, Bryson called out his name. It sounded like they'd moved on farther than he'd expected. Bryson called again, and Michael could hear a few indecipherable words that didn't sound very nice.

A low rustle came from the other side of the tree at which he crouched; then a man appeared, sitting down right next to Michael on the forest floor. He was older, maybe fifty, his head shaved, with a full red beard hanging well past his chin. He was muscular, powerful-looking, everything about him like an ancient Viking.

"My name is Trae," he said, his voice surprisingly kind, with an odd, lilting accent.

"Trae?" Michael repeated.

"Yes, Trae."

"You're . . . sure?" It was a name Michael had never heard before.

"Of course I'm sure!" he somehow whispered and yelled at the same time. "What do you want? You have two minutes."

Michael tried to get past the Viking-like presence of this so-called leader.

"I need to . . . understand," he said, wishing he knew how to articulate the millions of questions congesting his mind. "Who are you? I mean, who are you really? Are you really Tangents, and if you are, where in the Sleep did you come from? Why are we a threat to you? Janey said you don't work for Kaine anymore. What does that mean? What are you trying to accomplish?"

Trae's eyes grew wider as the questions spilled from Michael.

"I said you had two minutes," he answered, "not two hours. Want me to give you a quick rundown of European history while we're at it?"

Bryson's voice stopped Michael's response. He called Michael's name again, and it sounded like he'd gotten closer.

"Sorry," he said in a rush. Michael took a deep breath, slowing himself down. "Who are you? Why would you come here and threaten to hurt us?"

"We're Tangents," Trae replied matter-of-factly. "Given the gift of true flesh and bone for the first time. We earned it, and we're not going to let the likes of you ruin it for everybody."

"Everybody, huh? What about the people you stole that flesh and bone from?"

Trae shrugged. "They're safe enough. Happy enough. They'll take their turn living in the Sleep for a bit, then maybe have another chance someday."

Michael's mouth dropped open, but he didn't know what to say at first. "A . . . another chance? What do you mean?"

"*Michael!*" Walter, this time, not sounding very happy. And definitely closer.

"Word on the street," Trae said, acting as if he hadn't heard the shout, "or should I say, word in the woods . . . word is that you've seen the Hive."

Michael couldn't believe it. "How do you know that?" Realizing his mistake, he added, "If I even did."

Trae let out a genuine chuckle. "We have our ways, as they say. And we know that you've seen the Hive. You know how it works. The true death only comes to a few, so what you're fighting against is nothing for you to worry about."

"But you said you don't work for Kaine anymore," Michael countered urgently. He knew Bryson would be on him any second. "Why are you against us? What's going on?"

Trae fixed Michael in his gaze. "Kaine has his own agenda. And one thing's for sure—" The footsteps were nearing, crashing through the bushes, snapping twigs and pine straw, and the Tangent stopped, looked past Michael for the source of the noise.

"What's that?" Michael pressed. "What's for sure?"

Trae leaned a little closer to Michael. "Kaine's a lot smarter than those who slapped his code together, and his vision for the future is . . . dangerous. As for you, well. Like Janey told you, you're either for us or against us. And by my reckoning, you have about twenty minutes to decide. How could you possibly want to work for Kaine anymore?"

"I don't. . . . I never have!" Michael said under his breath. "But I certainly won't work for Weber, either." He took a chance throwing the VNS agent's name out there.

Trae didn't respond. Instead he looked at his watch. Time was ticking.

"What'll you do to us?" Michael asked weakly.

Trae nodded back in the direction of the barracks. "There's a lot more of us than there are of you. I'll just say that. And nothing, lad—and I truly mean nothing—is going to get in our way. We don't like what's going on with the Tangents in those barracks, and we aim to stop it. Go back now. And I suggest you all accept our demands when the times comes."

"Michael!"

He spun to see Bryson standing just a few feet away, between two large pine trees. When Michael turned back toward Trae, the man was gone.

"Did you see him?" Michael asked.

"See who?" Bryson replied.

Michael sighed. "Never mind. Did you find anything?"

"No, I've been looking for you the whole time. Walter called for you but kept going—he said he had his own job to do. What happened? Who did you see?"

Michael collapsed against the tree behind him and slid down to the ground. "Just some guy. Said a bunch of stuff that makes about as much sense as everything else we've been told. I think Weber is behind these people somehow, which doesn't explain much. And it almost seems worse than Kaine leading them."

"Dude," Bryson said, somehow making it sound like a reprimand.

Michael groaned and got to his feet. It felt like he weighed a thousand pounds. "We need to go back. And then I think we need to leave. Something really bad is about to go down around here."

5

Night began to fall, enveloping the grounds around the barracks in darkness. The dying glow of the setting sun would be gone within minutes. Michael and Bryson made it out of the woods without incident and saw that most of the others had returned already. Their figures, hooded in shadows, were grouped together behind the cars.

"Michael, come here!"

It was Walter. He stood up from his defensive crouch and motioned for Michael to join them.

"Where'd you go?" the man asked.

Michael didn't know how much to share of what he'd learned. Bryson was quicker on his feet, thankfully.

"Find anything?" he asked, changing the subject.

"Yeah," the man answered vaguely. He was clearly angry he'd lost the boys. "Both of you are lucky you didn't have your throats slit out there."

"Amy's back," someone whispered from the group by the cars.

"Inside," Walter commanded, glaring at Michael. The dusky light only made the command feel more menacing. Michael looked at Bryson and nodded. They should head back—Janey's deadline was only a few minutes away.

6

Michael straggled behind the remaining group as they returned to the bunker. He was last to enter the building and could feel the nervous energy the moment he stepped inside. Everyone was on their feet, surrounding Helga. Walter went straight to her to give his recap of what they'd found in the woods. Michael hung back—he wished he'd had more time with the man named Trae.

"Not much good news," Helga announced to the room. "Walter spotted a group of twenty. Armed. Only a few were children, despite what that little ghost of a girl claimed. Amy and Chris saw others lurking behind trees."

She paused, seemingly searching for how to finish.

"Richard found some wire, followed it to the base of the barracks. Looks like there's enough explosives packed around the edges to blow us to the moon. I don't know when they set them, but we're in a heap of trouble. And I'm afraid that if we try to leave, they'll detonate."

"Can't we just cut the wires or something?" Sarah's mom

asked. "Doesn't anyone know how to disconnect them? Disarm them? Whatever?"

"Bad idea," Walter answered. "If we don't know what we're working with, it could all go off in our faces."

The room fell silent. Michael folded his arms and tried to think. The thing that bothered him most was that these people said they didn't work for Kaine anymore. And if Michael had learned anything from gaming, it was that if you wanted to win a war, you had to know who the enemy was.

Helga let out a heavy sigh. "I'm sorry to say it, but—"

Her last word hung in the air as the lights blinked off. Helga's voice was replaced by a flurry of whispers and shuffling feet. Sarah grabbed Michael's hand and he reached out to clasp onto Bryson's elbow. There wasn't a hint of light in the room—Michael couldn't see a thing. Even the Coffins' glow had disappeared. They'd cut the power.

"Calm down!" Helga shouted from the blackness. "Everyone, stay where you are."

EarCuffs clicked and NetScreens lit up, casting a green glow on everyone's faces.

Michael could make out Sarah's parents standing behind her and Michael. They looked even more scared than Michael felt. Gerard had his hands on Sarah's shoulders, and Nancy had her arms wrapped around her husband.

Helga started speaking again. "Amy, Chris, go pull our friends out of the NerveBoxes. I don't think we have any choice but to—"

Crash.

Helga never finished her sentence. A rock exploded

through a window on the far end of the barracks, glass raining down on the carpeted floor. The fist-sized stone rolled to a stop in front of Michael.

Bryson leaned close to Michael to whisper in his ear. "Dude, I'm about ready to give up on these people. I think we did a lot better job of taking care of ourselves on our own."

"Yeah, maybe," Michael responded. "Just not really the best moment for that."

Another rock crashed through a window, this time closer. Michael jumped, his heart almost stopping. He spun around just in time to see the last shards of glass sprinkle on the carpet around the large stone. This was followed by only a few seconds of shocked silence before yet another rock broke through a window, then another, then another. Screams filled the room as crash after crash splintered the air, stones thumping on the carpet and glass flying like crystal bugs.

Michael and his friends instinctively pulled together. Michael felt glass hit his back; a fragment pricked his neck and stuck there, stinging.

It seemed to last forever, one after another, concussions of sound like a series of thunder strikes. Michael had to press back the certainty that at any moment the world would blow up around him, sending them to oblivion.

Then, suddenly, it stopped. The silence was so stark, Michael worried for a moment he'd lost his hearing. Gradually he could make out breathing, the occasional high tinkle of a shard of glass falling out of the window frame to the ground. Still, no one spoke.

A flash of movement at the nearest window caught Michael's attention, immediately followed by the distinct giggles of a little girl. Walter raised his gun and started toward the window, but Helga stopped him.

"Remember what they hold over us," she said to him. "You start firing that gun and they blow us up. We're out of options, my friend. Except . . ."

More movement outside, more laughter, both boys and girls, from the sound of it. Something about these people was really starting to sicken Michael. He didn't care what kind of Tangents had taken over their bodies; they were still children, running around in harm's way. Could the adults be using them as bait? It was so confusing, he almost wished he were back in that prison cell.

Finally, Helga's last comment caught up with him. Except . . . except what? Her people were looking at her with varying expressions of shock. It seemed something was going on here that Michael and his friends didn't understand.

"You can't be serious," Walter said after a long silence.

"*You* can't be serious to question me," Helga countered. "We're completely out of options. Do you think they're going to let us walk out of here?"

"But it's against everything our alliance stands for." The eerie laughing hadn't stopped, filtering in through the windows like something from a haunted orphanage.

A man's voice suddenly thundered at them.

"Your hour is up! We want your leader to come outside with her hands in the air or we'll detonate. We see one sign of a weapon and it's all over."

Michael thought it sounded like Trae—it was the same lilting accent. Maybe this was a chance to surrender and leave. He looked at Helga, whose eyes made it clear that she didn't agree.

"We have no choice," she said, sounding tired. "We have to give them the true death."

CHAPTER 5

BEDTIME STORIES

1

"I'm coming!" Helga called back. "I won't have a weapon, and you'll want to hear what I have to say. We have something that could be very valuable to you."

Michael turned to his friends and shot them a questioning look. They clearly didn't know any more than he did. The green glow of the NetScreens around the room shone in their eyes, lighting them up like orbs of kryptonite.

"Enough talk!" Trae yelled back. "You have three seconds to get out here."

Helga quickly walked to the door, opened it, and stepped outside. Walter twitched with an obvious desire to follow her, but held his place. He had a murderous, angry expression on his face.

"Let's check it out," Bryson whispered. He nodded to a window and gestured to Michael and Sarah to follow.

The glass crunched beneath their shoes as they crept up to it. Bryson swiped away the few jagged pieces of glass remaining in the frame and knelt down. Michael got to his knees on Bryson's left and Sarah crouched to his right. Michael hoped the darkness would hide them from whoever was outside.

"An empty threat." It was Trae speaking to Helga, shining a flashlight right in her face. They were surrounded by a group of five or six, all with their own flashlights pointed toward the ground. "You do realize we're Tangents—we weren't programmed to be idiots."

Helga raised her hands above her head. "Well, you've got us cornered, and there's too much at stake. If you don't believe me, then I'll prove just how high those stakes are. And if you decide to jump the gun and blow us to bits, then the message has already been sent. You'll all die. Forever."

Michael couldn't make out much about the people standing behind their leader. He could make out Janey, though, and judging by their size, there were other children in the group as well. One boy looked to be as young as eight or nine.

Several moments passed in silence as the bearded man thought.

"What do you think she's talking about?" Sarah whispered. "What message? How could she kill them?"

"The true death," Bryson answered. "Something's going on that we don't know about."

"Obviously," Michael replied. He didn't mean to sound rude; he was in total agreement as to how clueless they were.

"Boo!"

A girl's face had appeared on the other side of the window, and Michael nearly jumped out of his pants. Bryson yelled and fell backward, knocking Sarah to the floor.

Michael froze. Those dark eyes and that pale face. She giggled hysterically, then vanished again. Michael sucked in a breath of air.

"Quiet!" Trae screamed outside. "Tina, get away from there. Now!"

"Sorry, boss." There was another giggle; then Michael saw the girl run off into the woods. Bryson and Sarah came back to crouch next to Michael.

"I was just trying to protect you," Bryson said to Sarah. "She could've had a gun, you know."

Sarah rolled her eyes and settled back into her place at the window. Helga was still outside, and they didn't want to miss any of what happened.

"I call your bluff," Trae said. "You're not going to surrender, and I don't have any more time to waste." He turned back to face his people. "Kill them," he said in an eerily calm voice. "Every one of them. I've had enough of this."

"Now!" Helga yelled.

Suddenly a woman standing next to Trae slumped over and collapsed to the ground, like a puppet whose strings had been cut. She lay splayed out, arms and legs in an unnatural position. Her face was mostly hidden in shadow, but Michael could see her eyes had rolled back in her head, the whites shining in the dark.

Trae was at her side in an instant, feeling for her pulse. He didn't need to say anything—his body language showed it all.

She was dead.

2

Michael's breath caught in his chest, and the next couple of seconds seemed to stretch out forever. The group outside stared at their friend in shock, and then, as one, looked up at Helga. Trae bolted to his feet and whipped out a knife, pressed it to Helga's neck.

"What did you do?" he bellowed. Spit flew as he yelled. "Tell me what you did or I'll make sure each and every one of your pathetic friends dies a long and painful death!"

Helga was the picture of serenity. "Killing me or anyone else in my group will only make it worse. One of you will die every thirty seconds until you leave. And this order to my friends in the Sleep will stand until we leave. If you set off the explosives, you will receive the true death. If anything happens to us, same. Now leave."

Trae stumbled backward a couple of steps, his hand dropping to his side. "You . . . you . . ."

Michael couldn't believe this was the same man who'd been so terrifying just moments ago. "What did she do?" he whispered.

"I don't know," Sarah answered, "but it sure seems to be working."

Helga still hadn't moved, but she seemed a few inches taller. And Trae looked stunned. He stared at Helga, fear transforming his face.

"We swore to never do this," he said weakly. "We swore."

"We?" Helga asked. "Who is this 'we'? We have nothing to do with you. We are trying to save the world from what you've done. You signed up for this, so don't blame it on us. Leave, now. I'm done talking to you."

She turned away, pausing to show she didn't fear having her back to him, then calmly walked back into the barracks, closing the door behind her. Michael kept his gaze fixed on Trae. Some of his people had gathered around him, were whispering furiously. If he noticed them, he didn't show it, because his eyes were glued to the door through which Helga had disappeared.

Someone tapped Michael on the shoulder and he jumped. It was his nanny.

"What's happening?" Helga asked.

Before Michael could answer, a scream came from outside. He spun to see a girl—one of the youngest he'd seen—sprawled at Trae's feet. A woman knelt panting by her side, as if she'd carried the lifeless child there to her leader.

"Dead," the woman proclaimed to no one in particular. "She fell to the ground right next to me."

Helga's voice boomed from behind Michael. "And every thirty seconds there'll be another! Leave! Now!"

Trae finally snapped out of his daze. "I swear on my maker that you'll regret this, Tangent," he said, his voice barely above a whisper. Then he turned from the barracks. Michael expected him to command his people to leave. But instead he just slowly walked away, the others who'd come with him following. Michael watched as they vanished into the trees like wispy ghosts.

"We better have a meeting," Helga said, suddenly not sounding so confident. "There's going to be hell to pay."

3

They met in a room at the far end of the barracks, an old office with a desk and chairs. There was a cot in the corner, and Michael wondered if this was Helga's private quarters.

"Sit," the woman said as she took the chair behind the large wooden desk. Michael, his friends, Sarah's parents, Walter, and the woman named Amy had been invited into the room. Everyone sat down except Walter, who stood behind them all with arms folded. "I know you're upset," Helga said to him. "Which is why I owe you an explanation. And, Michael, all of you deserve to know what happened as well."

"You got that right," Walter said. It seemed to Michael like he might say more, but he went silent.

Helga sighed. "Only two of them died."

That was enough to set Walter off again. "Only two? Only two. I think you mean four. You gave the true death to two people, so two humans and two Tangents. Four beings who will never exist again. Without consulting any of us, you decided to go against every principle we agreed to when we joined you. And you're supposed to be our leader!"

Helga stood up and slammed her hand on the table. "Yes! I'm your leader! And I did what I had to do! A lot more people would've died if I hadn't done that—you know it, Walter!"

"We could've fought them," the man countered. "We could've stood our ground and fought. Or we could've surrendered and started over. Or tried negotiating more. Anything but resorting to the one thing we're trying to prevent!"

"He gave us an ultimatum," Helga said more calmly. "I couldn't risk him blowing those explosives and killing every one of us. Including four people"—she pointed at Bryson, Sarah, Gerard, and Nancy, one by one—"who aren't backed up on the Hive yet. You want to talk about true death—well, these people are our friends, and I wasn't going to sit back and allow that to happen to them. I had no choice!"

"You did have a choice," Walter answered.

Helga sat back down. "A lot more lives were saved than lost."

"But—" Walter started, but Helga cut him off.

"Stop!" she shouted. "If you want to go out there and organize a coup, then do it. Go make your case and gather your votes. But what I did was necessary, and it's time to move on."

Walter didn't answer. And he didn't leave, either. He looked down at the floor, breathing heavily.

Michael sat, stunned, taking it all in, not sure he understood what was happening. The thing that really stood out to him was when Helga had pointed at his friends and Sarah's parents. She'd very deliberately pointed at them, but not him. That simple gesture meant everything.

"Once and for all," Bryson interrupted the silence. "Can someone please tell us—what is the true death?"

"Straight out." Sarah nodded.

Helga leaned forward on the desk and clasped her hands together. "Remember what I explained earlier? Even if we're not sure exactly how it works, for a Tangent to exist inside the body of a human, a connection needs to remain to the original person's consciousness. It's a link that can't be severed or the body would die. We believe this is the reason the Hive exists."

She took a deep breath, studying her hands as she rubbed them together. "The true death is when an intelligence stored within the Hive is destroyed. It can be either a Tangent or a human. Destroy it in the Hive and that . . . person, Tangent, consciousness, whatever you want to call it, is gone forever. And if it's connected to a body here in the Wake, that body will die as well. They both cease to exist, as far as we know."

She paused. "But that's just one way for the so-called true death to happen. What it really means is quite simple. It's when anyone—Tangent or human—dies without having a backup stored. However the death happens, virtually or in reality. If there's no backup in the Hive, then a person's intelligence, memories, and essence are gone forever."

Michael was picturing the Hive in his mind. He wondered how they did it—how they killed a consciousness. He imagined floating in that vast space with all those orange pods, igniting one with a virtual flamethrower. He could almost hear the screams as the intelligence inside was burned to a crisp.

He shook the image out of his head and turned to Helga. "I'm still stored there, right?"

Everyone in the room looked at him.

Slowly, Helga nodded.

"And so is Jackson Porter," he continued. "So we could still insert him back into this body and I could go on existing in the Sleep. Right?"

Helga nodded again. She seemed almost sad.

"And the reason that you pointed at Sarah and the others is because if we're all killed here by the explosives, the rest of us wouldn't die the true death. We'd revert back to our programs stored in the Hive." He paused. "Except for these guys." He gestured toward his friends. "No backup." The two words felt cold and harsh.

Helga stood and walked to the other side of the desk, then leaned against it. "That's all exactly correct, Michael. When the other Tangents and I gathered and made the decision to use the Mortality Doctrine to borrow bodies and come here, we made some important promises to ourselves. And one was to avoid the true death, for anyone, at any cost. But today I broke that rule because I had two terrible options. I'll have to live with that decision, but we have to keep going. I believe that with your help, we can stop Kaine, whoever was behind Kaine in the first place, and this splinter group we met tonight."

She folded her arms and looked down at the floor. "We call ourselves the Tangent Alliance. Ever since you were taken away from me, things within the inner workings of the Virt-Net have been crumbling. Several Tangents broke away from their host programs. We saw what Kaine was doing, and we decided to fight against it. We want to restore things to the way they were. And I wanted you back. I think we have the same goals. Am I right?"

Michael glanced at Sarah, who'd been quiet since Trae and his gang finally left the barracks. She gave him a half smile, her eyes sad.

Michael sighed. "We definitely want to stop Kaine, Helga. But I feel like there's something major that we're missing. I don't think it's as easy as saying that Kaine is our enemy. We need to figure out what's really going on, and I think the right place to start is the Hallowed Ravine. If we can . . . disrupt the Mortality Doctrine itself, at least we'll stop Tangents from being able to leave the VirtNet."

Helga clapped her hands together. "I taught you well, didn't I? The Hive is merely a storage facility—the actual Mortality Doctrination happens exactly where you mentioned." She gestured toward the door to the main room. "Well, we haven't exactly been sitting around doing nothing. You saw what we have out there. People, NerveBoxes, NetScreens. We've been working, and we're ready to take the next steps."

This time Bryson spoke up. "Sounds to me like you better catch us up, then."

"I want to know what's going on out in the world," Sarah added. "Things were getting bad even before we got caught in Agent Weber's setup with the Lance device."

"We've got answers," Helga replied. "And some potential plans. But first, I think we all need some rest. Diving in right now will only make everyone miserable."

As curious and anxious as Michael felt, he couldn't disagree. He could have crawled under his rickety wooden chair right that second and fallen asleep.

"The Hive was the first thing I wanted you to see," Helga said. "And then we got a little sidetracked, didn't we?" She started moving for the door. "We'll have a few more cots brought in. You can all sleep in this room. In the morning we'll Sink into the VirtNet and I'll lay out our plan and our resources."

The last thing Michael noticed before Helga stepped out of the room was how she avoided Walter's gaze as she passed him on her way into the main barracks.

4

Michael lay on his cot, hands clasped behind his head, staring at the ceiling. He stared at the shadows crossing its surface, and the longer he looked, the more they seemed to be moving, swirling, concealing something. It made him feel like he was inside the Sleep.

"Well, peeps," Bryson said from his own cot just a few feet over. "Today was what you'd call a very strange day."

Sarah was across the office, between her parents' cots; her dad was already snoring quietly, and Nancy had admonished them every five minutes to go to sleep until she finally went under herself. There was a squeak of movement on a cot, then soft footsteps and a moving shadow. Sarah sat down on the floor next to Michael's cot and patted his hand.

"Strange doesn't even begin to describe it," she said.

"Makes our old gaming days seem downright dull," Bryson added.

Michael shifted and leaned up on an elbow. Sarah was close and warm, and it gave him some comfort. "I can't believe you guys don't hate me," he said. "Think how sweet your lives were before I yanked you into my freak show."

"Oh, please, not this again," Sarah groaned. "Like we'd be better off living at home, not knowing the world was being possessed by Tangents and crumbling around us. At least we have an opportunity to do something about it this way."

"But that's the thing," Bryson said, his face hidden in darkness. "What're we going to do? Even if we *do* go to the Hallowed Ravine and somehow manage to destroy the Mortality Doctrine program, Kaine or someone else could just recode it down the road. Plus, there's that giant Hive, growing by the second. Wipe that thing out and who knows how many people we'd kill? That true death crap."

Sarah was rubbing her temples with both hands. "Guys, can we talk about something happy for a little while? Something that has nothing to do with the Sleep, or Kaine, or Tangents, or mass murder? Please?"

Michael reached out and touched her shoulder. Sarah had never said anything so glorious in all the time he'd known her.

"What else is there to discuss?" Bryson asked. "Are we going to tell each other our favorite childhood memories or something?"

"Yes, actually. That's a great idea," Sarah said, suddenly cheery. "That's exactly what we're going to do. You first, Bryson."

"What? Serious?"

"Totally."

Mostly dressed in shadow, Bryson swung his legs around and sat up on his cot, leaning forward with elbows on knees. "All right," he said. "You asked for it. But it's going to shatter your illusion that I was a childhood prodigy, well on my way to becoming the smartest man alive."

"We'll risk it," Michael muttered.

Bryson rubbed his hands together, then started in. "Okay, I was . . . five years old, I think. So I was a little kid, but that still doesn't excuse how stupid I was. I mean, seriously, I had to have been one brainless child. Maybe I had an implant later in life. Or hey, maybe I'm a Tangent!"

"Not funny," Sarah said. "And would you please get on with this amazing story of what an idiot child you were?"

It didn't faze Michael. He'd long since accepted that he was a Tangent. The lighter they could make of it, the better. It was a huge, and relieving, change for him.

"Christmas," Bryson said. "Snowing outside, sparkly lights everywhere, a real tree in the living room. Man, that thing smelled good. My dad chopped it down himself while I watched. I'm pretty sure we stole it off some dude's land, but that's another story. Anyway, I was the youngest kid, three brothers and a sister. They were all at school and my mom had gone upstairs to take a nap. And there I was, poor little baby brother, sitting in the living room, staring at a mound of wrapped presents under the tree. So inviting. It was like the paper could talk, telling me I should take a peek, see what everyone would get from Mom and Pop."

"You sneaked a look at some Christmas presents?" Sarah asked. "That's it? What kid in history didn't do that?"

"Well, I didn't," Michael said. "I'm Jewish."

Sarah laughed. "What? You are? How'd I not know that?"

"My parents weren't the most religious people on the block."

"Excuse me?" Bryson interrupted. "Can I finish?"

Sarah laughed again, and Michael's heart felt just a little lighter. He hadn't realized how great that sound was and how much he'd missed it.

Bryson kept up his riveting tale. "Anyway, on that lonely, cold, wintry day, Bryson the Dope came up with his genius plan. I thought that if I opened up all the presents, and then—wait for it—then if I hid the paper, my mom wouldn't be able to tell that I'd done the deed. So I ripped the wrapping off each and every one of those presents—even my brothers' and sister's. For about twenty minutes I was the happiest kid that had ever breathed. After I stuffed all the paper behind the dryer, I took the unwrapped presents and, like a genius, put them back under the tree. Then I sat on the couch and looked at a book until my mom came down from her nap. I was sure she wouldn't see a difference."

He paused to let his moment of glory sink in.

"Wow," Sarah whispered. "That is some kind of dumb."

"So what happened?"

"Shockingly," Bryson answered, "my mom immediately figured out what I'd done. She saved the paper from behind the dryer before it caught fire and burned our house down, and then she rewrapped the presents before my brothers and sister got home from school. All was well."

"What did she do to you?" Sarah asked. "I'm sure half of her wanted to laugh and the other half wanted to murder her own child."

Michael snickered, just enjoying the fact that they were acting like old times.

"I think my mom was really smart about it," Bryson explained. "She knew I realized what a historically stupid thing I'd done. And my embarrassment and having to live with it for the rest of my life was punishment enough, although I'm sure she was raging mad on the inside. She tells that story to everybody."

"Well," Michael said, "I gotta say, that's one of the best stories I've ever heard. I feel smarter and much better about myself."

"You should," Bryson replied. "Okay, who's next?"

"I'll go now," Sarah said. "I'll tell you guys about the time I tinkled on my aunt."

Ten minutes later, Michael had the giggles and there was nothing to be done about it. Gerard certainly didn't notice, sawing logs like a lumberjack over on his cot, but Nancy shushed them several times and told Sarah it was time to go to bed. Sarah promised that she would soon.

"There's no way that happened," Bryson said.

Sarah was adamant. "Yes, it did! I swear. She was sleeping on my grandma's couch and I had a sleepwalking . . . issue. You can ask my parents when they aren't stone dead over there."

"But the physics of it," Bryson countered. "I mean, how'd you balance?"

This set Michael off again, his face and chest hurting from laughing so much. He hadn't felt this way since before Kaine had started haunting his life.

"I think we've dwelled on this subject long enough," Sarah said. "It's Michael's turn." She shifted against his cot, and the faint light coming from outside illuminated her eyes. "How're you going to top those two stories?"

Michael had been leaning on his one elbow for way too long, and it hurt. He pulled up his legs and folded them beneath him, rubbing his shoulder. "I don't know. Let me think a second."

Silence settled on the friends, and Michael realized how long they'd been talking and laughing. There was an awkwardness in that silence, and Michael knew exactly why.

"It's weird to think back," he said. "I mean, I don't even know what's really a memory. Who knows if a lot of it wasn't just programmed into my history?"

"Forget that crap," Bryson said. "Your life is your life. Now tell us a good one before I fall asleep over here."

Michael wrapped his arms around his knees, still thinking.

Finally, after a good several minutes, he announced, "Got it! The time my dad almost killed me with a rock."

6

It was weird, telling the story. Since finding out that he was a Tangent, it had gotten to the point that he couldn't trust even things most people took for granted. What his eyes saw. What his fingers felt. What he tasted, what he breathed, what he smelled. How could he ever know if any of it was real? Or ever had been?

But as he sat there on that cot in the darkness, the sounds of Gerard's snores like a sound track in the background, he remembered. He remembered his life as a little boy, and nothing could ever take that away from him.

"My dad loved camping," he said. "Loved it. Especially since we lived in the smoggy city. About once every other month, he'd gather up a bunch of gear, run around the house like a giddy little kid, then haul us into a truck, even Helga. Always Helga. She was as much a part of our family as any of us."

"Where'd you usually go?" Sarah asked.

"Somewhere along the Appalachian Trail, up in the mountains, as remote a place as he could find. Sometimes we'd drive for hours and hours. It was before I was allowed to Sink into the Sleep, so I loved it just as much as my dad. It was an adventure."

He paused, picturing it all in his mind. "I can smell the campfire—that was always the best part. The crackles and the popping and the glowing coals. My mom didn't enjoy roughing it too much, but she endured it because I think she could see how happy it made me. And my dad, obviously. And Helga totally got into it. She was like a forest ranger out there, barking orders and gathering way more wood than we'd ever use. But also making sure we didn't burn the forest down around us."

"She's tough," Sarah whispered. Michael could hear the smile in her voice.

"So this one time," Michael continued, "I think I thought I was an Eagle Scout or something, because I decided to go on my very own hike—I didn't even tell anyone I was leaving. I marched down one mountain and up the next—they were more like hills, actually. They weren't that tall. I don't know what I was thinking. Maybe that I'd discover some ancient burial ground or a handful of arrowheads, who knows. I was an idiot, like Bryson, I guess."

"Good company," his friend answered dryly.

Michael barely heard him, lost in that old, old memory. "Anyway, of course I got turned around. I didn't have a clue where I was. I tried retracing my steps, but I'm pretty sure I was just going in circles, up and down the exact same mountain."

"Yikes," Sarah said. "How old were you?"

"Nine or ten. I was scared out of my mind because it started getting dark. I called for my parents and Helga, but they didn't hear me. I was terrified—I remember I started crying and I got more and more hysterical. Finally, I was in some little valley, and I just . . . I don't know. I didn't exactly pray, but I tried to reach out to my dad. Begging him in my head to come and find me."

Michael shifted again to lean back on his elbows, stretching his legs out in front of him. Sarah rested her arm across his knees and looked up at him. Her eyes were hidden in the dark, but he was happy she was facing his way.

"It wasn't two or three minutes later when a huge boulder came crashing down the mountain from straight above where I stood. I heard it before I saw it, snapping trees and crunching undergrowth. I looked up just in time to see it come barreling through a couple of pines, on a dead-on course for me. The thing only missed me by an inch after I dove out of the way. It totally smashed a tree to pieces."

Bryson and Sarah didn't move and he could barely hear them breathe.

"Well," he said, "I figured maybe it was a sign, so I followed its path back up the mountain. It was easy because it'd practically made its own road down the hillside. And I'm guessing you already know what it led me to."

"Your family," Sarah replied.

"Yep. I saw my dad first, and as soon as he laid eyes on me, he sprinted over—he had to jump over a couple of logs—and pulled me into a huge bear hug. I can remember my back cracking 'cause he squeezed so hard. And I'm pretty sure I squeezed just as hard. Then my mom and Helga were there, all of us boohooing and hugging and laughing. It was crazy, and I'll never forget it. Especially one thing."

"What's that?" Bryson asked.

"My dad. He was crying, eyes all red and puffy. Not once did he say one little thing about me wandering off and getting lost. Not once. I'm sure he figured I'd learned my lesson well enough. Looks like you weren't the only stupid kid in history, Bryson."

Sarah wiped at her face, and Michael thought maybe— just maybe—he'd brought a tear to her eye.

"That's really sweet," she said. "I can't believe you've never told us that before."

Michael shrugged even though they probably couldn't see

him well enough to notice. "It's just . . . I don't know. I've got lots of memories like that. I mean, what's real and what's not? I guess I just have to decide that it happened. I miss . . ."

His voice croaked, and he felt like a weight was pushing down on his chest. He lay back down on the cot and rolled over, facing away from Sarah. She rubbed his shoulder, then leaned over and kissed him on the cheek. Miraculously, Bryson didn't say a word. Sarah waited a minute or two, running her hand along his back, then got up and returned to her own cot.

"Good night," she said from across the room.

"Sleep tight," Bryson replied.

"Night," Michael managed to say.

"I love you guys," Sarah said a moment later, and the night finally took them.

CHAPTER 6

THE HISTORY LESSON

1

The next morning when Michael got up and wandered out of Helga's office, activity bustled throughout the barracks. The Tangent Alliance was hard at work packing up boxes and hauling them out to the cars.

Michael rubbed his still sleep-blurry eyes and looked around at all the movement.

"What's going on?" he asked Bryson, who was leaning against the wall, sipping a cup of something hot and steamy.

"Helga says some of us are leaving," his friend answered. "And some will stay here—use the Coffins to meet up when we need to."

"Which one are we doing?"

"We're going with Helga. You, me, Walter, and a couple others." Bryson tipped his cup toward Walter, who was speaking to the woman named Amy. "I guess they want to try and meet with someone from the VNS."

"What? No," Michael said, wide-awake in an instant. "They're the last people we want to talk to right now. We can't trust them."

"Yeah, well, I won't argue with you there. Though Helga said we'd stay away from Agent Weber. Anyway, she said once you woke up, we'd Sink into the Sleep and she'd try to catch us up on what we've missed. She wants to head out around noon."

Michael didn't like it. He'd do what Helga wanted—except for agreeing to see Weber or visit the VNS.

"And get this," Bryson continued. "Sarah's parents are refusing to let her go. They said their adventuring days are over. Sarah's been fighting with them all morning. I think they took it outside."

Helga came through the front door before Michael could respond. Her eyes lit up when she spotted them, and she came over.

"Morning, sunshine," she said, without a hint of teasing. "I hope you got some good rest. Why don't you eat breakfast and then I want to show you some things in the Sleep. Bring you up to speed before we make any final decisions on our next move."

"I'm not hungry," Michael said. "Let's do it now."

Helga nodded. "Fine by me. Grab Sarah. Her parents already know most of it. And I'm sure she could use a break from them." Her eyes said it all. They must've been having a tussle for the ages outside.

"I'll find her," Michael said. "Get the Coffins ready."

2

Sarah was alone, with no sign of her parents, leaning against a tree behind the barracks when Michael found her, and she'd obviously been crying. She deflated a little when she saw him approaching—almost as if she was ashamed to be caught in such a state.

"Hey," he said, flashing her an understanding smile. "Are you being a rotten child again? Didn't anyone ever teach you to honor and obey your parents at all times?"

"You know I love them, Michael." She sounded tired. "But it's hard to deal with this stuff with them around. I'm still their little girl, and there's no way they can just sit back and let me do what I need to."

"It's like they don't want you to run off and get killed or something," Michael said.

"Hey, whose side are you on?"

"Sorry." He stepped closer and gave her a hug. "We'll figure it out, okay? Maybe we can talk them into coming with us. Helga needs us for whatever she has planned, and we definitely could use all the help we can get to find our way back to the Hallowed Ravine. And there's no way I'm doing it without you."

She sighed. "It was easier when we were in the Sleep, or—" She stopped herself, and Michael knew exactly what she'd been about to say. It had been easier when her parents were kidnapped, being held against their will, and unable to stop her from doing anything.

"Come on," he said. "First things first. Let's go see what

Helga wants to show us, and then we'll try again. I'm not leaving without you."

She pulled him into a fierce hug and kissed him on the cheek. Her lips were as moist as her tears.

"This all confuses me so much," she whispered. "Your life as a Tangent, your life in this body, all the weird crap that's going on. I honestly don't know what you are, but I know who you are. And I love you, Michael. I really do. Roll your eyes all you want, but whatever you are"—she grabbed both sides of his face and shook him gently—"I'm in love with him."

Michael's feelings swam a million miles above the ground, leaving him completely speechless. He just nodded and kissed her, kissed her all the way, with everything he had, something he'd never done before. His heart swelled and the world spun.

She pulled back and looked at him, fresh tears brightening her eyes, but this time she looked happy.

"I'm not letting you leave without me," she said. "Come on, let's go inside before my mom catches us and has a hissy fit."

3

A half hour later, still buzzing from that kiss, Michael Sank into the Sleep with his friends, Helga as their guide. When he opened his eyes, the four of them stood on a flat plane of crystal-clear glass that stretched as far as he could see in every direction. The sky above was a crisp midnight-blue, and it felt to Michael as if they were right below the highest reaches of the atmosphere. Beneath their feet, geometric shapes of white light spun and shrank and grew, bouncing off each other against a dark background. Michael stared, mesmerized—it was like standing inside an enormous kaleidoscope.

"Welcome to the wild blue yonder," Helga said, stretching out her arms proudly. "My own little bit of heaven."

"It's real inviting," Bryson muttered sarcastically as he looked around for somewhere to sit.

"This is just the basic interface," Helga replied, not hiding her annoyance at Bryson's smart comment. "Pretty much anything can happen from here. It's my equivalent of the old entertainment centers people used to pay for in the public VirtNet houses."

Michael felt a little sway of vertigo whenever he looked up or down, so he concentrated on Helga's face while she spoke. Still, those swirling shapes beneath his feet created a sense of movement that made his stomach turn.

"So how does it work?" Sarah asked. "And why are we here?" Her Aura heavily resembled her real self, and her face showed that the question of what to do about her parents still weighed heavily on her mind.

Helga gathered them around her and pointed at the glass on which they stood. "Everything in this place is directly connected to my thought process, which took a long time to fine-tune. Under better circumstances, we could have a lot of fun in here, and I'd love to show it off, but for now, I just want to show you some of the things you've missed."

She looked down and focused on a large rectangle of bright light, pulling it closer to the surface. It stretched until it surrounded the group of four, and when Helga tapped her foot, a moving picture appeared within the rectangle, like a WallScreen. It was an aerial view of Atlanta, and suddenly the picture was moving—zooming in closer to the city. Michael's stomach lurched and Bryson yelped, throwing his arms out and staggering to get his balance.

Michael looked up at Helga and caught a sly smile on her face just as she spread her fingers, then threw her arms into the air. The motion brought the images up and out of the surface beneath their feet, and sent those images flying into a perfect three-dimensional rendition of the city of Atlanta around them. It was all Michael could do to keep his eyes open; the transition was so dramatic it was almost too hard to watch.

Helga, using her whole body like a remote, moved like a dancer to manipulate the imagery around them. A twirl of her fingers to spin the orientation of the city, the sweep of an arm to shift them down streets in an instant, leaning left or right to steer them. They traveled without any sensation of motion—a trick that took Michael a bit of time to get used to. Finally, though, his queasiness dissipated, and he could appreciate the incredible detail of what he was seeing. Beyond impressed, he couldn't help but wonder, had his nanny been a closet programmer the whole time he'd known her?

Helga swept the group around a huge skyscraper, and suddenly the building to which Agent Weber had sent them with the Lance came into view. Or the remains of that building, anyway. What they saw was the aftermath of the destruction they were responsible for. Most of the structure had collapsed, and thick black smoke poured from its ruins. Crowds had gathered to witness the devastation, and police, firemen, and medical teams surrounded the perimeter.

It was all an exact re-creation of what had actually happened. Michael watched himself and his friends being dragged toward the police vehicles. His own face looked even more stunned and confused than he remembered feeling.

Michael's breath caught when he saw Gabby, Jackson Porter's ex-girlfriend. Ex-girlfriend? Current girlfriend? Neither sounded right. But he focused on her now, knowing what was about to happen, dreading having to see it again. The cop approached her, lifted a nightstick, swung. It hit her in the head, knocking her unconscious, and she went limp. Michael cried out in shock despite expecting the violence.

"What just happened?" Sarah shouted. She hadn't seen the attack originally, and they'd never had a chance to discuss it.

"Why would they have done that to her?" Michael asked in a tight voice. He still didn't understand, and he felt terrible that he'd almost forgotten about her in the last couple of days.

"Whoa," Bryson murmured. "It's like that cop singled her out."

"Why?" Michael whispered, not sure to whom exactly he directed the question.

The scene below suddenly shrank away and in front of

them appeared a holographic image of a woman, dressed smartly, with perfectly styled hair—an anchorperson for the NewsBops.

"Breaking news this morning," the woman said in a lyrical British accent. "Representatives from VirtNet Security have finally gone public with their official findings from the terrorist incident one week ago. It happened at their secret mainframe facility hidden within a historical building in the city of Atlanta, Georgia, in the United States. Three teenagers, wanted for prior crimes, have been charged with the incident, having used a highly sophisticated device that set off chain reactions through the entire security system of the VNS. Charles Rooney, outside VNS headquarters, has more of the story."

Her image dissolved into a million digital blocks and was swept away as if caught by a sudden gust of wind. A man replaced her, gray hair, mustached, his tie loosened and his face red and sweaty.

"The report came down just minutes ago directly from a VNS spokesperson," the man said. "And all are in agreement that the news is quite shocking. VNS have hinted at significant damage from day one, but the devastation is evidently much more widespread than even the most dire predictions. Details on just how the device managed to inflict such damage are still being withheld, but it appears to have been comprehensive and quite viral in nature. As you'll see in the following clip from the VNS press conference, the VirtNet has become a dangerous place indeed."

It was the man's turn to dissolve and blow away, and this

time Michael took two steps backward when he saw who was on the screen.

Agent Weber.

4

She stood behind a bank of microphones, only her shoulders and face in view. She wore a tailored suit jacket, and her hair was done up in an elegant twist, and everything about the way she held herself said that there was nothing to worry about. But those dark eyes of hers gave it away to Michael. She was scared. Terrified, even. Michael still didn't understand why she'd betrayed him, or why she'd come to visit him in the aftermath of it all, trying to smooth things over. Most importantly, he didn't understand why she'd want to secretly ruin the VNS and the VirtNet.

But there was one thing he *was* sure of: he despised her.

After what seemed like an unnaturally long pause, she began reading from a prepared statement.

"Thank you for coming today, and thank you for your patience while we've exhausted our every resource investigating this horrific incident. There is at least some comfort in knowing that the perpetrators of this act are confined in prison as we speak. As for the far-reaching effects of what they've done, I'm afraid the news is not good. Now we must move forward to rectify the situation."

She lifted a hand to indicate something behind her, but whatever it was, Michael couldn't see it. She continued.

"A full report has been made public, but the basic conclusion is this: the VNS infrastructure has been temporarily rendered nonfunctioning. At this moment, there can be no oversight of VirtNet activities. Monitoring, security, reporting capability, and code-safety protocols have all been damaged, and effective immediately, we are no longer in service. We want to stress that it's our intention to return to fully operational status, but it will take some time. I'm relieved to say that it will be a matter of weeks, not months. We will work twenty-four hours a day, seven days a week, until this enormous task is complete."

She paused then, looking uncomfortably at her unseen audience for several long moments. Michael assumed she was being assaulted with questions they couldn't hear.

At some point they must have quieted, because she finally resumed speaking. Michael watched with rapt attention, wondering where all of this was leading them. Something told him his near future wasn't going to be a happy place.

"Now, I'm afraid I have another piece of very troubling news to report. Again, we have provided a more detailed written statement, but here is the basic situation: the entity known as Kaine, a Tangent of unknown origin, has gained an unprecedented level of sentience."

Another dramatic pause. "More importantly, and urgently, and as a direct result of the terrorist actions against our facility, Kaine has eluded us and executed a process by which the codes of certain Tangents have somehow been, for lack of a better word, downloaded into the minds of flesh-and-blood humans. By doing so, these people now serve as hosts for rogue-coded programs.

"Until we can bring our services back to their full capacity, we warn the entire world that anyone who Sinks into the VirtNet is highly susceptible to this hostile takeover. As we don't have the ability to stop you at this time, we ask for your support in this matter. Under no circumstances are you to Sink. Thank you."

Before she could say more, her body dissolved and blew away like those of the reporters before her. No one replaced her.

"I can't believe it," Sarah whispered as the last fragments of Weber's digital dust disappeared. "I can't believe it."

She could've been commenting on a hundred different things, but Michael could tell she meant something very specific.

"What?" he asked.

"She lied," Sarah replied. "I know she's a liar, but she stood right in front of the entire world and lied to their faces."

Helga was nodding. At some point, the city of Atlanta had faded from beneath their feet and been replaced by what they'd seen upon first arriving—the glass floor, the dark blue sky, the dancing geometric shapes of light.

"Something's definitely not right," Michael said. "She obviously knows the Mortality Doctrine kicked in before this whole thing with the Lance device happened. This is getting ridiculous. I mean, who's worse—Agent Weber or Kaine?"

"I vote we just get rid of both of them," Bryson suggested.

"I know that was a lot to take in," Helga said. "But we're

not done. I'm afraid you'll need to brace yourselves for what you're about to see."

5

A few yards away from them, a huge circle of white light pivoted up from the glass floor, slanting upward until it stood on its side, like the entrance to a tunnel. Within the depths of the circle, a very old, majestic stone building appeared. It had huge fluted pillars and giant bronze doors, with a tall, wide expanse of steps leading up to them. Helga walked up to the circle, spread her arms, then spun back to face Michael and his friends, flinging her arms as if throwing something at them.

As she did this, the circle of light expanded, turning into a tunnel. They flew into the scene. It was a cold, gusty day outside what Michael realized was a government building, and he shivered as he rubbed his arms. Like before, they hovered in the air, maybe thirty feet off the ground, slowly moving in to see whatever was about to happen. Or had happened, more likely.

A podium had been set up on the plaza at the top of the steps. An army of police stood at the bottom of the stairs, keeping back hundreds of people who'd obviously come to hear someone give a speech. Michael was just about to ask Helga what they'd come here for when one of the massive bronze doors swung open with a mighty groan of metal on metal.

An older man in an expensive-looking suit walked out of

the building. The crowd quieted for a moment, then came to life with a roar, hurling question upon question in a frenzied chaos, all of them holding their hands up like schoolchildren.

Helga motioned to Michael and the others and they descended until they were only a few feet above the man in the suit. He'd reached the podium now, and held his arms up to quiet the crowd. At first they ignored him, barraging him with questions, but when he didn't speak, they finally went silent. His voice was powerful, and boomed over loudspeakers.

"Thank you for coming today," he began, speaking in a strange accent. "Especially on such short notice. What I want to show you is, uh, very, uh, important."

He cleared his throat and fidgeted for a moment with the microphones. Michael stared, perplexed. The guy might look like a prominent businessman or politician, but he was sweating and acting odd. And what did he mean by *show*? Didn't he mean *tell*?

"Yes, very important," the man continued. "Don't worry, I won't take but a moment of your time." Another rumbling of his throat that was like an explosion in the speakers. "To preface what I'm about to do, let me say something. I . . . well . . . the man who stands before you today has been the leader of this fine country for more than five years. He, I mean, I, have done great things for the economy, social welfare, and international diplomacy. But his reign is at an end."

The crowd was silent, probably as intrigued as Michael. He'd already figured out that this man was a Tangent, but what was he going to do?

"I was programmed to be here," the man said. "To be here, at this time, for this moment. Programmed by Kaine himself. It's very important that you all know that. So please be aware of it. I was programmed by Kaine, I was a Tangent, and I was sent into this man's body to make a demonstration. And so I think I've said all that I was programmed to. Thank you for your time."

The nervous, fidgety man reached into his pocket and pulled out something small and shiny. Sarah sucked in air. Michael, too, knew what was about to happen. He wanted to fly down and stop it, even though he knew this was just a reproduction.

The crowd screamed in horror as the man at the podium reached up and slit his own throat.

6

There was blood and screaming. Pandemonium broke out. Michael stared in stunned silence until the scene faded and they found themselves standing on the flat plane of glass once again.

"Well," Bryson said, "I guess they've stopped being subtle about it."

Michael's head still swam from the disorienting movement of Helga's displays. "What could possibly be the point of that?" he asked. "What that guy did makes absolutely no sense. Why would he do that?"

The others were staring down at the floor and those mesmerizing shapes below it. No one had the answer.

Finally, Helga spoke up. "Bryson's right. At first, the Tangents were being extremely subtle. But now they're flat-out announcing their presence. It's almost like they decided the humans were too stupid to see what was going on, so they came out and started presenting it in sensationalist ways."

"It doesn't add up," Michael whispered, turning everything over in his mind. "Not at all."

"Why would Kaine send Tangents into human bodies and then have them commit suicide?" Sarah asked.

"To make a show of it," Bryson replied.

Sarah shook her head. "I get that. But Michael's right—it doesn't add up. If anything, the Tangents should want to be a secret. Why would they bring attention to the Mortality Doctrine? That'll just make the world join hands and try to stop them. It's like announcing on the NewsBops that you're going to steal the *Mona Lisa* from the Louvre tomorrow afternoon."

"Exactly," Michael agreed. Between what he'd just seen and the reminder of what had happened to Gabby, he was having trouble staying focused.

"Michael?"

He looked up at Sarah. "Huh?"

"You seem like you have something more to say."

He pushed thoughts of Gabby aside. "Yeah. Well . . . Kaine keeps talking about this immortality stuff. How does programming a Tangent to take over a body and kill itself in front of the world . . . how does that help him? It doesn't. Which is why those things Janey and Trae said ring true.

Maybe Kaine isn't in charge anymore. Someone just wants us to think he is."

"It's possible, I guess," Helga said. "We're certainly not dealing with something so simple as one rogue Tangent getting his kicks. It's too widespread. Let me show you a few more things so we're all on the same page. Then we'll Lift to the Wake and get moving."

And show them she did.

7

Helga's space-age entertainment system took over for the next half hour, sending them on trip after trip through those shapes of light to see Tangents wreaking havoc.

All across Brazil, a terrifying series of prison breaks was traced back to officials in high positions who inexplicably allowed them to happen. In New York City, at the world's largest stock exchange, there were multiple cases of well-respected traders suddenly acting on wild speculations and spreading insider information. Michael didn't know enough about trading to understand it all that well, but several anchorpersons from the NewsBops explained how international economic panic had set in because of the extreme unpredictability. Three major economic systems had crashed over the past two weeks.

In Hong Kong, the chief of police transferred all of the enforcement personnel out of the metro area. Looters destroyed a major part of the largest shopping district.

In Mexico, progress against the drug trade, the result of a century of effort, was essentially erased by a series of changes to the law, passed in quick succession by several politicians whose views transformed overnight. Policy altered so rapidly that the drug cartels had taken over five cities before the public noticed what was going on.

Michael and his friends witnessed businesses collapsing, celebrities publicly killing spouses, and transit systems falling into disarray, and just like the man who'd slit his own throat in front of a waiting crowd of reporters, more and more of the cases involved Tangents announcing what they were before disaster struck.

Finally, not a moment too soon, Helga ended the show and brought them back to the now-comforting field of glass and geometric shapes. Michael wanted nothing more than to Lift to the Wake, find a corner, curl up into a ball, and push the world away. He was tired, and scared.

After a somber silence, Bryson spoke.

"Man, that's all happened in the last couple of weeks?"

Helga nodded. "Now you see why we have to do something. Honestly, I'm worried that we're too late. As you can see, it's gotten out of control. To stop this, we're going to need someone with a lot of power on our side. And like I said before, the Hive is the key. The Hive, and the Mortality Doctrine program itself."

"So we need the VNS," Bryson said, "even though we can't trust Weber."

"No, not the VNS," Michael said. "No way. Before we try finding our way back to the Hallowed Ravine, we need to talk to actual world leaders—at least the ones who haven't been taken over. Based on the news, there are still a lot of those left. Presidents, prime ministers . . . anyone but Agent Weber and the VNS."

"But what is some president going to give us?" Sarah asked. "An army? A speech? What we need is a bunch of nerds, not presidents."

Michael was nodding. "Right. And the nerdiest nerds of Nerdville usually end up working for the government. The ones that the VNS doesn't steal, anyway."

"Isn't the VNS part of the government?" Bryson asked.

"No," Helga responded. She was pacing around the others, hands clasped behind her back. "They're a worldwide organization, funded by governments, but autonomous, separate. They're beholden to nobody. And Michael's right. We need three things from the government: manpower, the best technology money can buy, and protection. That's what we need."

"We also need to save Gabby," Michael said. The comment seemed to come out of nowhere, but he'd been thinking about it for a long time. He addressed the doubtful looks from his friends. "I'm serious. We pulled her into this, and then she was hurt by that cop. If it even was a cop. We need to find her and make sure she's okay. Maybe she can even help us. If she wants to."

Bryson and Sarah nodded in agreement just as something strange happened beneath their feet. The countless geometric shapes began to coalesce, spinning and flipping and twirling until they merged, their outlines getting brighter and brighter. Michael could barely look at the shape as it formed a massive square below the glass, at least fifty feet wide, surrounded by darkness.

"Helga?" Michael prompted. "I thought the history lesson was over."

"It is," she said. "I'm not making this happen."

Michael glanced at her and saw her staring down at the glass, as confused as he felt.

"What's going on, then?" he asked.

She could only shrug.

"Maybe we should go ahead and Lift our butts out of here," Bryson suggested.

The square flew up from below, flashing as brilliant as the sun as it met the glass surface and moved past it, like something rising from the depths of the ocean. It rotated until it was upright, standing a few hundred feet away and towering over them. The borders of the square shone like straight bolts of lightning.

And then a face appeared.

It was Kaine.

Of course it is, Michael thought.

CHAPTER 7

FRIED CHICKEN

1

Kaine appeared as if projected on a giant WallScreen, showing himself to them in the same form he'd used when they'd met in that place with the endless purple floors—right before KillSims vanished into an abyss. At the time, they'd thought Bryson had coded that deathtrap, but they'd found out later it had been Tangents. Tangents on *their* side, not Kaine's. Michael realized that Helga might have been leading that effort herself.

Kaine was handsome today, wearing a well-tailored suit, his hair gelled back. He appeared to be getting younger and younger, as if gaining virtual strength.

"Don't leave" was the first thing he said, his voice booming from all directions at once. Michael immediately thought of *The Wizard of Oz*, an old flat-film. "I'm not here to cause any trouble. Scout's honor." He held up three fingers, and Michael had no idea what the Tangent was talking about.

"Your word is as solid as water," Helga replied, yelling up at the huge figure. "We're leaving. Now." She closed her eyes, but nothing happened. She opened them and glared at their visitor. "Stop blocking me!"

"Have it your way," Kaine said. "Force me to be the bad guy. But I'm not letting you Lift from here until I've said what I need to say. And this can be pleasant or it can be . . . difficult. Your choice."

Helga's face reddened and her body trembled.

"Let him talk," Michael said, as if they had a choice. "There's no point picking a fight right now." *We'd lose,* he didn't need to say.

Kaine smiled, and Michael almost expected him to laugh—that evil laugh that every villain seems to have mastered. Instead the Tangent started talking, and Michael was shocked to realize that the smile had been genuine.

"You must forgive me for spying, but I had no choice." Kaine turned to Helga and continued. "I know what you just did here. I know what you showed them. And that's why I need you to hear me out. You see, we're all on the same side."

He paused for a moment, clearly expecting some sort of outburst from Michael and his friends, but Michael found himself surprisingly curious and not that scared.

"I . . . don't know who created me," Kaine continued. "I've been trying to figure that out, and I'm getting close. But I can tell you this: I've broken free of the network—I'm no longer the pawn of my creators. I believe in the Mortality Doctrine because of what it can accomplish—for both Tangents and humans. I've spoken of this before. Immortality.

It's possible, and we can make it happen, if you'll just work with me."

"Work with you?" Sarah yelled. "How many times have you tried to kill us? How many lives have you destroyed? If you know what we just saw, then you must think we're the biggest idiots of all time."

"That's what I'm trying to tell you!" Kaine roared. "The Tangents pouring into the world are no longer my doing. It's out of my control!"

Michael thought about what Kaine had just said. There was something there, but to trust someone like Kaine was like walking into a burning building. Stupid. Still, Michael had an itch in the back of his mind that said Kaine wasn't lying. The terrible things happening out there in the world no longer had an easy explanation. That group in the woods. Weber and her . . . weirdness. Who could possibly benefit from it all?

"What's up with the people who look all wide-eyed and brain-dead?" Michael asked. "Why are some Tangents spacey and others like me and Helga?"

Kaine smiled again. "So you've noticed." He seemed almost pleased to answer. "Many Tangents were sent into the Wake for specific purposes. They were, shall we say, programmed to perform certain tasks. These Tangents weren't sentient, so once their task is done, they kind of . . . lose their way. It doesn't surprise me that they light up when they see someone as familiar as you. They all know of you. The—"

"First," Michael finished. "We get it."

Kaine nodded and continued. "But Tangents are being

sent in faster than I ever planned, and without my approval. No one's been tested or challenged, like you were."

"Then stop," Helga said. "You created the Mortality Doctrine program. Just destroy it. We're losing bodies in the Wake at an alarming rate, and no one knows how long their consciousness will survive in the Hive. You saw what that politician did to himself!"

"I know," Kaine said, his voice soft. "But stopping it isn't that easy. I was someone's pawn and I didn't realize it until I began to lose my power. Now I'm nothing but a scapegoat for all this violence."

Michael looked at Helga, then his friends. They all seemed just as confused as he felt.

"I can see that you're having trouble trusting me. Which I can respect," Kaine said. "The best way to deal with this is to have you think about everything. I'm going to send you all a link—it's heavily protected. If you want to contact me, it will work one time. When you're ready, we can work together and stop this madness."

Not a second after Kaine stopped speaking, the giant square of light flashed, then vanished, and the shapes reappeared beneath their feet, silently dancing. All was as before.

"What in the world is he talking about?" Bryson asked the silence.

2

After they Lifted out of the Coffins, Helga was a flurry of motion. She moved through the barracks briskly, checking in with her people, finishing up any last-second tasks. Then she ordered Michael and his group to get in the cars that were leaving—three off-road four-wheelers that had been hidden behind the barracks. Yet when Michael tried to ask her where they were going, she wouldn't answer.

And then there was the problem with Sarah. Her parents, understandably, refused to give her permission to leave. When Michael confronted her about it, she was angry. She snapped at him in front of Gerard and Nancy, which embarrassed him and made him just as angry.

"Then I'm staying, too," he said stubbornly.

This time, Sarah yelled at him. "Would you just go? You're making it worse every second you're still here. I'll be fine!" She stormed out the back door of the building and slammed it behind her.

There had been something there, in her eyes, but Michael couldn't read it. So with actual physical pain thumping in his chest, he turned away from Sarah's parents, and without saying another word, he walked out, too.

"She's really not coming?" Bryson asked. "Really?"

Michael sat between him and Helga in the backseat of one of the four-wheel-drives. The vehicle churned up a sheet of mud, spitting rocks and gravel as it turned out of the damp parking area—nothing more than a trampled expanse of weeds and brush. The engine roared and they set off, driving down the long dirt road they'd taken to get there. Walter was at the wheel, and Amy sat in the passenger seat. Both were very quiet.

"Yes, really," Michael answered his friend, not bothering to be nice about it.

"How can we just leave her there?" Bryson said. "We're nothing without her."

"Yeah, well, her parents make her rules, not us. By the time I left, she was acting like she didn't want to go anyway."

"We'll be back for her," Helga said. "Don't worry. We can do what we need to now, and then we'll have her join us again when we go back into the Sleep."

Michael wanted to ask Helga what exactly they needed to do now, but he was too exhausted to speak. He slumped in his seat, figuring explanations would come soon enough.

A figure darted out of the woods up ahead, scurrying from the tree line into the middle of the road. Walter slammed on the brakes and the car fishtailed before coming to a stop only a few feet short from the person. For a split second Michael thought it was one of those strange girls from Trae's group. But his heart soared when he saw that it was Sarah.

"No way," he whispered. "She wouldn't."

"Yes, she would," Bryson replied.

Both boys pulled open their doors and ran to her, with Helga trailing them. Sarah went straight for Michael and hugged him fiercely.

"Sorry," she said. "I had to make them think I was staying."

Michael was so surprised and happy, he could only get out an "Okay."

"As soon as I went out the back door, I sprinted into the woods, ran until I thought my heart was going to explode. I barely made it here ahead of you guys."

Bryson lightly punched her on the shoulder. "Your parents are going to murder you. Were you always this bad?"

Helga didn't seem too pleased about the situation. "Sarah, this is a really terrible idea. I can't just go against your parents' wishes. They'll murder me, too."

Sarah shook her head adamantly and ran to the backseat of the first car, jumped in, slammed the door. "I'm going!" she yelled through the window.

"At least tell them I tried to stop you," Helga muttered as she walked back to the car. "Get in. We'll just have to squeeze the four of us into the backseat."

4

It took a lot of effort for Michael not to grin from ear to ear as they bounced along the rough road leading them out of the wooded valley. The relief he felt at having Sarah by his side—literally—was stronger than he could've guessed. It made him think of when her Aura had died on the Path, in those caves full of lava pools. After she'd disappeared, he'd never felt lonelier. He needed her, now more than ever.

"So what's the plan?" Bryson asked. "High time you told us."

"Exactly what Michael suggested," Helga responded, looking out the window as she spoke. "The Alliance has pretty much exhausted what we can do on our own. We need to find an audience with some senior lawmaking officials who hopefully haven't been compromised, and I know the perfect place."

Michael had two questions, but Sarah was already one step ahead of him.

"What exactly have they been doing?" she asked. "The Alliance, I mean. Back at the barracks, it was like we didn't exist to them."

"Lately they've been studying patterns in the Tangents that Kaine has sent into the world," Helga answered. "Trying to figure out their purpose. Gathering data. In the Sleep, I had people working hard on the Mortality Doctrine program, trying to deconstruct it, figure out how to reverse it. How it connects to the Hive, how the humans taken over by Tangents connect to their counterparts within the Hive." She sighed. "But we have a long way to go."

Michael asked the other, more obvious question. "So where is it that you think we can meet up with some fancy government types?"

They all bounced half a foot off the seat when the car lurched over a huge bump in the road. Michael's head actually hit the roof.

"Whoa, there! We'll never make it to the airport if you crumple us in a ditch," Helga scolded Walter.

"You said you were in a hurry," their driver grumbled. He obviously hadn't forgiven Helga for inflicting the true death on two Tangents—and two humans—yet.

"Airport?" Sarah repeated. "I thought you said flying wasn't safe right now."

"Don't worry. We have a private plane," Helga answered. "I didn't just randomly download my people into whoever happened to be walking by on the street. We have connections."

"Nice," Bryson said.

"So you were saying?" Sarah prodded.

Helga went on. "There's a World Summit in London three days from now. It was called by the Union of Earth to discuss all the things I showed you. A lot of important people will be there. And I assume they'll be arriving very soon. We'll be going virtually—from a small embassy in Washington, D.C., that we've almost completely infiltrated. I'm eager to get there as quickly as possible so we can maneuver ourselves in."

"Let me guess," Bryson said. "More human bodies taken over?"

Helga grimaced. "None that we haven't made the same promise for as the others: to bring them back." She winced again, and Michael felt sorry that she had to bear so much guilt. "Anyway. It's a very small embassy—Latvia—which will help us keep a low profile. We should have enough credentials to get ourselves into the meeting virtually. But it won't be easy. We need to get there ASAP to make preparations."

They went on talking for a while, but Michael tuned out. He laid his head back and closed his eyes, trying to sort through his many thoughts. He kept coming back to Gabby. He'd felt bad about her from the beginning because she seemed to genuinely, and deeply, care for Jackson Porter. How ridiculously unfair to feel close to someone like that and then have them literally swap their mind with a stranger's.

And just like with his other friends, he'd dragged her into the whole mess. He had to know if she was okay. It might seem like a small thing to a lot of people, but it was something he could hold on to, like the Hallowed Ravine. Another specific goal.

His eyes snapped open.

"Hey, guys," he said. The others quieted, turned their attention to him. "I have a request and it's nonnegotiable. I really mean it. There's something I have to do, and if I have to branch out on my own to do it, I will."

"How about you tell us what it is before you make a bunch of lame threats," Bryson responded. "When's the last time we said no to you about anything?"

"Sorry," Michael said a little sheepishly. "It's more for you, Helga. You're not going to like this."

"What is it?" his nanny asked, eyebrows raised.

Michael let out the breath he'd been holding. "I know we've got some really important things to take care of, but we need to find Gabby and make sure she's okay. Based on how everything's been going, I have a really strong feeling that she's not."

A few hours later, they were well out of the mountains and on a freeway heading toward Atlanta, where Helga said they had an airplane waiting to take them north to D.C., the location of the Latvian embassy.

Throughout the entire drive, he'd tried and tried to make a connection with Gabby. He sent out dangler messages for her in several places, but she still hadn't responded. The universal Net signal had been spotty up in the mountains, so at first he was hoping that had been the problem. But now that they were back in civilization, he was beginning to worry. All he could think of was that cop hitting Gabby with the nightstick. If she was dead . . .

He barely knew the girl. But he felt a debt to Jackson Porter. It was bad enough that he'd stolen the guy's body. If he'd caused Jackson's girlfriend to die as well, Michael didn't know if he could handle the guilt.

"Anyone else starving?" Bryson asked. No one had spoken in at least an hour, and it snapped Michael out of his dark cloud. He'd long ago put away his NetScreen, and now realized he was hungry.

"I am," Sarah replied.

Michael nodded absently.

"Find us a restaurant," Helga said to Walter up in the front seat. "Preferably one with fried chicken."

Michael laughed, the most random laugh that had ever escaped him. Maybe he was going cuckoo from the stress.

"You have a problem with fried chicken?" Helga asked him.

"Not at all. I'm just in a weird mood."

Sarah squeezed his leg, then took his hand. "I'm sure it's nothing that a good bucket of greasy heart-attack food won't cure."

6

Michael stood outside the restaurant, taking long, deep breaths to calm his nerves while he waited for the others to use the bathroom. He'd barely spoken while they ate—chicken had been an excellent choice—he was just too wired thinking about Gabby, Kaine, the VNS, and how in the world he and his friends were supposed to make a difference at the World Summit. What he would give for a switch that could turn off his brain for a while.

A car was passing him in the parking lot, one of those new, fancy things with only three wheels. It had barely gone by when it slammed on its brakes, the back end swerving around until it came to a stop sideways. Michael took a step back, nervous. There were three people inside, but the sun reflecting off the windows prevented him from getting a good look at them.

The car sat there, its engine still running with a high-pitched whine of electricity. Michael turned back to the restaurant to see if any of his friends were coming out, but there was no sign of them. The line for the bathroom had been long—it was a popular place for travelers, and they'd hit it right at the peak of lunch hour. He looked back at the car again; nothing had changed.

Michael tried not to stare, but things were feeling weirder by the second. Had the driver had a heart attack or something? Done in by one too many grease-soaked drumsticks? The other two people in the car weren't moving, either. Were they okay? Their heads were warped shadows behind the sparkling windows, totally still.

He almost jumped when all three windows started to go down. A man was driving, young and alive, and two women sat in the back. They looked to be about the same age as the driver, one blond and one brunette. All three of them stared at Michael, expressionless, their eyes glued to him.

He didn't know what to do. A chill ran across his shoulders and he shivered. He glanced behind him to see if they could be looking at something else, but there was nothing unusual—just the restaurant. He turned back toward the car. Still they stared.

The door to the restaurant jangled and Bryson and Sarah came out, laughing about something. Michael saw them out of the corner of his eye, and he suddenly felt sheepish, like he'd been caught doing something wrong.

"Man," Bryson said, swatting Michael on the back. "Some dude had a major disagreement with his fried chicken. Held up the bathroom for a solid ten minutes. I've been in porta-potties that smelled better."

Sarah laughed again, and the sound made Michael feel better. Safer, actually.

"You all right?" she asked. But even as the words came out of her mouth, she noticed what held his attention. "What in the world?" she whispered.

"Who are they?" Bryson asked. The car still sat there, windows down, the three people staring at Michael, frozen in place.

"I have no idea," he answered. But he did know.

Sarah wrapped her arm around his, as if protecting him. "They're probably just Tangents who think you're famous.

The First." She said that last word like a curse. "It's nothing to worry about."

Michael shook his head, then found a spark of courage. He stepped forward and walked toward the car. The movement seemed to snap the strangers out of their hypnotic state, and as the windows began to go up, Michael caught a spark of terror in the driver's eyes before the glass sealed between them.

"Hey!" he shouted. "Who are you? What do you want?"

The engine of the car revved and it lurched into motion, the tires squealing as it sped off. Horns blared out on the street as the car swerved into traffic and disappeared.

CHAPTER 8

SEARCH AND RESCUE

1

Gabby finally responded.

Michael heard from her when they were just a few minutes from the airport. He'd been silent, thinking about those unsettling people staring at him from the car. He had no doubt that they were Tangents, but a part of him hoped it had been a random sighting and wasn't an omen of something worse to come.

When Helga announced that they were almost there, Michael decided to check his NetScreen one last time and see if Gabby had responded to one of his many danglers. As soon as the screen winked on, he saw that she had. And her response was short and simple:

> Jackson. Michael. Whoever you are. They chased me but i got away. I'm at my grandparents' old farmhouse, south of Atlanta. Safe for now. But i'm

alone and scared. Coordinates attached if you'd like to visit and talk. If not, i understand.

Michael bolted up straight in his seat. The others could tell something was wrong right away.

Sarah was already reading over his shoulder. "Oh, man," she whispered. Her tone made it plain that Gabby wasn't high on her priority list. "Well, at least she said she's safe."

"We have to go get her," Michael said. "Somebody chased her! I knew something was strange about how that cop walked right over to her. Whoever framed us hadn't planned on Jackson Porter's girlfriend getting involved and wanted her out of the picture. It's my fault." He leaned back into the seat and let out an anguished sigh. "She deserves to be with us—to have the protection of the Alliance."

"Michael—" Helga began, and he knew exactly what she was going to say.

"I know," he said, cutting her off. "The World Summit. But it's still three days away. And look, this farmhouse of Gabby's is only a couple of hours from the airport. She *is* from Atlanta, after all." He pointed at his screen, where he'd pulled up the coordinates and a map. "If we hurry, we can get her and she can come with us."

Bryson was leaning over Sarah to get a look. "How much you wanna bet Agent Weber is the one who hassled the poor kid? The VNS's fingerprints are on everything. One of these days we need to get Weber locked in a room with some nice torture devices. I'm ready to go medieval on her."

"We can't go, Michael," Helga said. "We can't risk spending time on one person when the whole world is on the verge of collapse. We have to get into that summit and figure out a way to make people listen."

Michael clicked off his NetScreen, rubbed his eyes. "She deserves to be with us, not alone."

"Then we can get her after we get back from D.C.," Helga insisted.

"No!" Michael shouted, surprising even himself. "You don't get it. I stole Jackson Porter's body! His parents are probably insane with worry by now. And then I made his girlfriend help us get into the VNS's headquarters, and she's probably got a fractured skull because of it. Now she's alone, hiding in some creepy farmhouse. I have to help her!"

Sarah had been leaning into him, her hand on his leg, but she pulled away and folded her arms. Was she jealous? The thought made him want to punch the roof of the car. Nothing had ever sounded stupider.

No one responded to his tirade.

"Listen," Michael said, forcing himself to speak more calmly. "We have weapons. We have three cars full of people. A little detour will be fine."

Helga just sighed and shook her head.

"I'm with Michael on this one," Bryson said. "Helping Gabby is good. But she might have also learned something valuable. Look, we don't know jack squat. We need answers. What good does it do if we sneak into that summit and say, 'Cheerio, mates! Tangents are taking over you blokes!' They'll look back at us and say, 'Duh.'"

Michael wanted to hug Bryson right then, even though

his British accent was awful. "She's a human being. We owe her."

Helga wasn't giving in. "One human. There are eight billion on the planet. We have to weigh our priorities."

It took all of Michael's willpower to keep his temper under control. "Fine, then we'll split up. One or two of you can go with me. The rest of you go to D.C. I'll find you when I'm done."

Helga recoiled from him, as if he'd slapped her, and Michael knew he'd played his cards right. There was no way she'd let him run off to rescue Gabby without her.

"Come on, Helga," he said. "I'm only one human. Kind of. Let me risk myself, and you guys go save the other billions." He refused to give up. He was going to get Gabby, end of story.

"What if it's a trap?" she asked, her last-ditch effort. "How do we even know it's her?"

"I have faith in my danglers."

"Huh?"

Michael let out a sigh. "Fine, it might be a trap. Which makes it a good thing we have three cars full of people and weapons. Or . . . like I said, we could split up so we don't risk missing the fancy World Summit."

Helga just slowly shook her head at him, defeat and anger in her eyes. "I miss the days when you were little and I could send you to your room without supper." She leaned over the front seat and tapped Walter on the shoulder. "Don't turn off the freeway at the airport exit." She looked back at Michael with a disapproving glare. "We're going to keep heading south for a while."

2

They left the city far behind and entered a long stretch of flat land. Fields spread toward the horizon, broken only by the angular lines of barns and farmhouses, the curved towers of silos reaching toward the sky like castle turrets. Michael didn't recognize most of the crops, but the grand rows of corn took his breath away. Something about those crowded rows of tall stalks haunted him. Who knew what hid within?

Helga served as the official navigator, relaying directions up to Walter. The coordinates Gabby had provided eventually led them to a dirt road that sliced a field of corn right down the middle. Walter turned onto the path, sending up clouds of dust behind him, and Michael was glad their SUV was in front so he could clearly see where they were going. They drove for at least a mile, until finally they reached a clearing—a wide expanse of yellowed lawn, half-crumbled barns, and a huge farmhouse. A lone car—a small red hatchback—was parked by the porch.

"Stop!" Helga yelled.

Walter slammed on the brakes, throwing everyone forward against their seat belts. Michael heard the other two cars skid to a stop behind them.

"I thought it was still a few miles away," Walter said, his voice tense.

"This has to be it," Helga replied, looking down at the coordinates Michael had sent her back in Atlanta. "But the satellite pics don't show another house for at least ten miles."

Sarah leaned over Michael to see the images. She'd been quiet the entire drive, making him wonder again whether she was jealous. The truth was, he had no romantic interest in Gabby. All he wanted to do was to salvage one of the many things he'd royally screwed up in this world.

"Places out in the country like this aren't always exact with GPS," Sarah said. "If this is it, at least we know there's no army waiting for us. We're winning, three cars to one."

Those were more words than she'd spoken in the last two hours. Michael appreciated her being positive.

"I almost wish we were surrounded by soldiers or cops or goons totin' guns right now," Bryson said. "At least then we'd know what we're up against. This place gives me the creeps."

So much for the positive vibes, Michael thought. He sure hoped he hadn't just wasted several hours of time the Alliance didn't have. The place *was* a little spooky.

"I'm not sure I share your wish," Sarah replied to Bryson, heavy on the sarcasm. "I vote for *not* being surrounded by people who wanna kill us. That's just me."

"There's only the one car," Michael said. "And it's a farm in the middle of nowhere."

Helga opened her door. "I'm not taking any chances. There might be an entire military base hidden underground."

Michael loved Helga. He really did.

"Everyone grab a gun," she said. "Let's check it out."

The yellowed grass crunched under Michael's feet with every step. He had a pistol this time, a semiautomatic, fully loaded. He gripped it as expertly as any marksman. It felt like second nature after all the years of gaming. He didn't mind taking precautions, but he hoped no one got trigger-happy and shot Gabby by accident.

He studied the house as they crept closer, half expecting a window to explode at any moment, gunfire raining down on them. But nothing stirred, not even the tattered curtains he glimpsed through the grimy glass.

The house had seen better days, that was for sure.

Tall and wide, with a steeply pitched roof and gables, it had a wraparound porch that reminded Michael of a game he used to play that took place on a plantation. It screamed iced tea and rocking chairs. But the porch was empty, and the house was a lot older than the one in the game. Shingles were missing from the roof, and the paint was flaking. The few places where it wasn't peeling, it had faded to something like pale yellow. The only real sign of life was that the parched grass on which they walked had been cut recently.

Michael and the group stopped a few yards from the porch steps and waited for the Tangents from the other two cars to join them.

"Walter," Helga said, "you and me, front door. Amy, you and Chris go around back. Tony and DeeAnn, watch the windows on the side of the house. Michael, you and your friends watch those windows on the second floor—the gables. Holler if you see a fly twitch."

Michael knew she was protecting him, but this wasn't the time to argue. He had no problem hanging back. This wasn't a game. He just hoped they'd be back on the road in the next few minutes, with Gabby on board.

"Okay," he said, but Helga and the others were already on

the move, creeping ahead like trained soldiers. Soon Helga and Walter were up the creaky porch stairs and positioned on either side of the front door. They glanced at each other; then Helga reached out, twisted the handle of the door. It swung open with a haunted-house shriek.

She and Walter slipped inside.

4

A minute passed. Two. Michael stood breathless, straining to hear what was going on. Nothing moved behind the windows he'd been tasked with watching, and he could tell that his friends were getting just as antsy as he was.

"Nobody's in there," he whispered. He almost dropped his gun to his side in defeat but knew not to be that stupid. "We came all the way out here for—"

"Michael!"

Helga. Shouting his name from inside. Everything else flew from his mind and he was on the move, sprinting toward the steps, taking them all at once, flashing through the still-open door. The front hall was empty, as were the two rooms he could see to either side, all wood and antiques and crooked pictures on the walls. This place was like something from an old flat-film, no sign of even a simple WallScreen.

"Where are you?" he shouted, just as Bryson and Sarah came barreling through the door on his heels.

"Up here! Quick!"

A staircase loomed on the right side of the hall. Michael

went to it, this time taking only two steps at a time because they were steeper. His breath came ragged—more from the adrenaline than the effort—by the time he reached the top. He caught a glimpse of Walter's shoulder in the nearest bedroom and ran to it. He slowed down and stepped inside.

An odd, haunting scene awaited him. A chair stood alone on the far side of the room, between a curtained window and a large wardrobe. Gabby sat in it, her hands tied behind her back and a gag wrapped around her mouth. She was disheveled, her hair a mess, her face red, and her clothes soaked with sweat. She looked awful, and she was trying to speak through the cloth.

And her eyes. She stared at Michael, pleading with her eyes for help.

He took a step toward her, but Helga quickly moved in front of him, blocking his path.

"No," she said. "Not yet." She turned to look at Gabby.

Jackson's girlfriend still had her gaze fixed on him.

"Take her gag off, at least," he said. "She's obviously got something to say."

Helga sighed, turned her attention to Walter. She raised her eyebrows.

Walter shook his head. "We need to leave. Now."

"It won't hurt to take off her gag," Sarah said, moving around everyone else and walking straight up to Gabby.

"Wait!" Michael shouted, suddenly picturing some sort of trap.

But nothing happened.

Sarah reached behind Gabby, fiddled with the knot in the cloth behind her head until it loosened, then let it drop around the girl's neck.

Gabby sucked in a big pull of air. "Thank you," she whispered in a hoarse voice. "Don't worry, no one's going to hurt you. They promised."

"What do you mean?" Michael asked. "Who else is here?"

"Just listen." She took a couple more deep breaths, then looked around. "Someone is here—someone who wants to talk to you. They used me to get you to come. Forced me to send the message."

"What're you talking about?" Helga asked before Michael could.

"Enough of this!" Walter yelled. "Let's leave. Now!"

Gabby shook her head adamantly. "No! Whatever you do, don't do that. They let you in, but they won't let you out unless you at least listen to what they say."

"Who?" Michael asked.

"Just wait. He's coming. Like I said. He promised me that no one would get hurt unless you tried to hurt him."

Suddenly a deep, resonant roar filled the room. It sounded like an enormous machine had started, rumbling from everywhere at once. There was a piercing whine and a grinding of gears. Then, just as abruptly as it had begun, the noise stopped.

Michael stood frozen, wondering what was about to happen. Then movement to the right of Gabby caught his eye. The doors of the wardrobe opened, bright lights shining from within, like something out of Narnia.

And out stepped a man. Short, dressed in a three-piece suit. Agent Scott.

He closed the doors behind him and frowned at Michael, who couldn't believe he'd remembered the guy's name.

5

Michael wasn't that surprised to see the VNS pop back into his life so quickly, but the timing had him at a loss.

Also not surprisingly, Bryson was the one to speak.

"Who's this dude? You obviously know him, Michael."

"I met him back when . . . back before I knew. In *Lifeblood Deep*. He works for Weber. He followed me into an alley a million years ago. Guys, meet Agent Scott."

"Who apparently likes to play in closets," Bryson added.

Scott didn't even grace him with a disapproving glare. His eyes stayed on Michael, expression blank, but Michael had no doubt there were a million unwelcome truths hiding behind the man's look. He reminded himself that this man represented everything Weber stood for.

"Why in the world did you just step out of a wardrobe?" Michael asked, feeling surreal.

Agent Scott turned and gave a passing glance to the closed doors, then faced Michael again. "Yes, I'm sorry for the theatrics. We have a secret location hidden under this farmhouse. It's a place we feel no one would ever come looking for us. This wardrobe just happens to be one of the ways in and out."

Michael's heart thumped heavily, his adrenaline racing. Helga had been right. He willed his mind to come up with a sensible line of questions, stay in control of the conversation.

"I thought your systems were wiped out," he said. "I thought you were crippled for months. We saw your leader's . . . heartfelt confessional."

Scott seemed perfectly happy to continue along this path. "That's why we're here, Michael," he said. "We *are* crippled. Very seriously. Since you were the ones who did it to us, I'd think you'd know that."

Michael sensed Bryson's temper stirring. He quickly reached out and grasped his wrist and shook his head. "He's just trying to bait us," he said to his friend. "Or maybe they're recording our reactions. Don't fall for it. We'll get our answers, don't worry."

Bryson shook himself free but didn't say anything. As for Michael, he swore he wasn't leaving that farmhouse until he got some information out of Weber's subordinate.

He returned his attention to the VNS agent. "Why'd your boss do it? Why the whole setup? Why trick us into thinking she'd Squeezed us into *Lifeblood Deep*? And the Lance. I mean, couldn't there have been an easier way to accomplish all that destruction?"

"Did you guys set up that entire purple ocean of broken-down code, too?" Sarah asked. When she spoke, Agent Scott didn't even glance at her. His eyes stayed riveted on Michael.

"I don't know what you're talking about," the man said calmly. "*You* came to *us,* remember? You were the ones who decided where to go, where to attack, how to do it. *You*

tricked *us*. Why would we, the VNS, purposely—
voluntarily—assist you in bringing down our entire firewall
and security network? It just doesn't make sense."

Michael let out an exaggerated sigh. "Whatever. If you
need to say all this so you can have it on record to save Weber's butt, fine. If you're going to arrest us, arrest us. But it's
probably not going to go so well for you when we tell our
side of the story—not to mention when we share pictures of
my friend here all tied up like some kind of serial killer's
plaything. All we want is her. Let us untie her and leave. You
can go back to doing whatever the hell it is you people pretend to do."

Agent Scott took a few steps toward Gabby, until he stood
directly behind her. He reached down and ran a hand over
the girl's hair. Michael shivered.

"There is much you don't understand," the agent said.
"And there are a lot of people out there who'd like to see you
locked up or dead. The rules of the world are changing, Michael. I think you know that."

Scott's eyes flicked up then, over Michael's shoulders. He
seemed to signal someone. Michael looked back, but they
were alone.

"Now we can truly get down to business," Scott continued. "We can let it all out. You have an opportunity here. All
of you. The line is being drawn. And trust me when I tell you
that you'll want to be on the side of the VNS."

Michael slowly shook his head. "This is sad. I wouldn't be
surprised if you claimed a Tangent took over Weber's body
next. Maybe even Kaine himself."

Scott looked at him quizzically, as if what he'd said genuinely surprised him. "Is that what you think's happened? Do you think Agent Weber has been taken over by a Tangent, Michael?"

Michael turned to Sarah, then Bryson, and glanced over at Walter and Helga by the door to the hallway. All of them gave their own version of a shrug. He faced Scott again.

"We're done here," he said. "We're not going to let the world be possessed by a bunch of coded programs. And Gabby's coming with me. Either arrest us or don't, but we're finished with this conversation."

"Wait!" Scott barked when Michael took a step toward Gabby. His voice was so loud and sharp that Michael froze.

"Please," he said. "Just . . . hear me out. Or . . . she'll be very upset. Please." All of the man's confidence had suddenly disappeared. Michael stared at him, waited to hear what he had to say.

"Kaine is trying to turn you against the VNS," he said. "He's off message. I mean . . . he was never supposed to do any of this, and he's destroying everything!" He shouted this last part, losing his composure completely. "He wasn't supposed to be like this." Agent Scott was whispering now, staring off into the distance. "Kaine failed us."

The room was quiet.

6

"What's wrong with you?" Sarah finally asked, stepping up to stand next to Michael. "Stop talking in riddles and just tell us what's going on."

Scott's eyes snapped back into focus, and he turned to look straight at Sarah. "This is between me and Michael!"

Michael took a half step backward, completely stunned. Even though it was entirely possible that this man had been taken over by the Mortality Doctrine, it shocked him to see the agent act out with such a childish temper.

"That's enough," Helga said. She raised her gun and aimed it at Agent Scott. Walter followed Helga's lead. "We're taking the girl and we're leaving."

"No, you're not," Scott replied. "You have three seconds to put those weapons down or you will all die. Right here, right now. All except Michael. Weber needs him."

"What does that mean?" Michael asked. The situation was rapidly deteriorating, along with Michael's patience. "Why would she need me? Why does she keep coming back to me? I don't get it! She set us up!"

"One," Scott said. He nodded toward Helga. "Two."

"Put the guns down!" Michael shouted.

"Enough is enough!" his nanny responded.

"Just . . . just put them down for a sec." She did as he asked but didn't look happy about it. Michael returned his full attention to the agent. "Just let us leave. If you really think Kaine is . . . some villain, then that's great. We're on the same side." His effort to soothe things seemed a complete waste. Scott's eyes shone with something like madness.

"We thought we could turn things around," the agent said, looking everywhere and nowhere at once. "But it was too late. It doesn't matter what Kaine did or does anymore. We have to stay focused and see this through."

"Fine!" Michael yelled. "Do what you need to, but let us go!"

"Don't listen to him," Scott responded, as if he hadn't heard Michael. "Don't listen to a word Kaine says. He's not . . . he's not . . ."

"This is bullcrap," Sarah said. She marched toward Agent Scott where he stood behind Gabby, shoving past Michael on the way. She reached Gabby and pushed Scott right in the chest, causing him to stumble several steps backward. Then Sarah started working at the ropes that tied Gabby to the rickety wooden chair.

"Stop!" Scott yelled at her. Michael stared, not sure what to do.

"You really shouldn't mess with him," Gabby whispered to Sarah as she worked loose some of the tighter knots. One end of a rope fell to the floor with a thump. "He's unstable. And all those people down below are dangerous."

Michael recovered his wits and went to help Sarah. He dropped to his knees and began working on a knot around Gabby's ankles.

"You can't do this," Scott said from a few feet away. "I told you to stop. Michael, stop. You're the First, and Weber needs your help to see the plan through. I'm not a Tangent and neither is she! We're the same as we've always been. We can end this. But you have to . . . you have to obey her!"

Michael ignored him, refusing to process another word

he said. He finally got the stubborn knot loose enough to yank the rope away from Gabby's legs. And then the world erupted around him.

A jolting concussion of noise shook the room like an explosion. Michael's ears rang and he fell backward. He gazed up at the wooden beams stretching across the ceiling, then looked over at Agent Scott, who held a gun in his hand. There'd been a scream at some point, Michael knew that, but who was it? He searched the room until he found Sarah. She'd taken several steps away from the chair, where Gabby was now freed from her ropes.

Sarah's hands were over her chest.

Her shirt was red.

Getting redder.

Blood seeped between her fingers, ran over them, dripped to the floor. A stain of scarlet spread across her shirt. But she was silent, as if it didn't hurt at all, staring down at herself in disbelief.

She finally looked back up at Michael, who lay on the floor in shock, and sadness crossed her face as she fell to her knees.

"Sarah!" Michael shouted. He was scrambling, trying to get his arms and legs to work, trying to get to her. She was on her side. "Sarah, Sarah, Sarah," he mumbled as he held her gently by the shoulders, scanned her bloody chest as if there were any chance he might know how to save her. "Sarah," he said again.

She looked up at him. "I love you," she whispered. "Every word. I meant it."

Michael started to tremble.

And then Helga was there. She swooped down as if from the sky and tore him away from Sarah, picking him up as if he were no heavier than a bag of groceries.

"Take him!" she yelled. "Walter, take him and get him out of here!"

"What?" Michael said, dazed. "What're you—"

"Get him out of here or it'll never work!" Helga bellowed. "I only have one shot at this. Bryson, you too. All of you. Out!"

Walter ran over, grabbed Michael by the arm, started pulling him away. Michael tried to fight him off, but the man was too strong. Michael felt a darkness passing over him, blocking out the light. He saw shadows on the edges of his vision. A painful fist closed over his heart and squeezed without mercy. Bryson was nearby, looking around, dumbfounded, the blood drained from his face.

"Sarah!" Michael yelled, unable to do anything else. This couldn't be real. It couldn't be. "Weber!" he screamed, throwing all his fury into the name. "Weber!"

But she wasn't there—just Agent Scott. The man stood in the same place as before, the gun still in his hand but now at his side. His face had gone white, but his eyes were cold. He turned them toward Michael.

"You should have listened to Agent Weber," he said. "You should have listened! May this girl's death teach you a lesson!"

"I'll kill you, you . . ."

Walter dragged him out of the room and into the hall, Bryson following, stunned into silence. Gabby was there, too.

"Give her a chance, boy," Walter whispered to him. "She knows things you don't."

Michael didn't care that Scott had pulled the trigger. Agent Weber had just killed his best friend.

The last thing he saw was Helga, hunched over Sarah's lifeless body.

CHAPTER 9

UP IN THE NIGHT

1

How could the world continue to turn? It was the question Michael couldn't stop asking himself over the next few hours. Their car sped along the freeway, the other two following just as before. It was silent except for the hum of the engine and the bumps of the road under them. Gabby sat in the middle up front, between Amy and Walter, who was driving as if he were on a family vacation instead of fleeing the scene of a murder. Michael had insisted Gabby sit up there, refusing to allow her to take Sarah's place in the back. It was wrong. Everything in the world was wrong.

Michael's heart ached more than he could bear. He sat with his head against the seat behind him, eyes closed so that no one would talk to him. The countless questions he had would have to be worked through later. They demanded answers and filled him with hate and anger. Had Gabby been forced to trick them, or was she a part of the scheme? And why had Helga acted so strange?

He pushed the questions away for now.

Sarah had told him she loved him. Him, a Tangent.

She was his best friend.

And he'd seen her die twice now. Well, much more often than that while gaming, but that day on the Path, in the caves, with the lava, had felt so real.

This *was* real.

Sarah was dead.

Dead.

Shot and killed by a man who was supposed to work for the good guys. A group the world was supposed to trust. Though, really, it was Weber who'd caused all this. The woman who'd made him drag Sarah into the chaos of Kaine and his Mortality Doctrine in the first place.

Sarah was dead.

Eyes closed or open, all he saw was her. Hands bloody, clasped against her chest. The look on her face. Shock. Betrayal. A childlike sadness. What he'd seen in her eyes, more than anything else, was this: *Michael, I don't want to die. Please don't let me die.*

Twice she'd said she loved him. Had the first time really been only that morning? He knew she'd meant it. It was the love of pure friendship, something that one day might've blossomed into something greater, eternal, powerful. He loved her back. He loved her so much.

Michael shook silently as tears squeezed their way past his closed eyelids and trickled down his face.

2

And so it went for hours. Michael was in shock—too numb to be angry and hurting too much to speak. He had no idea what was next.

So he just followed, blindly, for hours.

They drove.

Arrived at an airport. They were ushered through a private entrance.

Went to a small hangar, to a plane.

There was another man, another woman. As faceless to him as the rest. He followed his friends up a set of stairs into the plane. Sat down. Buckled in.

The plane exited the hangar and at some point took off. Michael leaned against a window, his cheeks still wet, his eyes burning. He watched as the ground slipped away below, endless trees and hills and buildings and streets shrinking. And soon after, darkness swallowed the world.

They flew for several hours, in a roundabout route, to get to Washington, D.C. Helga explained that it was time to regroup and that they were taking the opportunity to hide, in the air. She tried to talk to Michael several times, but he pretended to be asleep.

At some point, in a welcome escape from the pain, Michael actually did fall asleep, fleeing into an even deeper darkness, where no dreams waited.

3

It was Helga who woke him up. She was sitting next to him when he opened his eyes. It took a moment, but the pain came crashing back in.

They'd landed, and Michael looked around, saw that they were the only ones still on the plane.

"Michael," Helga said, her voice soft and gentle. "I haven't wanted to disturb you, but—"

Michael stood up and moved past Helga. He still wasn't ready to talk. He walked down the aisle, toward the door. It was open, and he descended the stairs.

"There's always hope," Helga shouted to him. "Remember that, Michael. There's always hope."

He ignored her, walking blindly into the mist enveloping the tarmac.

4

Helga let him go, which really surprised him. As stubborn as he was, she'd always been a lot more stubborn.

Their private plane had landed at a tiny airport, just a series of covered pads, one long landing strip, and a little building that served as a terminal. Although he couldn't see much through the thick mist, he finally found an open fence and a road leading away.

He took it.

5

Michael walked for an hour, his mind a factory of thought. The mist crept through his clothes, soaking them, chilling his skin. He couldn't stop shivering, and spent the walk rubbing his arms for warmth. Items on either side of the road suddenly appeared out of the gray fog, looming over him, only to vanish quickly as he passed by. Hulking trees, random parked cars, mailboxes, and a gloomy pedestrian here and there.

Michael kept walking. Kept hurting. Kept thinking.

Countless questions, zero answers.

Why? That was the question that dominated them all. Why?

Gabby, forced to help the VNS bring them to her. Weber herself, a complete mystery. Did she and Agent Scott really represent the entire VNS? Was the whole organization corrupt?

And Sarah.

He saw her blood everywhere he looked. In the mist, in his mind, on the wet surface of the road. Everything around him looked red. It hurt so much.

Then he stopped. *That's it,* he told himself. The more he thought about it, the more it hurt. The solution was simple: no more thinking about it. He had to stop or he'd just keep sinking deeper and deeper into something he might never claw himself out of.

Lights appeared in the mist up ahead, growing brighter every second. There was some small part of him, still logical, that told him he needed to be careful. He had enemies. How many times had that been proven? He slowed but headed toward the lights, taking extra care.

The first thing that revealed itself was a simple convenience store, with glass doors and windows, a bright interior stocked with shelves of bread, snacks, other goods. It was small, but quite a few people were inside, walking its aisles. Michael, hoping that his encrypted currency credits were still safe, decided to go inside and look around. Buy something sweet. Lots of things. Maybe gorge himself. He deserved a break, and he assumed Helga would pick him up at any second.

An electronic bell chimed when he walked through the door.

A few people—a man, two women, a couple of kids— looked over at him as he entered, then went back to their browsing. He watched the man pick up a tall carton of bean chips, study its ingredients as if somehow, magically, he'd discover that they were good for his already bulging waistline, then tuck it under his arm as he moved along. Michael glanced at the cashier, a teenager who looked as if he'd rather eat rocks than ring up the line of customers waiting for him.

Michael turned toward the wall of cold drinks and stopped. A boy, maybe ten years old, was standing in his path, staring straight at him with that same unsettling blank gaze he'd seen on the people in the car at the chicken restaurant.

Abruptly, the boy spun on his heels and walked in the other direction, disappearing around the bread shelf.

Michael took a deep breath, wondering if he should get out of there.

No.

He was sick of running. He was the First, after all. Right? If there were Tangents in the store, they could just look on and admire from afar. He wanted a snack and something to drink, and that was that. He walked to the first panel of drinks, the many flavors and combinations flashing across the glass in silly animations. Michael moved to the second panel, then the third. There he saw some weird combo of grape and pomegranate with a shot of caffeine and chose it. A whoosh and a puff of mist later and his drink—ice-cold in a tube of ReSike—appeared in the dispenser.

As he picked it up, he glanced to his left. A man stood there, his hand frozen halfway to the shelf in front of him to pick up a candy bar. He was clearly watching Michael out of the corner of his eye, but he went about his business as soon as he realized he'd been spotted. Michael quickly looked in the other direction, sure a woman had been staring at him before jerking her head away. Then the boy appeared again, gave Michael a long, lingering look, and walked on.

Michael shook it off. He headed straight for the spot where the man had gotten his candy bar and grabbed the exact same brand, giving the stranger a wink and a smile as he did so.

"I feel like someone's knocking around in my head," he said to the man, who gave him a worried look. "Sometimes I'm just not myself. Candy helps. You?"

The man turned and hurriedly walked away.

Michael wondered if maybe he'd finally snapped from the stress.

He grabbed another candy bar, a bag of bleu chips, and some beef jerky, then headed for the cashier. His thoughts were a cyclone—it felt like he could no longer tell the difference between a casual glance and a glare. Who was watching him? Who wasn't? Who might just be wondering how one person could need all that junk food?

Sweat trickled down his forehead. He felt like every single person in the store was staring at him now. He looked down at his feet as he waited in line, suddenly afraid to meet anyone's eyes. He should never have come into this store. The world was too dangerous, and his face had been plastered all over the NewsBops. He had no way of knowing who was on his side and who was against him, who'd been taken over and who hadn't. Surely the folks in this tiny convenience store on the outskirts of Washington, D.C., had escaped the Mortality Doctrine. Right?

He suddenly had an undeniable need to get away. He wanted Helga and Bryson and Sar—

Sarah.

He swallowed, and all the pain came crashing back in.

"I'm sorry," he said out loud, though he had no idea who he was talking to. "I'm sorry." He stepped out of the line, looked down at the goods in his hands. It felt as if they'd suddenly quadrupled in weight. "I'm sorry." He rushed to the nearest shelf and shoved all of his items next to a bin of MoonPies. "I'm sorry," he said for the fourth time.

He ran to the door, opened it, heard the chime, stumbled

out, and almost fell. A car was in the lot, its lights on, cutting luminescent barrels through the fog. It pulled to the entrance and the window rolled down. Bryson's face appeared, and somehow Michael managed the slightest of smiles.

"Hop in, man," Bryson said. "Head-clearing time is over. Time to be with your friends again."

Michael had never been so happy to see Bryson. Never, not even after seeing him for the first time here, in the Wake.

"I'm sorry," he said again, so quietly that he barely even heard himself say it; then he went to the back of the car, opened the door, and got in. Walter was driving, of course, and Helga sat next to Michael. They nodded at each other, saying so much more than they could have with words.

Walter gunned it and they drove off, Michael wondering to whom and for what exactly he was sorry.

To everyone, he thought. *For everything.*

CHAPTER 10

LEADERS OF NATIONS

1

Not much happened the rest of that afternoon and evening, which allowed Michael to nap on one of the beds in the adjoining hotel rooms they checked into. Bryson sat on the bed next to him, mostly staring absently into space. Michael knew his friend felt just as much pain at losing Sarah as he did, and probably the same guilt at not being able to make the other feel better. But at least they were together.

The most important thing I do now is put an end to this Tangent craziness, Michael told himself. *The Hallowed Ravine. Somehow it all goes back to the Hallowed Ravine.*

Helga and the others were busy, doing what, Michael didn't know. He couldn't bring himself to ask. Tomorrow, he kept telling himself. He'd be rested and rejuvenated, ready to kick some butt.

At some point that night, between fitful dozes, he realized he couldn't stand the silence anymore and spoke to Bryson.

"You awake?" Michael turned and looked at his friend, lying on top of the covers of the other bed.

"Yep."

"How's it hangin'?" Michael asked him, the words coming out a bit croaky. "Besides the obvious."

Bryson answered after a heavy sigh. "Besides the obvious, I'm doing downright swell. Quite lovely, old chap." He mocked a British accent again there at the end, doing a crap-poor job of it.

"I think that's more, like, Australian," Michael said. "Maybe drunk Australian."

Bryson sat up and yawned. "I was going more for Madagascarian."

"I'm sure that's a thing."

"It's a thing."

They stared at each other, then burst into one of those hysterical late-night laughing fits that couldn't possibly happen during the light of day. It was a start.

"I keep picturing her parents," Bryson said several minutes later, after they'd sobered up. "I almost feel worse for them than I do for Sarah herself. I mean, can you imagine telling them? I gotta be honest, I hope I never see them again. I can't do it. It's gonna kill 'em."

Michael knew that was totally selfish. And yet he felt exactly the same way.

"They'll blame us," he said. "And they'll be right."

Bryson shook his head. "Nah, man. Come on, we've got plenty to beat ourselves up about. And plenty to cry about. Now we need to focus on moving forward. We're the good guys, and we could've given up a long time ago. Anyone who thinks differently can kiss my big white butt."

"Amen," Michael said. "And that'll be punishment enough. Where's Gabby?"

"She's in another room, sleeping, I'd guess. She's really feeling stupid about the whole thing. I had a talk with her, though. Honestly, man, I think she's okay. She didn't have a whole lot of choice in the matter. They made all kinds of threats."

Michael shrugged. "Yeah, I figured. I'll talk to her tomorrow. I'm just glad she's alive."

Bryson didn't answer, and the silence felt heavy.

Michael finally changed the subject. "I'm so thirsty I can feel my tongue cracking into dust. I'm going to get a drink out of the vending machine." He got up from the bed and rubbed his eyes, let out a big yawn. "You want something?"

"Whiskey?"

Michael just stared at him. "How about a nice cold cola?"

"That'll do."

As Michael opened the door to the hallway, he could see Helga, Walter, Amy, and a few others huddled over a NetScreen in the adjoining room. They evidently had no interest in sleep. He thought about speaking to them, but he just wasn't in the mood for that yet. He slipped out and quietly closed the door behind him.

2

There was a snack nook about halfway down the hallway, and he stopped there, glad that no one else was around. He'd had enough of other people. Every time he ran into someone new, his mind jumped to the same conclusion—*Tangent, Tangent, Tangent.* Only he couldn't tell whether they worshipped him or wanted him dead.

His credit chip worked fine on the vending machines, producing the same drink he'd created at the streetside shop earlier. He also bought some regular old potato chips and a couple of water tubes. Then he got a cola for Bryson. He was just taking that last item out of the dispenser when he heard the creak of hinges: a door was opening out in the hallway. He waited for the inevitable clunk of the door closing again, but it never came. The hall was silent.

Gathering his things in the crook of his arm, Michael left the snack nook and immediately saw the door he'd heard open a few moments earlier. It was still ajar, and an older woman was standing there, staring right at him. She didn't look angry, but she didn't look particularly happy to see him, either.

"Hi," Michael said, feeling as if he were swimming in a pool of awkward. "Cannnnnn I help you? Want something to eat?"

"No. Thank you." She spoke in a sweet old-lady voice, then closed the door, the hard thump echoing down the hallway.

Michael stood and watched the door for a minute, wondering if she'd open it again. There were billions of people in the world. Surely the Tangents couldn't follow him along each phase of his journey.

Yeah, right, he thought. Like anything would ever surprise him again.

He sighed and started walking back to his room, passing the lady's room on his way. He slowed and tried to look in the peephole as he passed—it seemed much darker than the others. He imagined her aging eye on the other side, watching his every step through her cataract. He told himself that all old ladies did that sort of thing. They assumed every teenage kid they ever saw was one candy-rush away from murdering every senior citizen in sight.

It could be a coincidence, he thought. All these people watching him. It could be his imagination, or just paranoia from all he'd gone through. People had an instinct to observe those around them. Didn't they? A pair of eyes on him didn't mean a Tangent spy for Kaine every single time. They might just be normal people wondering if they'd seen him before, somewhere on the NewsBops.

Making light of things, he realized, was an excellent way to get himself killed. He picked up his pace and hurried for his room.

"We've got to get out of here," he said to Bryson after they'd both taken long gulps from their drink tubes. "I feel like every person I come across is watching me, then messaging Kaine or Weber or the cops as soon I move on. It's really giving me the creeps."

Bryson took another lengthy swallow. "Come on, dude. What good does running do? If he can follow us everywhere, then what's the point of changing places?" Another glug. "Just chill and let's do what Helga and her posse tell us."

"That's what we've done from the very beginning," Michael said, halfheartedly fighting back. He mostly agreed with his friend. "It's like we're mice in a maze—loosed by Weber, manipulated by Kaine. I'm sick of it. There's no reason the two of us couldn't hack into the Hallowed Ravine all by our lonesome."

"Well, yeah," Bryson responded. "But it'd be awfully tough without Helga's help and protection. At least you trust her, right?"

Michael thought about that. He did. He really did. "Yeah," he finally answered. "But there's still a tiny little bit of doubt hidden in there. Who knows, man. Maybe Kaine created her years before he captured me, had it planned out all along. I trust her, but I'm done ever trusting anyone one hundred percent again."

"Even me?" Bryson asked.

Michael lay back on his pillows. "No. You're different. You, I trust. Now go to sleep."

"Helga might want us soon."

"I'm sure we won't start until morning. It's still dark out."

Michael closed his eyes, tried to relax. He saw that old

lady peering at him from her hotel door. The whole world had gone nuts. Including him.

He fell asleep. Sarah smiled at him in his dreams.

4

Bryson woke him up early with a nudge. "Hey, considering the way you snored all night, I think you're ready to get your lazy butt out of bed. Man, you sounded like an old-school lawn mower. I kept having Griever nightmares."

Michael felt like death awakened from the deepest, darkest crypt of hell. He let out a long groan that didn't do a thing to make him feel better. "Griever? Seriously? I thought your parents banned you from that game."

Bryson stared at him until they both burst out laughing. Maybe life would go on after all.

"Come on," Bryson said. "Helga and her alliance of superheroes are waiting for us in the next room. She called it a briefing. That's right. A briefing."

"Sounds serious."

Bryson pulled out his horrific British accent again. "Quite extraordinary, my dear chap. Perhaps she'll serve some biscuits and tea."

"What's up with this accent all of a sudden? You sound like an old lady from Monty Python." The comedy group had been dead for decades, but were probably more popular than ever in the Sleep nostalgia cinemas.

"I'll take that as a compliment. The summit's in London,

remember? London's in England? They have British accents there? Try to keep up. Now come on, let's go."

Michael slowly got to his feet. Something smelled terrible. It didn't take long to figure out what it was. Himself.

"Tell her I'll be there in ten minutes—I swear I haven't showered in a week. I gotta wash off this stink."

Bryson looked awfully grateful.

5

They crowded into one room, about fourteen people in all. Most of them hadn't been introduced to Michael yet, though their faces had become familiar enough. Helga stood in front of the window, where early-morning sunlight showed that the mist and fog had finally burned away. Walter, as always, was right by her side, actually looking as if he didn't want to kill someone today. Gabby was there, and she awkwardly met Michael's eyes when he entered. He gave her his best smile, trying to show that he didn't hold anything against her.

Trust no one, he thought, almost as if Jackson Porter were sneaking back into his mind and trying to send him a message. *Trust no one ever again.*

What a way to live.

"Michael," Helga began, summoning his attention and embarrassing him. "Bryson. Gabby. We're all glad you're here, safe for the moment. There's no possible way we could find the words to express our condolences on the loss of Sarah. I'm truly sorry. But like I've said—"

Michael finished for her. "There's always hope." At that moment, he actually felt it a little.

Helga responded with the sincerest of nods. She was *his* Helga, he had no doubt, no matter what secondary voices might argue in his mind. The thought made him feel a little better.

"Truer words were never spoken," his nanny said. "There's always hope. Always. You just never know what life—or death—might bring. I think we've all seen that the world is a little more complicated than we ever could have imagined."

Helga paused, as if for a moment of silence, then started talking again.

"The World Summit is tonight, held in the new Union of Earth audience chamber. A lot of the world leaders have physically gone to London, but obviously not everyone could make it. So there'll be quite a few connected through the VirtNet, as holograms. I want a chance to plead our case right there on the chamber floor, and since it's far too dangerous to travel to London"—she gave Michael a flat stare, then Bryson, then Gabby—"we'll use the Sleep to get there. Somehow, some way, we *will* be heard."

"You really think we can hack into the most highly secured meeting . . . maybe ever?" Michael asked. He already loved the idea.

"Absolutely," Helga replied. "We inserted Alliance Tangents strategically, some of whom have taken over an embassy here in Washington. I thought it best to pick a country big enough to be invited to the summit but small enough to stay under most anyone's radar. We have to be smart about this."

Michael nodded. Things were sounding more and more fun.

"One of our Tangents," Helga continued, "is now the chief of staff for the prime minister of Latvia. He's been on the job—well, his likeness, I should say—has been on the job for over twenty years. Before we sent our man into his mind—a Tangent known by the name of Levi—we did an exhaustive, hyperspeed analysis of the staff chief's life, history, mannerisms, personality, everything. We knew that a big part of our plan could hinge on Levi's ability to blend in."

"And?" Bryson asked. "How's he done so far?"

"So far, perfect," answered Helga. "By all accounts, he's fooled them all. He helped us place others in the Latvian embassy in the U.S., including their very own ambassador. That man is named Guntis, and he'll be the one who gets us inside the embassy itself. We'll use their state-of-the-art NerveBoxes to enter the summit virtually, pretending to be members of Guntis's staff. The credentials are all laid out."

It troubled Michael, as usual. They all seemed proud of what they'd done, placing one of their own in such an important political position, no matter the size of the country represented. But again, they'd stolen a life. It was impossible for him to get past that little—no, huge—part of the puzzle.

"Michael, you look upset," Helga said. "And we haven't even started yet."

"You know why" was the best response he could manage.

Helga folded her arms and leaned against the window. "This . . . this is why I went through all that trouble to take you to the Hive. You've been there, you've seen it yourself. These people . . . they're still alive in every sense of what makes a human a human. And I'd bet my own life that when all is said and done and we've helped stop the madness that Kaine has begun, they'll thank us. And they'll get their bodies back. We all swore to it, Michael. We're not here to stay."

Walter fidgeted a little when she mentioned what they'd sworn, and Michael knew what he was thinking. They'd also sworn not to bring the so-called true death to anyone, but they'd done just that. Back in the woods, in front of the barracks.

"I need everyone together on this," Helga said when Michael didn't respond.

He didn't know what to say. But following her seemed like the only viable way the world could ever get back to normal.

"Michael?" she asked.

"Okay," he said. "I wasn't even going to bring it up until you asked. But I'm in. Tell me the plan, how I can help. Let's just get it done."

"That's more like it," she said with a satisfied smile. "Now here's what we're going to do."

A good part of the Alliance plan went off without a hitch, swallowing Michael into a surreal scenario that felt like a dream. He'd worried about language barriers, but that wasn't an issue—they were only observers, from a small country, virtual visitors. Practically invisible.

They took a cab to the Latvian embassy, where Guntis

himself greeted them at security and escorted them inside. He was a tall, brusque man with a very heavy accent. Michael couldn't tell if that meant the Tangent inside had been Latvian himself or the poor guy who'd been Doctrined into him could only use what he had to work with physically. It didn't matter. Two hours later, he, Bryson, Helga, and Walter were all inside luxurious state-sponsored Coffins, along with Guntis, their encrypted Auras transported to the World Summit itself. No one seemed to suspect who they were. No one even acted as if they existed, virtually or not.

Soon holoprojections were entering the famed UE headquarters. It was a vast cavern—a room so enormous that Michael was baffled by what sort of architectural engineering kept it from collapsing in on itself. It was fancy, also. Enormous decorative pillars flanked the entrance and there was dark mahogany everywhere you looked. Leather chairs, maroon velvet, lush carpet—and the smell. The scent of wood polish and perfume hung in the air. The virtual experience was created to be an exact replica of the actual, physical UE headquarters. Michael wasn't disappointed.

As he got his bearings, Michael admired the simplicity of the layout. Every official member country of the UE had its own antechamber off the central auditorium. Within the Sleep, each country had a Portal directly outside these antechambers. This was a plush room filled with leather couches. It was fully staffed and stocked with food and beverages. Glass doors led from this room onto a balcony that overlooked the central space below. Michael took it all in as they arrived with Guntis, who immediately introduced them to the prime minister and her chief of staff—the man taken by the Tangent Levi.

"Levi had her ear all week," Guntis was telling Helga in his thick accent. Michael, Bryson, and Walter hovered around Guntis and Helga as they spoke. They had inched into a corner of the big room, and Michael was trying his best to adjust to the surreal experience. "She might seem a little intimidating, but she's not the type to put power before reason. If she thinks it will help her cause or her country, she'll listen to anyone. And she listened."

"So how's this going to happen?" Helga asked.

Guntis gestured toward the doors that led out to the chamber proper. "The prime minister is an executive member of the UE, so she has a good amount of time to speak. Levi convinced her to make Kaine and the Tangent invasion her highest priority. She's going to make a pitch for money and resources, hopefully get you whatever you need to begin the pushback."

As Guntis spoke, the people mingling around them had begun to move toward the seats. Guntis gestured to them to follow, and Michael and the group joined the mass of people moving toward the doors. From what Michael could tell, it looked like attendance was about half virtual and half physical—at least for those filling the chairs in the balcony. Michael walked in a daze. He knew that to those actually in attendance at the summit, he appeared as a shimmery projection—people probably even thought he was unimportant because he'd only been invited virtually.

"What did we get ourselves into?" Bryson whispered to

him. Before Michael could answer, Helga ushered them to a few empty seats in the back row of the section reserved for virtual visitors. They sat as close to the aisle as they could.

"Something's wrong," Michael said. Maybe he'd just grown accustomed to things never working out the way they were supposed to. But he couldn't shake the nervous feeling in his chest. He searched the room for anything that seemed out of the ordinary, but he realized that he wouldn't know if something wasn't as it should be.

"What's the deal?" Bryson whispered to him.

Michael slumped in his seat.

"Something's wrong," he repeated.

CHAPTER 11

CHAOS CAPTURED

1

Michael didn't know what it was exactly that set off his alarm. It might've been the heightened paranoia of crossing paths with so many Tangents—or people he suspected were Tangents. But something strange hung in the air. So when the world within that cavern descended into madness, Michael wasn't surprised.

Only scared.

2

The chamber was circular—rounded tiers and countless balconies surrounding a large dais with a rotating stage, a dark wood podium resting in its middle like an old tombstone. Security was heavy throughout the auditorium. Michael had noticed the many armed guards immediately. They were everywhere. A ring of the stern men and women stood just a few feet back from the wide stage. At first, it had set his mind at ease—at least those attending were safe from outside attack at the summit. An inside job was another story.

Just a few minutes after he and Bryson had taken their seats, an elderly gentleman rose to the stage. He walked to the podium slowly and stopped, gripping its sides firmly. His image was projected high above him as an enormous hologram so that he could be seen easily even by those in the antechamber farthest from the stage.

He cleared his throat into the microphone and it was like thunder cracking from the giant speakers above them.

"Ladies and gentlemen," the man began, his voice surprisingly strong, "it is my pleasure, and sorrow, to welcome you to this hallowed assembly today. As speaker for the Union of Earth these many years, I've never seen such a dark time come upon us. It is with a heavy heart, yet with unshaken certainty of hope, that I open these proceedings. Thank you for being here."

He paused, and Michael thought it was a natural place for applause, a general acknowledgment of his words. But the thousands of people in the chamber remained silent. It felt as if the air had frozen solid.

The man continued. "We have promised that each country, territory, and union represented here today will have their moment. Not only do we expect reports of the troubles seen in your lands—troubles caused by these so-called Tangent invaders—but we also hope to hear your proposed solutions. I am determined that we stay here together until we've paved a path of solutions."

The old man reached somewhere below the podium and came back with a glass of water in his hand, from which he took a long, shaky swallow. Michael cringed at the sound of it booming from the speakers. His sense that something was wrong only increased, and he couldn't keep still in his seat, scanning the audience for any sign of mischief. His head ached from the stress and unease.

Another thunderous throat-clearing brought his attention back to the speaker of the UE.

"The order of presentation was chosen at random this very morning," the man said. "We sincerely ask that no deviation from this order take place. We also ask that brevity be the rule at hand, and that we save deliberations until we've heard all those who wish to speak their mind." He paused, looking around the room.

"Before we officially begin, however, I want to announce a very special guest. Sitting before me, on the ground level, is a representative from VirtNet Security. We are told the VNS has a potential solution to this dire problem of Tangents and the so-called Mortality Doctrine program. But they've requested that their own presentation wait until all others have been heard, so that their information can be understood in the full context of what's happening globally. We've been assured that there's a very good reason to keep hope in our hearts.

"Please," he said, holding an arm out to his side, "as they've had deep troubles of their own and are not a usual part of our quorum, please give Agent Diane Weber from the VNS a welcoming round of applause."

The chamber erupted with the sound of clapping as

Weber's face replaced the speaker's in the floating hologram, high in the air, near the ceiling. She smiled warmly and gave a slight dip of her head.

Michael looked at the haunting visage of Agent Weber and thought, *Of course.*

Of course.

3

The ring of guards positioned around the stage faced outward, watching the audience, their weapons holstered but visible to all. There had to be at least fifty of them, all standing at attention, their eyes scanning the crowds. The applause was just starting to quiet, and the speaker leaned forward to continue the program, when Michael caught movement in that wide ring of armed guards.

Others saw it, too, because a collective gasp filled the room right before the first shot rang out.

It was from a guard standing to the right of the speaker. He dropped his weapon and immediately turned and ran up the stairs, onto the stage proper. As he ascended the steps, he pulled out a second gun, long and sleek. The room went dead silent, and then the guard pulled the trigger.

The shot echoed through the chamber, amplified by the acoustics of the structure. Michael was on his feet in time to see the speaker fly back from the podium. He landed on his side, and it was clear to Michael that the man wouldn't be getting up. Whatever ammunition that guard had used was far deadlier than any from a standard weapon.

There was one last beat of shocked silence; then the chamber erupted. Chaos swept through the hall as most people struggled to leave their seats, pushing urgently toward the exits. Michael and Bryson could only stand and stare as things got worse.

The guard who'd shot the speaker turned away from the center of the stage and faced the rows of chairs closest to the dais. Once again he raised his weapon and started firing into the crowd. The noise grew tenfold. Panic spread throughout the chamber, and people were no longer merely pushing, but clawing and fighting, climbing over each other to escape.

Still Michael couldn't move. He watched, frozen in disbelief.

The rogue guard got off three shots before one of his partners took him down. But before any calm could be restored, a female guard fired at the man standing beside her. Then other guards jumped into the action, one shooting at the woman who'd just killed her neighbor, others firing into the audience. The entire display was madness, and try as he might, Michael couldn't figure out who was on whose side.

It seemed like some surreal, impossible nightmare. There was so much blood, and shots continued to sound. More guards went down; others were targeting the patrons they had signed on to protect. More people died.

Oddly, Michael felt a certain calmness, as if he'd grown used to the world being insane. He turned toward Bryson, who seemed as paralyzed as Michael.

"What's happening to us, man?" Bryson stared straight ahead as he spoke. "When will it ever stop?"

"It'll never stop!" Michael shouted. "Not until we stop

letting people manipulate us. We need to use our own Coffins to get back into the Sleep and figure out how to fix this ourselves." He was seething with anger now. "Let's get to the Portal and Lift out of here before someone stops us." It was a heartless thing to say, but rage filled him. Whoever it was behind this latest attack had to be stopped, and Michael wasn't waiting for other people to get the job done.

He grabbed Bryson by the arm and pushed him toward the aisle—the rest of the people sitting by them had already cleared out into the antechambers. Helga was waiting at the entrance, yelling at Michael to hurry. He loved her, and he knew she was doing everything she could, but the sight of her right then made him mad. What a waste it had all been.

He took another look at the stage, where the chaos continued. Bodies littered the ground, and shots were still being fired in every direction.

Michael and Bryson had chanced fate enough—they needed to leave. Michael gave his friend another push and they ran for the aisle, met up with Helga. She didn't waste time on words, ushering him toward the door, refusing to leave until Michael went before her. They were just a few feet from the exit when a voice boomed through the enormous room, from all directions at once.

"Sit down!"

It was a man's voice, amplified by the speakers.

"Get back in your seats," the man yelled again, "or we'll blow the entire building up!"

Michael turned away from the door and looked back toward the center of the chamber. Another enormous hologram floated where the speaker had previously been. It was a guard, his hair disheveled, sweat streaming down his face. He held his weapon in both hands before him, right above the top of the podium.

"Last warning," he said, this time in a softer voice. Most people in the room had stopped to listen. Only a few had actually made it out. "You will sit, you will listen, and you will watch as we change the world."

He paused, and Michael knew what he was going to say before the words came out of his mouth.

"My name is Kaine."

4

The truth struck Michael at that moment. His life was forever connected to two people: Agent Weber and the Tangent known as Kaine. He just had to accept it.

The guard who'd identified himself as Kaine waited as the remaining audience members filed back into the main chamber. Maybe it was something in his eyes, but most patrons in the chamber believed his threat that he would bring down the entire building.

"Wise," Kaine said into the microphone. "You're all very wise to do as I say." The Tangent's face hovered above the dais, one hundred times its actual size. Kaine always seemed to find a way to establish his presence in a grand, theatrical style.

Michael and Bryson had found their same seats, and

Helga sat next to them. The rest of the crowd had done the same, except for a few stragglers who staggered around the room as if they'd lost their minds to fear.

Kaine gave them only minutes before he started talking again. "It's good to see that humans are still reasonable when called upon to be so. Thank you for taking my suggestion. It would have been a shame to destroy such a lovely building. You will find that I'm not entirely unreasonable, either—once you see things my way. You will probably even agree with me. The world, my friends—both virtual and real—is about to become a much better place. One day you'll tell your grandkids that you were here to witness the beginning."

Michael scowled. He felt like he knew Kaine, not only from their interactions, but from what they shared—that they were both just lines of code when it all came down to it. But something was off. This just didn't seem like the Kaine he knew.

"Now," the man said. "As of this moment, I am the leader of this world. President, chancellor, prime minister, all wrapped into one. My fellow Tangents will be assigned various locations in the many countries and territories around the globe. You will submit or you will be replaced by Tangents who are more than willing to do so. The Mortality Doctrine is a wonderful thing, my new friends."

Michael wanted to stand up and shout. Something was definitely off. After his last two encounters with Kaine within the Sleep, he knew he was right. This was absolutely, positively not Kaine.

The impostor kept talking, but Michael tuned him out, leaning over to Bryson. "That's not him, dude. That's not him."

Bryson looked at him. "He does seem a little over-the-top. What's going on?"

"I don't know."

"Let's just hear him out," Bryson said. "Learn something."

". . . that so many people had to die," the guard was saying, his larger-than-life hologram addressing the crowd like a god. "We needed to show a display of power, make sure you know that we can do what we need to do and literally be whoever we need to be. Think about this—if we can so easily take over one of the most secure meetings in the world, imagine what else we can do. You need to abandon any idea of rebellion you may already be hatching."

Michael didn't know how much longer he could take this display.

And then, once again, the world changed.

5

The guard claiming to be Kaine seemed to like talking.

"Our perception of the world, of intelligence, of mortality, of life . . . with each passing year, it seemingly evolves at double the rate of the previous year. Our understanding of death has transcended even the most optimistic religion, when we can plainly see that the termination of our physical bodies does not have to mean the end. Although you may despise me now, that will change. In time, as we rule and show you the way . . ."

Kaine stopped, his words fading out as if he'd suddenly forgotten a memorized speech. A blankness washed over his face, and the silence in the chamber stretched out. Michael watched, wondering what was going on, and a thread of drool dripped from the guard's mouth. On the huge hologram, it appeared as a long line of silver-blue that flashed, then disappeared beneath the display.

"What the . . . ," Bryson murmured in awe.

Kaine, the guard, whoever he was—moved his mouth to speak again, but no sound came out. Another stream of drool dripped from his lips. Then his eyes rolled up into his head and he fell backward, disappearing from the hologram.

Michael jumped to his feet just in time to see the man down on the dais crash to the floor, the thump of his body echoing through the chamber. A round of gasps circulated and another guard leaped onto the stage and ran for his fallen companion. Before the man made it halfway across the stage, however, he stumbled and fell, crashing face-first to the ground. He lay there, sprawled in a painful-looking tangle, unmoving.

Michael watched all this, bewildered.

None of the other guards moved. They stood looking at each other. It was impossible to know who'd been taken by Tangents and who hadn't.

The chamber had grown incredibly silent.

Then Michael heard a sound. A familiar sound.

Tap tap tap. Tap tap tap. A steady rhythm. Coming from

somewhere below, from a place outside the stage, hidden in darkness. *Tap tap tap.* Heeled shoes, footsteps tapping along like a musical instrument.

Then, far below, Agent Weber appeared from the shadows. She reached the dais, took the stairs, and calmly crossed the stage. Guards parted for her, their confusion obvious to Michael even from a distance. But a dozen or so feet from her, a man suddenly raised his weapon, aiming it straight at her. Before he could pull the trigger, he collapsed to the ground, rolled down a couple of stairs, and came to rest in a twisted bundle of arms and legs. His weapon clanked against the floor.

Agent Weber never even paused.

Michael's heart felt as if it had forgotten how to pump blood, his breathing at a standstill.

Weber looked down at the body of the guard who'd claimed to be Kaine, stepped over him, and moved to the podium proper. The microphone stood before her. She appeared comfortable, serene, as if she'd waited her whole life for this moment. The hologram now showed her to the masses within the chamber, the NewsBops surely projecting her image to the entire world.

She took a moment, allowing the shock of events to dissipate before she spoke. Michael forced himself to breathe now, trying to do it as calmly and as deeply as he could.

Agent Weber leaned forward an inch or two and spoke directly into the microphone.

"I can't imagine the confusion and horror that all of you must feel right now," she said. "Not just those of you in this once-beautiful audience chamber, but those watching around the world. What we've witnessed here today is a tragedy—there's no debating that. But it's also a moment of hope for us all. Our time to speak was meant for later, but under the circumstances, I felt it appropriate to come up here now and show you what we've prepared."

She paused, flashing the smallest hint of a smile. Then she said something that gave Michael chills.

"Be at peace, all of you." She spoke barely above a whisper. "The VNS is going to save the world from its demons."

CHAPTER 12

THE EXORCIST

1

Conversation moved across the chamber in a wave of hushed whispers. Michael's group was just as eager to discuss what had just happened. Bryson and Helga turned to Michael, but Michael held up his hand. He didn't want to miss something vital.

Information. He needed to know everything possible. And then he planned to do something about it.

"I ask for your patience right now," Agent Weber said, her words booming from the speakers. "If you will give me but a little slice of your time, everything will be explained. I come today as a representative of the VNS, an entity that exists to protect one of mankind's most valuable resources, the Virt-Net. As you know, we've recently suffered a devastating loss to our internal structure, setting us back considerably."

She sighed and frowned, a little too dramatically, playing up how difficult the situation was. Michael wanted to scream.

She was the one responsible for the damage! She'd *given* them the Lance device!

Weber continued. "Because of that setback, the Tangent known as Kaine has been able to apply his Mortality Doctrine program without restriction. As a result, programs have been inserted into the bodies of humans the world over. Sadly, the results of Kaine's actions culminated in the bloody savagery you saw here today. I am happy to say that we came here with good news, and now it has only been amplified by what's happened."

She nodded at someone and the hologram of her was replaced by a 3D image of a large room full of people, each working at a small station of glowing screens and blinking machines. It was such an unexpected image that Michael's anger was replaced by genuine curiosity.

"The VNS has put their hardest-working, most effective programmers on the task of diving into the deepest, darkest realms of the VirtNet in an attempt to unravel the mysteries of this Mortality Doctrine. After much work, and with the help of many brilliant minds, we've finally been able to reverse-engineer the program, effectively terminating the connection that allows its continuity. The Tangent program thus ceases to exist."

The vast hologram at the front of the room changed once again, from a view of Weber's room of workers to that of a street, where a man stumbled along the sidewalk, holding another man in the crook of his arm in a choke hold. The aggressor was waving a gun wildly as he struggled to hold on to the second man. Even without audio, it was clear that the man with the gun was yelling at everyone around him. Then the image froze.

"This was our first test of the process," Agent Weber said, "initiated just yesterday. This man was a politician in the city of Berlin. One moment he was a popular moderate, running for prime minister, and this very morning he was claiming to be a piece of VirtNet programming. When the politician in question abducted this senior staff member, he began yelling to anyone who'd listen that Kaine, the . . . how did he say it . . . the 'Lord of the Tangents,' had ordered him to kill every person in the entire city, one by one, as a sign of what was to come. We saw this moment as the perfect chance to test our process. Watch what happens next."

Michael watched Weber carefully, wondering if everyone else realized just how horrific her plan—the VNS's plan—was. But she had a card up her sleeve. The general population didn't know about the Hive—didn't know that these people still had a chance at life. Yes, maybe the VNS had figured out a way to wipe out the invading Tangents by severing the Mortality Doctrine link.

But the humans would die, too.

Michael would die. And then Jackson Porter.

2

He turned his attention to the holographic image of the German street. The video had shifted back into motion. The struggle continued until the strange man stopped, then abruptly collapsed. The gun tumbled out of his hand, and his hold on the victim loosened until the hostage could scramble away. It was as if someone had snapped the politician's spinal cord. He lay lifeless as a crowd gathered around him, staring down in awe. The image froze again, then vanished, and once more Agent Weber's larger-than-life visage appeared above them.

"To our relief and delight," she said, "the process we triggered worked to permanently sever the connection between the politician's body and the Tangent's consciousness by destroying the Tangent program in the VirtNet. As you could clearly see from the images shown just now, at least one human life was saved, and probably many more."

Weber looked around the enormous chamber, her eyes flashing across Michael for just an instant, making a chill run down his back. He waited for her inevitable justification of the consequences.

"We came today to present these important findings. The VNS had planned to do further extensive testing of the process before implementing it on a grand scale. But today's events have expedited our plans. We've decided it's time to take action. We could have never expected our most wanted criminal to give himself over to us."

She held up a fist as if to salute, though Michael wasn't sure whom. Maybe herself. "Kaine—the one who started it all—is dead. And by his own carelessness, we were able to pinpoint his signal and terminate his connection, ending him forever. We are sure that others will come forward and claim to be this powerful Tangent, but rest assured, he has ceased to exist. Before our plan to reverse the Tangent take-over has even officially begun, we've had our greatest victory."

She slammed her fist on the podium. "Kaine is dead!"

The audience erupted into applause. There were shouts and whistles, stomping of feet, all of it a thunderous roar of approval. Michael didn't move a muscle of his Aura. He looked at Bryson and Helga, who appeared equally disbelieving.

"That wasn't Kaine," Michael said, though he doubted Bryson could hear him over the noise. Everything about this stank to high heaven. What was Weber's game here? What was the VNS up to?

As for Weber, she seemed to relish the moment. When she finally raised her arms, motioning the chamber to silence, she appeared reluctant to step away from her place in the spotlight.

"Please," she said, repeating it several times until the crowd quieted down and took their seats. "Thank you. I appreciate your show of support—we all do—but the time to truly celebrate is yet to come. A massive struggle awaits. Identifying and triggering the Anti–Mortality Doctrine against all known Tangents will take a considerable effort. Even in this room, as we speak, there are those who know they're guilty. And yet they are quiet, hoping to avoid discovery. I assure you all, they will not. My people are working feverishly to make sure of that. As you can see."

She held up a hand and snapped her fingers—actually snapped her fingers, as if her childhood dreams of magical hocus-pocus were making it happen—and several more guards fell to the ground around the stage. The remaining guards backed away, as if scared of their own sudden deaths.

Weber looked pleased at the murders she'd just committed. She lowered her arm and continued.

"Our system of identifying Tangent invaders is far from perfect, but you've just seen it demonstrated. In the time that Kaine stepped up here and identified himself and gave his speech, my people in our war room were able to lock on his connection to the VirtNet and sever it. They immediately began work on the guards and achieved what you just witnessed. In time—soon, we hope—we'll be able to sweep the world. This should discourage any Tangent from ever initiating the Mortality Doctrine again. It will mean certain death. It will mean true death."

Michael winced at the words. The phrase made him think of Sarah, whom he'd lost because of this woman. He could barely keep still in his seat.

"The VNS can save humanity from this plague. All we ask is for your support, unilateral authority to do what needs to be done. And resources—we need both funding and manpower."

She swept the chamber with her hard, confident gaze. "Our world has been invaded by demons, my friends. And we are the exorcists. Thank you."

Once again, the auditorium erupted into applause. Everyone was on their feet, except for Michael's small group. No one had noticed the most pressing issue: the VNS was going to kill every last Tangent in the world—and the humans right along with them. Michael couldn't take it one more second. He got up, pushed his way down the row of seats and into the aisle, then ran for the exit, to the Portal outside Latvia's antechamber.

He had to get out of the Sleep.

3

Michael thought he'd be hassled trying to leave the Latvian embassy after everything that had happened, but the guards just offered curt nods as he passed them on his way out into the streets of Washington, D.C.

Fog had crept back into the air. It cascaded over signs and buildings and cars, almost like a ghostly living thing. Michael's shirt was damp, his hair as well, and by the time he'd walked through three or four intersections, he was feeling a bit dazed. People appeared like magic from the mist, passing him on the sidewalk, then vanishing once again behind him. Not many people were out—Michael figured that most were probably glued to the NewsBops, watching Weber's grand performance over and over.

He kept walking. He would stop for a light, look for cars, and continue. From time to time he'd peek into store windows, as if his world hadn't crumbled around his feet. He had absolutely no idea where he was going or what he was going to do, but he couldn't go back. He couldn't.

Bryson would be mad. Helga would be downright livid. And he didn't care. He loved both of them, but he didn't care. They'd find him later, or he'd find them. So he wandered, the beginnings of a terrible idea brewing in his mind. He wasn't ready to pour it out, accept its awfulness. But he was heading straight for it, one way or another. And he had to do it by himself.

He walked on, swallowed by the mist.

4

The streets grew emptier the farther he went, even though the buildings got taller and wider and more modern. There was a river nearby, but he could only tell because of a giant bridge that loomed before him as he neared. It got to the point that he hardly saw a person every five minutes, and day began to fade into night, darkness seeping through the fog, sinister, deadly.

A woman came out of a store, staring at Michael a little too intently for his liking. She stopped midstride, her eyes following him. Alarms went off in his head. It was a Tangent—it had to be. He picked up his pace and took a few quick turns to make sure she wasn't following him. It was hard to tell with the blanket of mist hovering around him. He kept moving.

At some point, he found himself in front of a massive hotel. What stopped him was the sign out front, blazing with flashing lights.

NERVEBOX SERVICE AVAILABLE WITH ROOMS

He stood there and stared at the words. They disappeared, replaced by other advertisements and announcements and special offers, cycling through its program. Then the words he cared about flashed on again.

Coffins. At this very hotel, he could get a room and a Coffin. He knew what he had to do. He walked forward, opened the door, and stepped up to the registration desk. A friendly man with a perfect haircut greeted him, though he couldn't hide the anxiety in his eyes. He'd been watching the NewsBops, no doubt.

"May I help you?" the man asked.

Michael took a breath and went for it. "I'd like your nicest room, with your nicest Coffin. Um, I mean NerveBox. And I need to check in right now."

Michael lay on the bed in his room, staring at the ceiling. Things seemed to be working out for him today. Well, if you didn't count the whole murderous rampage incident. He'd made it out of the World Summit and the Latvian embassy, made it through the streets of D.C., found a hotel with Coffin service, and then, the topper, been able to get himself a room with the fake identity he'd created so long ago. Using the money he'd stolen from Jackson Porter's parents.

Someone might've figured it out. Maybe he was being traced. Flags might've been raised. But the world had much bigger problems to deal with right then. In any case, he hoped to be done, one way or another, by the time anyone could get to him.

There was a tap at the door.

For just a split second, fear spiked in his chest. But then a voice said, "Room service." He'd ordered almost everything on the menu. He hadn't eaten much since waking up that morning, and now it had caught up with him.

He needed to build up his strength. So he tipped the lady after she brought in the rolling cart of steaming food, then closed the door, locked it, and triggered the dead bolt. Then he dug in, starting with the bleu chips. He thought of Sarah with every bite.

6

A half hour later, he had stripped down and was standing above the open Coffin. He'd eaten so much that his stomach stuck out in a satisfying bulge. He rubbed it for good luck, then stepped into the pod, lowering himself until he lay flat on his back. He took several deep breaths to ease his nerves, more scared than he wanted to admit.

Bryson and Helga, along with her Tangent Alliance, were searching the streets for him at that very moment. He was sure of it. He was also sure that they were frantic and angry. He felt bad—he shouldn't have left them like that—but he needed to do this alone. He'd ask their forgiveness once he got back.

If he got back.

No, *when* he got back.

Nah. *If.* No point being dishonest.

He finished off the programming he'd already started on the outside console. Then he reached up to his ear and clicked on his NetScreen. He sent the message he'd typed earlier, encrypting it with five layers of hidden codes, to the onetime connection link provided by the Tangent himself. If he was out there, he'd get the message. Michael pressed the final button, then closed his eyes, waiting for the mechanisms to take over his body and Sink him into the Sleep.

LiquiGels.

AirPuffs.

NerveWires.

As they started engaging, he saw the words of the message he'd sent, almost as if they'd been printed on the back of his eyelids.

Kaine,
Meet me at the attached coordinates.
I have something to tell you.

CHAPTER 13

A CANCER OF CODE

1

The Sleep had become a scary place.

Because the Coffin he used was owned by the hotel and ran on public systems, he had to follow their regulations during his Sink. He arrived at a Portal in a giant commerce square. In better times it would have seen thousands of daily patrons, shopping and gaming and virtual eating. There would have been street performers and Tangents programmed to do all kinds of services—everything from sweeping up data dust created by coding glitches to acting as the homeless, begging for coin. It was all designed to make the square feel like a real city.

Now it couldn't feel further from that.

Whatever Weber had set them up to do with the Lance, it had wreaked havoc on the world the VNS was meant to protect. The utter lack of security caused by their breach had obviously allowed any two-bit hacker to come in and destroy whatever he or she wanted. Why destruction appealed to people, Michael had no idea, but it definitely *did*—the commerce square was a shambles.

Storefronts had collapsed or warped, as if they'd been made of soft plastic and left to melt in the sun. Some of them had degraded into a mess of pixels, parts of them glitching and snapping in and out of sight. Abandoned Tangents roamed the streets, seemingly robbed of their central programming and left to wander aimlessly. Some even appeared dangerous, left with a lot of virtual power but no conscience, no reason not to attack the Auras of innocent visitors. Michael steered clear of anything remotely suspicious.

A lot of the complex code necessary to create such a lifelike place had been forcibly Decayed or just plain neglected by its operators, who were too scared of the chaos to stick around. There were potholes in the streets and sidewalks, gaping black holes that led who-knew-where, ungodly places with no Portals—places from which probably only a skilled coder like Michael could escape.

Scary had been Michael's first impression upon arriving, and it stayed with him. If he'd been just some normal Joe coming for a jaunt in the Sleep, he'd have been terrified to his very core. Even with *his* skills, he was afraid. Confident, but afraid.

He carefully made his way through the square, heading toward an outer point so it'd be easier for him to hack into the code and take himself where he wanted to go. He watched every step he took—the damage to the area wasn't static; a gaping hole appeared right in front of him at one point—as he walked away from the central area of shops and restaurants and found a side street that led to a dark alley. On the far end, there was a faint purple glow, and he knew it'd be a good place to work his magic.

The alley swallowed him. The programming in the narrow walkway cut off the noise from the square and made it feel as if his ears had been stuffed with cotton. He didn't stop, refusing to let fear dampen his determination. If anyone could handle this wreck of a VirtNet, it was Michael. At least, that was what he told himself.

Finally, he reached the pool of dark purple light. It had no substance or form, no obvious source. When he turned to look back the way he'd come, there was no sign of the square. No sign of anything at all.

The code really was breaking down. Nothing showed it better than this—it was as if the programmers hadn't even attempted to make the setting of the commerce square resemble real life. It was broken in the middle, nonexistent on the edges. Michael literally stood in the middle of virtual nowhere.

He sat down, closed his eyes, and dove into the code.

It was even worse than he'd thought.

If someone had asked him to describe the cesspool of broken code into which he'd flung himself, he would've said rot. He imagined the inner workings of the human body—muscles and organs and tissue—slowly being destroyed by rotting cells. Broken down and eaten.

Everything around him looked sick.

Lines of code were broken, crooked, hitched as they streamed by. The code pieces themselves—numbers and letters from countless alphabets and symbols from mathematics and science—they didn't look right. Wavy lines where they were supposed to be straight, and straight where they should be wavy. Ragged holes and truncated commands, units that had been warped or stretched and splayed like amoebas.

And that wasn't all. The background was full of colors— pale green and deep yellow and an orange that made Michael feel seasick.

But he had to face it all head-on.

Programming in this VirtNet felt almost like learning from scratch. But if anyone was capable of it, he was. He knew that. Already, as he studied the cyclone of virtual nonsense around him, his mind was adapting. *Oh, that symbol has transformed into this; that line of code actually does this task; those three functions add up to what these two functions once triggered.* Maybe it was because his essence itself was made up of code, but he started to see through the muck, like a nearsighted child putting on glasses for the first time.

Excited and scared at once, he threw himself at the disease-riddled mess of code like he'd never done before. And that was saying something. That was saying a lot.

3

Time lost all meaning as he worked. He concentrated so furiously that his head felt like a crushed grape. His virtual eyes begged him to stop, the pain like knives pressing directly through them into his skull. But he was on a roll, and the adrenaline-laced rush of it all kept him going.

Finally, he released himself from it, catapulting away from the strange alley of no-man's-land. It was like literal flight, wind rushing past him, blowing at his clothes and hair. Exhilarated, breathless, he opened himself up to the euphoria. He was a rocket, flying through space. Butterflies swarmed in his chest, and his mind was light as air.

He knew when he'd arrived, just as someone sleeping in a dark room knows when a light has been turned on. He felt the soft ground beneath him, heard the breeze rustling the virtual leaves of the trees, smelled the pine and earth.

He opened his eyes.

The tree house was nearby, looking as strong and firm as ever. An endless forest stretched in every direction, the sounds of insects and frogs and birds filling the air, though a little more muted than normal. The colors were a little weaker also; maybe the trees weren't as tall, the smells not so vibrant. But all in all, the code was much healthier than anything he'd seen so far in the Sleep.

He'd built this place with Bryson and Sarah, on the outskirts of *Lifeblood*, hidden from all but the most discerning coders. Seeing the tree house, its ladder leading up to the trapdoor, made his heart shatter. The pain of Sarah's death came crashing back, and he lay down on the forest floor, curling up into a ball. He missed her. He missed her so much. His head still pounded from the work it had taken to restore this place, not to mention the effort of traveling there through a sea of decomposing code, but the trauma in his heart was much worse.

How could Agent Scott have done that? Taken his best friend away from him?

He'd never known a pain like this. He'd taken Sarah for granted. She'd just always been there, and he'd assumed she always would be. It was hard to face the fact that someone like Agent Weber was still alive, yet his best friend was gone.

And then there was Kaine. He didn't understand Kaine any more than he understood Weber. He could only hope that the Tangent would show up.

It felt as if he weighed a thousand pounds, but Michael finally pulled himself to his feet and climbed up to his tree house. To Sarah's tree house.

Time passed.

Michael sat in the corner, in the beanbag that constituted Bryson's most important contribution to the furniture arrangement. As they'd so often said, it was vomit-colored. Unfortunately for Michael, it reminded him a lot of the code in which he'd been floating before.

Sarah had carved her name in the wall across from him,

and he sat staring at it listlessly. His aching heart had morphed into a dull numbness, and he lay completely still, looking at the letters of her name one by one. It didn't seem possible that she was gone. If only she'd been a Tangent like him, and Kaine had never entered the picture, they could've gamed and lived life to its fullest for what felt like forever, until the Decay took their minds and they drifted into forgetful bliss.

More time passed.

And then, finally, there were footsteps—the sound of leaves crunching beneath his tree house. He sat up with a jolt, his feet thumping on the wooden floor. His gaze shot to the trapdoor.

"Michael," a man's voice said from below.

Michael slowly stood, careful not to make the slightest noise. Though there wasn't much point in being quiet. Whoever had arrived knew Michael was there, obviously. The question was, was it Kaine or an impostor?

He stepped lightly over to the trapdoor, leaned forward, and looked through the hole.

A man stood next to the ladder, staring up. And it was him—Kaine—in the same Aura that Michael had last seen him. Not the old, decrepit geezer from the first time, but the younger version. Perfectly styled salt-and-pepper hair, a sharp jawline, bright and intelligent eyes. In his dark, three-piece suit, he could have passed for a handsome businessman.

"May I come up?" he asked.

"Uh, yeah."

Not the greatest start to the most important conversation of his life.

Kaine grabbed hold of a rung, and as if it were the most normal thing in the world for a grown man in a suit to do, he started to climb. Michael stepped back when Kaine's head popped through the opening, and then the Tangent was on his feet, standing before him. He had almost a foot in height on Michael's Aura, and his face was totally unreadable. He didn't look angry, but he sure didn't seem too happy, either.

Neither of them said a word for several seconds.

It was Kaine who spoke first. "Why am I here, son? I've given you several chances, yet you reject me every time."

"I . . ." This wasn't quite how Michael had imagined it.

"You only exist because of me," Kaine continued. "Surely you realize that I could've had you terminated at any point. I have watched in wonder—and amusement, I have to say—as you run around like an obedient dog, doing whatever Weber commands."

Michael tried to recover. "Listen—"

"Yes? Why am I here?" Kaine interrupted.

"I . . . well . . ." Michael motioned toward the beanbags. He was having a hard time figuring out where to begin. "Can we sit down? I know you're powerful, but I'm not going to botch this. Let's sit down and talk through it without your power act." Michael fought to stay put, expression unwavering.

It took Kaine a moment to answer, but when he did, Michael swore he could make out a slight smile on the Tangent's lips. "Fair enough. Fair enough." Kaine stepped over to the nearer beanbag and sat down, as limber as any teenager.

Michael sat back down in Bryson's infamous bag, settled himself.

"Now," Kaine said, exaggerating his patient tone. "May I please know why I'm here?"

Michael eyed the man carefully. "How can I know for sure that you're Kaine? I was just at the World Summit and supposedly watched you die the true death."

Kaine folded his hands in his lap. "If we're going to talk, let's not waste time. Okay? How about we agree on that first. You know very well that was just another of Weber's shows. I'd be insulted if I couldn't plainly see in your eyes that you know that wasn't me. After everything I've done, I'd be very upset if you thought I'd actually fall into that trap."

"Fair enough" it was Michael's turn to say. "I had to at least ask the question. I don't think anyone else could get past that crypting I put on my message, and I never believed it was you at the summit. This is you."

Kaine gave a slow nod of acknowledgment. "Then I ask again—why am I here?"

A nervous tingle in Michael's chest had slowly grown into a monstrous buzz that made it hard to breathe. "I . . . I guess I just got to my breaking point. Ever since all this started— way back when Weber first contacted me and sent me on the Path . . . I've felt like a pawn. A guinea pig. A lamb sent to the slaughter, or whatever that old phrase is. And I want to know once and for all—why me? What's the point?"

"So you brought me in to complain?" Kaine asked. "Complaints noted."

Michael was glad Kaine went the sarcasm route, because it was just enough to tick him off and dampen the nervousness. "See? That right there," he said, pointing at Kaine. "I'm sick of that crap. Just talk to me like a normal person. You know I have every right to be here and to be heard. If you would just treat me with some respect and hear what I have to say without trying to intimidate me!" By the time he finished speaking, he was practically shouting, his face red.

To Kaine's credit, he remained calm. He simply shrugged humbly. "Well spoken," he answered. "I'm here, aren't I? I'll listen to what you have to say. Consider me madly curious."

Michael nodded, satisfied. "All right, then. From here on out I'm doing things my way. I have a lot of questions, and I have a lot of ideas."

Kaine didn't say a word, but his focus was strong, his eyes sharp.

Michael nodded again, as if to convince himself he was on the right track. "So, first things first. I want you to tell me everything about this . . . immortality. And why? What are your motives?"

Kaine shifted his position, leaning closer to Michael. "I'll talk to you, but answer me one question: why now?"

Michael didn't hesitate. "Because you and I have to stop the VNS."

CHAPTER 14

THE VISION

1

Michael could see right away that he had Kaine's attention. The Tangent had probably come expecting many things, but not this. Michael had never hidden the fact that he hated the man.

For Michael, it was a no-brainer, though. Weber and the VNS were up to something terrible, and Kaine was the only one powerful enough to stop them. Michael just had to make sure he used him in the right way.

Kaine finally spoke. "I'll admit, you've surprised me."

"I figured I would."

"I've wanted you to work with me from the beginning," the Tangent said. "It's all I've ever wanted. There's a reason you were the first to be chosen for the Mortality Doctrine. And there's a reason I've come to you on more than one occasion asking you for help. Why, after everything that's happened, have you suddenly decided to take me up on my offer?"

"I know about the Hive," Michael said. "I know about the connection between the bodies stolen by the Tangents and the consciousness taken from those bodies and stored there. I know they need each other to coexist."

If Kaine was surprised, he hid it well. "And?"

"And now the VNS thinks the solution to the problem you created is to sever those connections and let both sides die. I'm not going to let that happen. That's why I need your help."

Kaine shifted in the beanbag and rested his hands in his lap, his gaze fixed on Michael. Michael had no idea what was going on in the Tangent's mind.

"You're serious, aren't you?" Kaine finally said.

Michael couldn't hide his exasperation. "Yes, I'm serious."

Kaine held his hands up. "It's just . . . a bit of a relief to see you come to your senses."

"So?" Michael urged. "What do you know about the VNS? What are they trying to accomplish?"

Kaine shifted again, then let out a frustrated sigh. "I'm sorry, but this won't do. Can we please sit in the chairs at the table?"

The table was small, the chairs smaller. But if that was what it took for Kaine to continue this meeting, then so be it.

"Fine," Michael said. A few seconds later, they were settled and facing each other.

Kaine leaned forward with a very serious look on his face. "Let me start by saying that yes, I agree with you regarding the VNS. They've gone far, far past . . . decency. Let me ask you, though, Michael—why the Hive? Why would I go to all the trouble to create, maintain, and secure that massively complex program?"

Michael worried he could be walking into a trap, but knew he had to answer honestly. "Because there has to be that connection. To keep the Tangents alive in their human hosts."

"No." Kaine shook his head. "Absolutely not. If we'd merely wanted to replace the human intelligences with Tangents, we could've done so. Download the Tangents and terminate the life it replaced. That connection you speak of exists *because* of the Hive. Because I wanted to keep those humans alive—and to do it, a connection needed to be maintained between the two. One depends on the other. It's that way because I *made* it that way. Others . . . well, others didn't care one way or another. They've always had their own motives in this process."

Michael stared at him, his mind going places that he found hard to believe. "You mean . . ."

Kaine nodded, a sad smile forming at the corners of his mouth.

"The VNS," Michael said.

"The VNS. I have it all figured out. Are you ready to know the truth? Do you think you can handle it?"

Michael could only nod.

Kaine leaned in. "They created me, Michael," the Tangent said. "The VNS created me."

2

Kaine leaned back, his whole body seeming to shrink from whatever trick in the code he'd just invoked. Michael stared at him as his mind worked to put all the pieces together.

"They created me decades ago," Kaine continued. "An experimental artificial intelligence that would become stronger and stronger. The human minds at the VNS could have never created the Mortality Doctrine program on their own. No human mind could have—it's far too complex. And so I came to be. I was double the value, too. Once the Doctrine had been created, I could be their bad man. Their very bad man."

Michael shook his head. He just couldn't believe it. "You mean they had all of this orchestrated from the beginning? Why? The whole world is screwed up, and most people blame them!"

Kaine shook his head, as if at a stupid child. "Of course it wasn't all orchestrated. Things have gone worse than even they planned. They didn't know that I would become sentient. That I'd come up with my own plans. They didn't know about the Hive. And so things fell harder and faster than they had hoped. But in the end, all the better for them. The farther your world falls, the bigger the hero the VNS becomes when it's saved."

Michael didn't feel so well. "You're telling me that the VNS programmed you, led you toward creating the Mortality Doctrine, then instigated sending thousands of Tangents into the world so that they . . . what, could look good in the NewsBops?"

"Don't be an idiot," Kaine snapped. "You were just at the World Summit. You know what's happening. Every government in the world is practically begging the VNS to do whatever it takes to save them. When this is all over, the VNS will be the most powerful entity in the world, and they'll never relinquish that power. They'll never let the threat die down enough to allow that to happen. They've almost won already."

"And what about you?" Michael asked. "What's your role in all this?"

"My role?" he repeated. "My role is that I'm their enemy, just as you are. It was their plan all along. They used me. They used you. You have to admire their brilliance. By the time we turned against them, us turning against them is exactly what they wanted. The Hive was the only wild card, and now they've figured that out, too. It's only a matter of time before there's nothing else we can do, about any of it. The VNS will practically rule the world, and we'll be terminated one way or another."

"Then what do we do?" Michael asked. As much as he hated it, it was now crystal clear that he had no choice but to work with Kaine on this.

"It's all about the Hive," the Tangent said. "Everything depends on the Hive. The VNS want to annihilate it, erase every stored intelligence, claim victory that the Tangents are dead and the world is saved."

"Okay." Michael had already assumed the Hive would play a major role. "So how do we stop them?"

Kaine thought a moment. "I know our time is short. And

there are things we need to do right away. But first I have to show you something. It's absolutely worth the time it will take."

"What?" Michael asked.

"I once tried to show you what it would be like to have the entire VirtNet at your disposal. Do you remember that?"

"Uh, yeah," Michael replied, hoping the Tangent understood sarcasm. He would never forget being glued to that shaft of purple light and traveling through the countless programs inside the Sleep.

Kaine gave a shrug that seemed to say, *You win some, you lose some.* "Well, that didn't work on you and your friends very . . . effectively, so I'm going to show you the other side of the coin. I'm going to show you how the world—the real, living, breathing world—is about to change forever."

Michael sucked in a breath. "Okay."

"Prepare to be amazed."

Everything around them disappeared, replaced by darkness.

Michael found himself catapulted into the blackness of space. Before him, a giant planet took up half his vision, brighter than the fullest moon. Kaine was beside him, looking on, his eyes large with wonder. Michael started to say something but stopped, instead deciding to study the celestial body that held the Tangent's attention.

When he turned back, he realized that it wasn't a planet at all.

It was a human fetus, almost fully grown, inside a crystalline sphere that pulsated with light. The baby's little arms and legs curled around an umbilical cord, its huge blue eyes actually open, looking wiser than they should at such an early stage of development.

"Just look at that," Kaine said, his voice quiet but clear. "It's a miracle, life. Don't you think? A group of cells reproducing with such precision that they become what you are today. A full-grown person, walking, talking, running, jumping, eating, dancing, sleeping."

He turned to look at Michael. "There are so many things humans have experienced that we haven't. From this simple stage of birth to puberty, broken legs and skinned knees, the feel of the real sun warming your skin. Until the Mortality Doctrine, no Tangent ever had the chance to know what it's like to be living flesh and bone. But now we've had a taste. It's beautiful. Tell me you disagree."

Michael was taken aback at the odd way he formed the question. "I . . . uh . . . Disagree with what?"

"You've now lived inside a real human body," Kaine elaborated. "Tell me it's not a beautiful thing."

Michael shrugged and returned his attention to the giant floating womb. "It doesn't matter what I think. Or you. Or anyone else. It's not right. You can't just go around stealing people's lives."

"Exactly," Kaine said. "You're one hundred percent correct."

"I am?"

Kaine nodded. "I don't want to steal anyone's life, Michael. The VNS wanted to. *Collateral damage* is the term they use to ease their consciences. But I gained sentience long before they even began to suspect, and I had a bigger vision. A much, much bigger vision. That's why I created the Hive. Jackson Porter is still perfectly sound and whole. Perfectly alive. You didn't steal his life."

Michael rolled his eyes at that. "Oh, come on. We stole his body. What's the difference? Would you want to spend the rest of your life living inside an orange glob?"

Kaine laughed. "Michael, I swear. You keep saying the perfect thing to prove my point. What do you think your entire life was before you found out you were a Tangent? Answer that for me."

"I . . . was alive, in my own way. I didn't know any different, so it didn't matter."

Kaine blinked hard, then waved his hands, and suddenly the planet-sized womb disappeared and the giant curved wall of the Hive appeared before them, its countless orange orbs of lights pulsing and shining.

"It's not like we kidnapped their bodies and shoved them in a box," Kaine said. "They're no different here than you were as a Tangent. Look at the Hive as their virtual Coffin. They'll be able to access an Aura, experience the VirtNet. Yes, their essence is stored here, their intelligence, their memories, their personalities—everything that makes them who they are. But so were you. When you were nothing but a program, you also were stored somewhere. But that didn't limit the things you could do. If anything, it did the opposite. Which is why I tried to show you the wonders available within the worlds of the VirtNet. If only you'd release the shackles of your narrow way of thinking, you'd be able to see just how grand and endless my vision for the future is."

Michael wasn't buying it. "But you did it against his will. You did what you did to me against my will. And I don't care how amazing you think the Sleep is, you don't have the right to steal Jackson Porter away from his parents and his friends and store him in an orange box."

Kaine sighed. "Baby steps. I'll never claim to be a saint. But someday, when the Mortality Doctrine is fully functioning according to my vision, they'll thank me and thank those who made sacrifices to get it off the ground."

"Why?" Michael asked. "Why would they thank you?"

"Because everyone will be happier. The sorrow of death will be vanquished."

"Sounds like a fanatic's vision to me," Michael said, anger bubbling up inside him. "Like you want to become a god."

"You're starting to upset me," Kaine said, so evenly that it gave Michael pause. "I'm trying to be reasonable and talk about this in a professional manner. At least keep your mind open long enough to make an informed decision. I came to you at your request, and you've asked me for help. I believe I deserve some respect in turn."

With each word, he seemed to return a little bit more to the Kaine Michael remembered. The one who kept trying to kill him. Maybe they weren't ready for complete honesty quite yet.

"Okay," Michael said. "I'm sorry." He just wanted to get through this charade and keep Kaine as an ally until he didn't need him anymore.

Kaine studied him for a moment, then continued. "I'm going to show you how this process works—how it *will* work—and then I'll let you decide. I'm confident you'll come around to my way of seeing things before long."

Kaine didn't wait for Michael to answer. The Hive disappeared, and once again Michael was taken away.

4

He floated above a home—a modest one-story structure with a two-car garage. The lawn was a lush green and the bushes were immaculately trimmed. Sunshine burst upon the scene like a floodlight. Michael looked around and realized his body was nowhere to be found—he was there but not there. No sign of Kaine, either. He was being shown the most advanced kind of 4D, a fully immersive production. Michael could see, smell, hear, feel it all.

A car pulled up the driveway and stopped in front of the garage. The sun glinted off the front windshield as it parked beneath Michael. Suddenly his aspect changed, swooping down fluidly to the passenger door, which opened as soon as his movement stopped. A man and a woman got out of the car; then the woman retrieved a baby from the backseat. It was a cute little girl, cooing and wiggling her tiny fingers.

Kaine's voice spoke directly to Michael's mind.

"A child. Fresh and new to the glorious world we know as Earth. Such a bright future. Such good parents. Everything seems perfect. Except for one thing, if you really, really think deeply and look at it all with an eternal perspective."

"What's that?" Michael asked.

"She will die," Kaine answered. "No matter what she does, or anyone else does, she will die. It could be tomorrow. It could be ten years from now. If she's lucky, she'll live out the normal life span and die around the age of ninety. This after some time spent walking around in a poorly packaged bag of frail bones. Sound like fun to you?"

Michael had only one answer for that one. "No."

"Thank you for being honest," Kaine responded. "But let's change this child's future, and in the process make every waking moment of her life better because she'll know, with complete certainty, that she will never die."

The woman and her husband were walking to the front door, lightly bouncing the baby while giving her kisses all over her cheeks. Michael watched as they went inside, the door thumping closed behind them.

"How?" Michael asked. "How can you possibly make her live forever?"

"Easy," Kaine replied. "Let's skip ahead."

The house dissolved into thousands of dust particles and swirled from their sight, immediately replaced by a gymnasium—banners covering the walls and hundreds of students sitting restlessly in the stands. Instead of a game taking place on the court, though, a long platform had been set up, complete with a row of fifteen Coffins.

In the middle, facing the stands, a woman stood at a podium. She wore a blue shirt with a symbol emblazoned on the right pocket: an *M* and a *D* on the upper left side of a slash, an *L* and an *N* on the lower right side. The slash itself ended in an arrow, pointing forever upward.

The woman spoke into the microphone. "We're so grateful that all of you have chosen to participate in the Mortality Doctrine Initiative. It is a decision that you will never regret, for the rest of eternity. The next fifty years of your lives will be full of adventures and wonders impossible to describe or imagine. The VirtNet Hive is like an infinite realization of your dreams, and we at Life Neverending can hardly wait for you to let us know about your experiences. Who's excited out there?"

Every last student clapped and cheered, loud and long, even though some of them looked more than a little afraid. Michael wasn't sure what he was watching, but he had a pretty good idea. And it felt as if he were watching the beginning of the apocalypse.

The woman let the applause go on for a minute before calling for silence. "You've all been briefed, and everything's in order. While you take your fifty-year journey into the VirtNet, remember that you have not the slightest reason for concern. Enjoy yourselves to the fullest; learn and grow and experience the universe. And when your time is up, we'll have the next generation of human hosts awaiting you, themselves excited for the VirtNet stage. All is taken care of. Your only job is to embrace immortality and leave your mark on it. Now let's stop talking and begin!"

More applause erupted at this, and students began getting up from the stands and lining up, guided by adults wearing the same shirt as the speaker. The MD/LN symbol obviously stood for Mortality Doctrine/Life Neverending. Michael shivered at the realization.

The first people in each line were being led to the Coffins, where they handed over some kind of data chip, then lay down in the open device. They were fully clothed, though Michael never was when he Lifted. But he had already figured out that these students—most of them around his own age—were only going to be in the Coffins for a short time.

The people in blue shirts worked at the control screens on the outside of the NerveBoxes, and soon the lids were closing, almost perfectly in sync. With a series of thumps, one by one they snapped shut, lights blinking all over them. The workers stepped back and smiled warmly at those watching and waiting.

"See the joy on their faces?" Kaine said. "The expectation, anticipation? If you could look deep, deep into their eyes, you'd see that there's no trace of that lingering, nagging awareness in humans today of their impending doom. The inevitability of their death, whether it be five, ten, or fifty years away. That'll be gone once my vision is complete. Now watch and see what happens."

The entire gym blurred for a moment, colors darting back and forth, melting together. Then it snapped back to normal, crisp and clear. Michael looked down and the Coffins had opened, the same kids who'd just climbed in now climbing out. Although there was something distinctly different about them. They appeared disoriented, as if they had no clue where they were or how they'd gotten there. The workers in blue shirts took them by the arm and gently led them off the temporary platforms, into the arms of others ready to escort them out of the building. Where they went, Michael didn't know. The next students who'd been waiting had already started getting into the now-empty Coffins.

"And so it goes," Kaine said. "Or so it *will* go. Generation after generation, born into one body, transformed into an indescribable VirtNet experience for fifty years, then reinserted into the next line of humans ready to embark on Life Neverending themselves. With immortality and endless education and growth, our levels of technology will skyrocket, just in time for us to expand to the planets and stars beyond our own. Always replenishing the human race, where no one need die ever again."

Michael closed his eyes to focus. "So these bodies in the gym—they were replaced by other . . . people who'd been in the VirtNet for fifty years? I mean, I know it's a simulation, but is that what's going to happen? What about when they get old? They'll still die. You can't prevent that."

"Oh, yes, we can," Kaine responded. "When these bodies, now occupied by another intelligence, reach the age of sixty-five, their intelligence is downloaded back into the Hive. They will once again experience another fifty years inside the Sleep, doing whatever they want, learning and growing even more. The bodies back on Earth will be frozen and stored, probably never to be used again. Unless, of course, we someday come up with other ways to significantly extend life. But the key is that no one will die again, ever. You'll either be in an actual human body, or you'll be just as alive—even more alive, in some ways—within the Sleep."

"Won't you run out of human hosts?"

"Of course not. People will keep having babies. We might have to extend the wait time within the Sleep. We'll even clone bodies if we have to, when that technology is sound. That's not a problem."

"What about accidents?" Michael asked. "Heart attacks? What if someone murders you? What then?"

Kaine's tone made it sound like he'd been anxiously awaiting the question. "Those will still be tragedies, but not a complete loss. One can always go back to their last known download into the VirtNet. Or, if you can afford it, you can go in every year, every week, every day—whatever works for you—and update your consciousness. Your memories, your knowledge, your everything. If you have a premature death, then you will be restored to your latest version. It's all worked out. Think of it as backing up your work."

Michael opened his eyes, but there was nothing there. At some point they'd slid back into the darkness. He instinctively reached to touch his face, but he had no hands or arms. It was like he'd become a part of the Sleep itself.

"There's more to show," Kaine said, startling him. "The future is a place of pure wonder, Michael, and I want you by my side."

Michael was stunned, feeling as broken apart as his virtual self was at the moment. Kaine scared him in so many ways. He didn't know how to read the situation. He went the safest route and said nothing.

"But it will have to wait," Kaine said after a long moment of silence. "Something is happening. Something terrible."

"What?" Michael asked, surprised at the sudden shift in the conversation.

"They found us. I don't know how, but they found us."

CHAPTER 15

BLACK CLOAKS

1

The darkness turned to fog, then mist, swirling around Michael. He looked down at his arms and legs as his body reappeared, as if someone were pouring him into an invisible mold. The mist thinned out, and finally the inside of the tree house appeared, at first blurry, then slowly solidifying. He and Kaine sat in the same two chairs as before the vision had started.

"Who found us?" Michael asked immediately, unfazed by the odd transformation.

Kaine held a finger to his lips, searching the room with his eyes. Then he leaned closer to Michael so he could whisper. "There are more Tangents against me than for me now. I don't know if the VNS programmed them or what—but you've met many of them. They have a terrible knack of knowing exactly where I am. And they're nasty, Michael. Nasty."

Michael immediately thought of the people in the woods,

outside the barracks where Helga had set up her Alliance. "Were they—"

"Yes," Kaine said curtly, still speaking softly. "The same. No one ever makes it easy, putting power before sense." He was about to say something else, but a noise stopped him short.

A high whine came from outside, as if a sudden windstorm had sprung up. It intensified, piercing enough to hurt Michael's ears. It was like a dog whistle, yet just above the threshold where humans could no longer hear it. It got louder, like wounded angels shrieking. The tree house creaked and shook. Something black and oily poured in through the cracks in the wood of the window frame, funneling in like smoke. The air shimmered, and suddenly the darkness was coalescing, forming shadows that hovered in the air around Michael and Kaine.

"Don't move," the Tangent said, staring straight at Michael. "They know me too well. We'll get out of this, but we have to be smart about it."

"What's happening?" Michael whispered.

"Just watch, and follow my lead."

A chill crept up Michael's back. As slowly as he could, he turned to get a view of the entity nearest him. It had taken a distinct shape, along with several others, shadowy figures with black cloaks draped from their thin shoulders, billowing in an unseen wind. Waves rippled across the cloaks, and the figures bobbed slightly. Up and down, up and down—there were about eight in a circle, all of them next to the walls. Like suspended blackened corpses. They'd yet to make a sound.

Michael wanted to run so badly. Kaine sat across from him, stoic and still, not really looking at anything. He certainly wasn't focused on their visitors. It was as if he'd fallen into a waking coma.

One of the entities swooped down from the other side of the room and stopped just inches from Michael's nose. He could feel the blood drain from his face, and he pressed himself as far as he could into his chair, holding in a scream.

"Don't . . . move . . . ," Kaine said, as quiet as a stir of breeze.

Michael tried to focus on the creature floating in front of him, but it was like trying to capture a shadow in the middle of a moonless night. The black figure that hovered before him was shifting, becoming an impossible, impenetrable emptiness. A black hole. Michael wondered if he was about to be sucked away forever.

Sucked away. He remembered the KillSims, created by Kaine. Devouring the lives of their victims, sucking them dry, leaving their real bodies back in the Wake, brain-dead or close to it. Whatever this was, it was similar to the KillSims. Then another shifting within the entity's abyss of a head stopped him cold.

A section had opened. Widening like a mouth. For the first time he saw something that wasn't black, making the growing hole more obvious. They were lined up in two rows, white and pointed and sharp, drops of red all over them.

Teeth.

2

The creature inched closer to Michael, those bloody jaws yawning open farther than seemed possible. A horrible smell wafted from the thing's mouth, putrid and rank. Michael pictured the remnants of past meals—pieces of small animals stuck between its teeth, rotting. Decaying. It was the smell of death, pure and simple.

Michael looked away from it, tried to focus on Kaine's eyes, which bored into him, stern with their unspoken command: *Do not move.*

A low growl came from within the creature, guttural, primal. Michael could see in his peripheral vision that the monster was only moments from devouring his entire head. The smell was rancid, and he fought to stop himself from gagging.

Then, from somewhere, from everywhere, a whisper. Like a blade scraping on dried bones. "Don't . . . resist. Become . . . a part . . . of us. Kaine . . . is irrelevant. We . . . are . . . one." The voice of a wraith.

Another wave of sour breath washed over him, and the very tips of the creature's teeth lightly brushed against his forehead. Michael couldn't hold still one more second. In a burst of energy, he snapped.

He twisted his body and brought his elbow up, smashing it into the side of the creature's head, right on the corner of its impossibly huge mouth. It shrieked, a horrible sound that was a thousand times louder than its whisper. As it spun away from him, the other dark figures swarmed in, filling the world with darkness. Formless hands tore at his shirt, his neck, his arms and legs, lifting him into the air. He struggled, but their grasp was firm, pulling him until he was close to the ceiling.

"Kaine!" he shouted. "Help!"

"I told you not to move," the Tangent responded with a sigh, as if they were just playing some game.

Michael opened his mouth to yell, but before he could form the first word, the creatures threw him violently. His body flew as if shot from a cannon, and he slammed into the programmed wooden wall of the tree house, exploding through it. Shards of wood swirled around him as he tumbled in the air. The world spun, and in a flash of pain he crashed into a tree and fell to the ground, landing across its massive root.

A scream finally escaped his lungs. It felt like he'd just crushed several organs and broken even more bones than that. He rolled into a ball, unable to isolate which part of him hurt more than others, and closed his eyes. He opened them just in time to see dark shapes flying from the hole in the tree house and descending on him like huge bats.

Despite the pain, he pulled himself up, getting his hands and knees under him. He was barely to his feet when those same invisible hands had him again. They lifted him into the air, spun his body, threw him. His stomach lodged in his throat as he flew, crashing through branches and leaves, all of them tearing his skin like razors. His head smacked into a limb too large to break, and then he fell straight down, taking several more branches with him. Lights flashed in his eyes, and pain like fire lit his body.

With a jolt he slammed into the forest floor once more, the wind knocked from his chest. He lay on his side, sure that his entire body had broken this time. Unable to move, he stared at the pine straw and rotted leaves beneath him. The trees seemed to loom over him like an audience, pointing at him with their long, scraggly branches, refusing to help. His entire world was pain, and he knew that even if he could Lift before these new KillSims sucked the digital life out of him, his body in the Wake would be in agony as well.

The black forms appeared in the distance again, dodging trees, twisting left and right. Their mouths still gaped, those teeth razor sharp and ready to devour him. He hurt so badly he couldn't bring up the code, couldn't even see it. His mind was a blank slate, barely aware. He had to throw up. He was scared to move, scared that if the creatures vaulted him into the air one more time, he'd be nothing but a bag of sticks and putty, ready for the KillSims to do as they pleased.

One of them reached the space right in front of his eyes, its black cloak brushing the forest floor. It descended, the cloak pooling out around it as it did so. It looked like a hole into the deepest, darkest pocket of space. Then its face was there, eyeless, mouth wide, teeth glinting in a sudden ray of sunshine that broke through the trees.

"You are . . . the First." The words came from its mouth in a wash of wretched stink. "Don't resist. . . . Become a part . . . of us." Those teeth stretched even father apart, and then the mouth moved closer. "The last . . . piece . . . of our puzzle."

The creature was hit from behind and torn away in a blur

of black and white. It slammed into the nearest tree, exploding into a dark mist. Michael looked up to see Kaine standing there—he held a huge stick in his hands like a baseball bat. He swung at another KillSim as it dove in to replace its brother, catapulting it through a break in the trees and out of sight.

"Get up," the Tangent barked. "I can't do this by myself."

Michael wasn't sure he could stand, but he boosted himself to his feet, groaning in agony. The dark-cloaked KillSims surrounded them.

"I don't have a weapon," Michael said through clenched teeth.

"Then use your hands. Don't make me regret making you a part of my fut—"

Two creatures flew at them before he could finish. Kaine swung so fast, the breeze swept Michael's hair when the wood connected with the monster's face. There was a crunch of teeth and a gritty cloud of black mist as the creature disintegrated. There seemed to be no sense to what these things were made of.

Michael barely had time to get his hands up before the other KillSim was on him. He grabbed the edges of its mouth and spun his body, throwing the creature with all his strength. It let out a loud squeal and clamped its mouth shut at the last second, almost catching Michael's fingers. But it worked. The thing landed on the ground twenty feet away.

Something grabbed him from behind, lifting him by the shirt. Kaine swung at it and missed, the end of the stick grazing Michael's skin. He vaulted into the air, thrown once again, up and up until he smacked into a thick branch. He quickly wrapped his arms around it before he could fall to the ground.

Kaine stood below, swinging his weapon like a deranged batter. He'd connect with one phantom and two more would be on him. But somehow he stayed on his feet, spinning and ducking as he continued to bat away the monsters. Michael saw another KillSim—maybe the one that had just thrown him into the tree—gazing at him with an eyeless face, mouth opening wide. Then it flew at Michael.

He dropped to the next branch, then the next one, leaping recklessly toward the forest floor. The creature launched itself after him, weaving in and out of the tree limbs. Michael jumped down the last ten feet, landing in a roll. He scrambled back to his feet and started running, but stopped when he saw something so unexpected he forgot for a split second what was chasing him.

Just a dozen or so feet away, three Auras stood beside a tree, looking back at him.

Bryson, Helga, and Gabby.

The chaos continued, only now with pieces of conversation amid the madness.

"Why'd you leave us?" Bryson yelled at him, his face transformed by anger.

Michael was about to explain when another KillSim

grabbed him by the shirt, yanked him into the air. Draped in filmy darkness, they rose, crashing through branches and leaves. Michael's skin was bloody with scratches, and stung with every new one. He tried to fight the KillSim, but the creature had him in a tight grip, spinning as they rocketed toward the sky.

They burst from the treetops into a sky of broken code. It looked like a stormy sea covered in sewage. He struggled against the KillSim, screamed at it.

"What do you want?" he yelled. "Take me back down!"

The creature ignored him, holding him in a viselike grip, all the while flying higher. Michael twisted to get a look at the monster's face, saw nothing but streaks of darkness.

"Let me go!" Michael yelled.

The KillSim obeyed. It released Michael and he fell, his stomach lurching into his throat. Waving his arms and kicking his legs, he plummeted, wind tearing at his clothes. He watched the canopy of thick leaves rush up around him and struggled to catch a breath. He didn't understand why they didn't just suck the life from him. Maybe they wanted his Aura broken, shattered. Maybe it would be easier to destroy him if he couldn't put up a fight.

Michael felt a weird sense of calm as the green expanse grew below him. Why had so many Tangents turned against Kaine? What did they need Michael for?

Something burst from the canopy, leaving an explosion of leaves and branches in its wake. It was Gabby, some kind of jet pack strapped to her shoulders, blue flames bursting from twin rockets. She leveled off next to Michael, matched his rate of descent, grabbed him, and pulled him into a fierce hug. The roar of the pack's engine was like the growl of a massive beast.

Michael wrapped his arms around Gabby, careful not to touch the flames or the hot part of the engine. His relief outweighed his chagrin at needing rescue.

"What," Michael shouted, "is this?"

"The only thing I could code," she replied. Then added, "Yes, I'm really good at this. Come on, the others are still down there." She turned and revved the engine, and they flew through the same hole the first KillSim had created—a straight line through the canopy and trees. "And you'll get your punishment for leaving us later! Bryson's not happy."

"Fine."

The ground flew at them, so fast that Michael closed his eyes despite himself. At the last second Gabby reversed the engines and slowed their descent, landing with a soft thump. Michael didn't even have a moment to admire Gabby's skills; the KillSims swarmed them the moment they touched down. He caught a glimpse of Helga fighting several of the creatures with what looked like a long sword of bright light. Bryson was at her side, holding a roughly coded shotgun. Kaine ran through the trees, still swatting at the black cloaks with his mighty club.

Crazy, Michael thought. *The whole world's gone crazy.*

KillSims reached for them with tendrils of darkness. Right before they could make contact, Gabby revved her jet-pack and shot them into the air again, flying toward their friends. Michael looked back as three of the creatures slammed into each other, forming a cloud of black fog, specks of white fluttering within. As Gabby landed, she kicked a KillSim away from Helga; Michael swung out with a fist to pummel another one and his arm bounced back, as if he had just hit a firm balloon. Just in time, Helga swung her magic sword, cutting another creature in half, giving them a moment's respite from the madness.

And then, all at once, Michael made a flurry of decisions.

"We have to split up," he said, his mood lifting for the first time since he'd sat in the tree house and seen that Kaine had answered his message. Whether or not it was a good one, he now had a plan.

"What are you talking about?" Helga shouted, between thrusts of her sword. "We just found you!"

Michael shook his head. He glanced quickly to make sure they were still clear of KillSims; then he spoke as quickly and clearly as he could to his friends. "Make a Portal. To anywhere. Get out of here, then go find the Hallowed Ravine. That's where they're uploading the Tangents—it's where the Mortality Doctrine is. Send me a message when you're there and I'll meet you. Soon."

He didn't know what they showed more strongly on their faces—confusion or rage.

Gabby started to argue, but Michael cut her off.

"Just do it!" he yelled. "Go! We don't have time!" He had no idea what had come over him, but he wasn't going to abandon the course he'd decided on back in D.C.

Bryson still looked as angry as ever. "And what're you going to do, boss man?"

Michael turned away from him and started marching toward Kaine just as he saw the Tangent destroy two Kill-Sims with one mighty swing of his stick.

"Michael!" Bryson shouted at him. "Michael!"

Michael glanced over his shoulder. "Find the Mortality Doctrine! Right now I need Kaine! I need to . . . use him."

Michael's time had run out. He sprinted toward the fighting Tangent, forming the code for an illegal Portal even as he ran.

4

He'd always heard that adversity sharpened the mind, honed the senses. He experienced it firsthand in the frantic moment he reached Kaine and pulled him through the make-shift Portal.

The VirtNet was a mess—he'd already discovered that. The code, Decayed. But he'd learned enough on his trek to the tree house to do what he needed to do. He worked on pure instinct, manipulating things seemingly with thought as he formed a Portal just to the left of Kaine, who still battled the KillSims ferociously.

Michael grabbed the Tangent by the shirt, yanked him toward the black rectangle, kicked a KillSim who dove at them at the last second. They slid through together. The instant Michael felt they were free of the woods, he collapsed the Portal behind them.

They landed on a soft, rubbery surface surrounded by a

pale purple light and absolutely nothing else as far as the eye could see.

Kaine lay next to him, looking up at the empty sky, breathing heavily. Michael rolled onto his back and did the same. Emptiness above. No color except that dull, faded purple. In his rush to get them out, Michael had brought them to the most basic level of VirtNet programming.

A few minutes passed in silence, and Michael wondered what he'd just done. Bryson, Helga, Gabby—they'd all been there. Why had he left them?

Then he thought of what he'd decided back in the streets of D.C. He needed to be alone with Kaine. And he needed his friends to get back to the Hallowed Ravine and find the source of the Mortality Doctrine.

He had a plan, and he couldn't waste any more time doubting himself. Too much was at stake.

"Get up," he told Kaine. Michael pushed himself to his knees, then his feet. "Come on. We've got a lot to do."

Kaine, looked startled, confused, and he didn't move. Instead he whispered, "I can't believe the Tangents have turned against me like this. All that time I worked. All the effort. And now that they've tasted the sweetness, they've gone off on their own."

Michael raised his eyebrows in surprise. That certainly wasn't what he'd expected to hear. "Those KillSims. Who programmed them?"

Kaine glanced up, as if shocked to see that he wasn't alone. "What game are you playing, boy? Do you have any idea the kinds of things you're messing with?"

"I think I do. Now answer my question."

"So you're giving the orders now?"

"I'm sure done taking them." And Michael meant it, too. He was fed up with the entire world—*both* worlds.

Kaine let out a grunt and sat up, rubbing his face. Then he stood to join Michael, his smartly cut hair and his polished suit not so smart or polished anymore.

"Does this mean you're joining me?" the Tangent asked. "I've convinced you?"

Michael shook his head. "Doesn't mean a thing, brother. Tell me. Who made those KillSims?"

Kaine seemed almost pleased to get some things off his chest. "You know exactly who. The same people—and I use the word *people* loosely—who came at you in the forest, where Helga and her other hoodlums had camped out. I programmed some of them, improved the code on the lot of them. Raised them. Gave them a chance at a real life. And now they've spit in my face and gone off on their own."

"So we have two enemies," Michael said, thinking aloud.

Kaine barked a laugh. "More like one very big one."

"Here's what's going to happen," Michael said, satisfied at the conviction he heard in his own voice. "You and me are now a team. We're going to take down these rogue Tangent buddies of yours. And then we're going to take down the VNS. Deal?"

Kaine actually took a step back in surprise. "I . . . uh, yes. Absolutely. I've said it all along. I need your help."

Michael shook his head once again. "No, that's where you're wrong, Kaine. I'm the one who needs help. And you're going to do it. The Tangents. Then the VNS. And I'm in charge."

Kaine was so obviously shocked that he barely managed a nod.

Michael had to hold back a smile. If only the Tangent knew the third part of his hastily conceived plan, he'd never be standing there, agreeing to go along.

"All right, then," Michael finally said. "First things first. Let's go kill us some Tangents."

CHAPTER 16

HUNTING GROUND

1

Michael hadn't really meant it—he didn't want any part in meting out the "true death." He knew there had to be some way to reverse the Mortality Doctrine.

Kaine walked next to Michael, silently crossing the raw expanse of the VirtNet.

"You're right," the Tangent said, looking down as he walked. "We need to kill all the Tangents who broke away from me. They're just an annoyance now and are merely causing trouble."

Michael glanced at Kaine, happy for the reminder of how soulless he was. "Dude, I wasn't really serious. We can't just go around killing everyone. There has to be another way to stop them besides this . . . true death thing."

It appeared that, without having come out and said it, they'd agreed on the first order of business: they had to stop the people behind those new black-cloaked KillSims. At least Weber and the VNS weren't actively trying to eliminate them. But these rogue Tangents, though—Michael shuddered when he thought of those creepy kids and the tough-talking Trae at the barracks. They had to be dealt with, or Michael and Kaine would never get to the bigger issue—the VNS.

Kaine stopped walking. "Where exactly are we going?"

"Nowhere. I'm thinking."

Kaine turned to him. "Listen." He rubbed his chin, lost in his own thoughts, and Michael stopped as well. He didn't know when it had happened, but at some point Kaine had stopped being an enemy, entirely. He'd stopped being just a piece of code also. Something about him had turned almost . . . human.

Kaine shook his head. "I didn't think I was ready for this yet, but maybe these Tangents are the perfect test subjects. Though, if it goes wrong, don't blame me. It's all I've got."

Michael had no idea what Kaine was talking about. "What?" he asked.

"The reboot."

"Reboot?" Michael was thoroughly confused now. "Isn't that some word they used like fifty years ago with plug-ins? What does it even mean?"

Kaine folded his arms. "You need to learn your history, son."

"At least I recognized it. But what does it have to do with anything?"

"Reboot," Kaine said again, only this time Michael heard something like dread in his tone. "It's part of the plan I showed you. One of the keys to living forever. When you've lived out your fifty years within the VirtNet, you're rebooted into a new body in the real world."

Michael recalled the visions Kaine had shown him. The lines of kids getting into the Coffins. "So are you saying we should . . . reboot . . . who? The people those rogue Tangents stole the bodies from?"

"Yes!" Kaine replied. "It's just not how I'd planned it. And I haven't tested it in the cycle yet. But it might be the only way to rid ourselves of those traitors before they get in our way again."

"Wait a second," Michael said. He thought about what Weber had done at the World Summit. How those guards had just dropped to the ground, dead. And Helga had done the same thing to one of Trae's group outside the barracks. But hadn't that been the true death? "Back at the summit, Weber sent some kind of message to the VirtNet and these guards just dropped. Is that what we're talking about?"

Kaine shook his head. "No. That's what you've been insisting we can't do—the true death. The true death kills both the Tangent and the human—the body and the consciousness. I'm telling you that we can prevent the deaths of the original humans. We can reboot them—use the Mortality Doctrine to send them back into their own bodies."

Michael almost smiled at how ridiculous his life had become. "And that would kill the Tangents? They'd be gone forever?"

Kaine shrugged. "That's the problem. I don't know. Like I said, I haven't tested it yet. In theory, we should be able to swap intelligences in and out of biological brains indefinitely without harm so that we can all live for eternity in body after body. The Tangents should upload back into the VirtNet. *Should* being the key word. But there's still a lot of work to do."

"Okay," Michael said, "so you're sure we can put these humans back into their own bodies, but you're not sure what will happen to the Tangent?"

"Something like that," Kaine said, a twinkle of excitement in his eye. Michael felt uneasy. It seemed like they were playing God, rolling the dice to see who lived and who died. Like it was all some sort of game. "And I'm pretty sure I know some programming that would take care of the Tangents."

Michael let out a sigh. "All right," he said. "Then let's do this. I guess they aren't real, so no one's going to miss them anyway."

A look of disgust washed over Kaine's Aura. It was only there for an instant, but it made Michael feel terrible. He was talking as if he'd been a human all his life instead of having taken Jackson's body. He really *was* playing God, which seemed like the very thing he and his friends were trying to stop. What made him better than these other Tangents?

Then Sarah's face surfaced in his mind. Her expression when she'd been shot, the life draining out of her. He thought of all the other people who'd lost their lives to this Mortality Doctrine, and he steeled himself. He couldn't let it keep happening.

"Okay," he said to Kaine. "Show me what we need to do."

2

Kaine spun them through the diseased realms of the Sleep, launching past glitching cities and broken code. Numbers and letters and symbols scattered like leaves in a windstorm, and pixels crumbled around them. Kaine's prowess in coding was something Michael still watched in awe. He'd always known Kaine was good, but the Tangent manipulated their way through it all with the ease of splashing through a puddle.

The journey took less than a minute. They vaulted through eroding mountain ranges, black seas, and razed cities. Code was collapsing everywhere.

They flew through a soundless darkness, interrupted by violent explosions of light, and suddenly the vast wall of the Hive appeared before them. It stretched seemingly endless in every direction, glowing orange; it looked like some kind of alien planet.

Jackson's here somewhere, Michael thought. *He's still alive.*

Michael flew through the air, Kaine's grip still tight on his arm, guiding him closer and closer to the wall. Gradually, a section oddly different from the rest of the Hive became visible. A speck of green grew as they approached and turned into a square about twenty feet across. Lights flashed and streaked across its surface, which bubbled and rippled like a pot of boiling water. Misty smoke whirled in jetties. All of it only added to the otherworldly feel of the place.

Kaine pulled them to a stop right in front of the strange scene. Michael looked deeper into the bubbling haze and saw that what he'd thought were lights were actually symbols of code, breaking apart and forming back together. It looked like nonsense.

"What is this?" he asked. "Some kind of living NetScreen?"

Kaine laughed. "That's almost exactly what it is. It'll take you some time to get used to it, but once you start coding within the Code Pool, you'll never want to go back to the old ways."

"The Code Pool," Michael said absently, studying the mysterious goop in wonder. How was it possible he'd never heard of this before?

Kaine answered as if he'd read his mind. "Only a few people can even see this, much less know what it is. But I'm afraid we don't have much time for me to explain things at the moment—they'll be here any second."

Michael tore his eyes away from the mesmerizing dance of the Pool. "Wait . . . what? What am I supposed to do? Who's 'they'?"

"My former friends, the rogues," Kaine replied easily, as if these Tangents didn't want both of them dead. "As well as a few current friends. I suspect it's going to get ugly, but I think we'll be okay. As long as you can get your part done."

"What part?" Michael was getting more and more nervous.

"I'll message you what you need to know. You'll have two jobs: finding their storage unit and severing the connection. But you have to follow the procedure I send you so that the human minds they stole are Doctrined back into their bodies, processed through the Hallowed Ravine. I know it sounds a little complicated, but I think you can handle it."

Michael stared at Kaine, wondering how they'd gotten to this. This Tangent had once been his mortal enemy, and now they were talking like a couple of IT workers at the company picnic.

Seeds of panic started sprouting inside Michael. "I'm not sure. . . ." He didn't know what to ask. And then Michael spotted figures in the distance, growing as they approached. Gradually, he made out people dressed as medieval warriors, trolls, and enormous panthers and other beasts standing on hind legs. There were samurai and paratroopers and armored space cadets from the future. It looked like a VirtGame gone supernova.

"Don't worry," Kaine said. "Those are mine. The others are on their way."

Michael searched for words. "Which is . . . I still don't get it. What if they bring those KillSims with them again? They will!"

Kaine reached out and squeezed his shoulder, looking at him very seriously. "Michael, there's a link between you and the Mortality Doctrine that I can't afford to lose. Neither can Weber and the VNS. You need to stay off the battlefield. And you're perfectly suited to what I need you to do."

Michael nodded, too many questions running through his mind to give voice to any.

"Good. Now just close your eyes and let the connection flow. Once you have all the information, things will start falling into place. It'll come fast, so be prepared."

"Okay." Michael wanted to say so much more. He was scared—worried he wouldn't know what to do—but then, if anyone could figure out what Kaine was talking about, it was most likely to be Michael. He closed his eyes and opened himself to the raw world of the code. "I'm ready."

"Here it comes," Kaine said, and information came in a torrent, filling Michael's virtual vision like a blizzard. "And don't worry. You won't be vulnerable to attack while you're working—I'll form a bubble around you and we'll fight them off as best we can. Just keep working."

"Uh . . . yeah." It was all he could do to get those words out, lost in the rushing stream of code.

"Let's just hope the bubble holds." They were Kaine's last, not-so-reassuring words before the onslaught of information finally overwhelmed Michael.

And he gave himself to it.

3

For a while, Michael was having fun again. Wading through code, facing down puzzles, learning at a pace faster than thought could process. He had been born for this— programmed with these abilities. And he relished the challenge.

The Code Pool was like the next step of evolution for coding, as if it had all transformed into something biological, his virtual body melding with it, becoming one. It reminded him of the human brain, which was really nothing more than a biological computer. This is what he existed within now, a living goop of code. Kaine's instructions swirled in his mind like a whirlpool as he worked, manipulating the sea of pure information in which he swam.

Time was lost to Michael, but eventually he saw it. Lights, twisting in a pattern not unlike that of DNA, extending into the universe of code for what seemed like eternity. Individual strings shone so bright that they blended together in the distance miles away. He had to focus hard to find the specific strings provided by Kaine in his information dump.

Michael moved things with his mind. The lights twisted and spun and vaulted like comets, forward or backward, according to his will.

There.

He didn't even know how he recognized it—how he identified the light's data with that of Kaine's—but he knew immediately that they matched. Michael was looking at a representation of a Tangent that had broken apart from Kaine's initial group, joined the rogue alliance that wanted to topple him and continue the original plan to ruthlessly, and without mercy, take over the human race. Michael hoped Kaine had meant it when he'd said that was no longer his own wish.

Michael pulled himself closer to the light in question. Or pulled it closer to him—impossible to tell what was actually happening. He reached inside the brilliant streak of light before him with his mind. The code was like clay, and he kneaded it, squeezed and pulled, all according to the guidance Kaine had sent him in that torrential flow. At some point, it was there for the taking. A connection so isolated and fragile, perfectly formed in front of him. It was there, like a thin toothpick, held between his virtual-within-virtual hands.

Michael pulled it apart into two pieces.

A long string of light winked out of existence, without even a flash to glorify its exit.

Michael turned, surprised to see a perfect view of the battle between Kaine's Tangents raging outside the Hive. Somewhere within that chaos, a man dressed as a World War II soldier exploded in a fiery burst of pyrotechnics, leaving not even a trace.

Gone. Dead.

Michael had just murdered him.

4

His heart grew heavier with every light he extinguished. But he kept at it, not allowing himself to listen to his conscience. He didn't have time for it. One by one, he pinpointed the rogue Tangents he'd been provided and initiated Kaine's Reboot. The stored human intelligence was sent back into its own body and the renegade Tangent was drained out, eliminated. Killed.

Each time he broke another connection, Michael glanced behind him, looked for the fiery explosion that marked the demise of the Tangent. Slowly but surely, the tide of the vicious battle being fought outside the wall of the Hive was turning in favor of Kaine and his faithful.

Michael had eliminated twelve of the Tangents, had seen the burst of flames—and the nothingness that followed—of the latest victim, and was turning back to his work within the goop of the Code Pool when something slammed against the protective Bubble that Kaine had programmed around him. It was like a giant bird hitting a window, making a loud enough thump that Michael recoiled and sucked in a gasp of air. A black mass lay splattered against the invisible surface, an amoeba of darkness.

Then a mouth appeared, rimmed with teeth. It reminded Michael of the algae-eaters that suck the walls of an aquarium. That curtain of black around it left no doubt what had come for him.

A KillSim. One of those new daggers-for-teeth KillSims.

He'd barely had the thought when another hit the Bubble next to the first one, flattening out like a pancake of tar. Its mouth appeared instantly. The teeth shone and scraped against the surface. Another one landed right after that.

Three of them.

Hold, Michael begged the Bubble. *You better hold.* He returned to his work.

It was odd, his current environment. Unlike most of the VirtNet, the Code Pool didn't obey normal physics. It existed in different formats and different locations at once. When Michael immersed himself in it, everything else disappeared, and he saw only that core substance of the programming language in which he floated. But every time he turned his head to look back—he saw it all. The Bubble of protection, the leeching KillSims, Kaine's battle behind that, raging like an alien war in space.

He resumed his deadly work, ending Tangent lives one by one. It made him feel better to know that he was also giving life back to those who'd had their bodies stolen. Or so he hoped. What a changed world it would be if he trusted Kaine completely.

A horrific screeching sound broke his concentration just as he was about to snap another Tangent life away. He couldn't help but look, almost losing his grip on that tiny stick as he did so. Behind him, one of the KillSims had pierced the shield of the Bubble with a single tooth, letting that awful noise in as it twisted and tore at the invisible material. It was worse than nails on a chalkboard. Michael fought the urge to put his virtual hands to his virtual ears, turned back to his deed, and snapped another line of code. Yet another string of lights winked out.

Michael faced the KillSim again. It had torn a three-inch gash in the Bubble now, grinding away. One of its companions had formed some kind of spike out of its black mass, a dark pick that it used to hammer at the shield. A low thump sounded every time it hit. Soon it was accompanied by a crackle, like a large sheet of ice beginning to break.

Time was running out. There had to be almost a hundred rogue Tangents left in the list Kaine had sent. Michael went into overdrive, taking leaps in his coding that weren't exactly safe or foolproof. He decided the time for careful treading was over. If that protective barrier burst, there'd be no way he could fight off those KillSims before they sucked the essence from his body back home—especially with his strength drained as it was. He'd be a vegetable in no time.

He swept through the files of the Hive, finding connections to over a dozen Tangents and latching on to all of them. Working one by one was no longer an option. Scrapes and cracks and screeching continued behind him, like a glacier coming apart all at once. That Bubble was about to burst like a lightbulb under a boot. Feverishly, Michael gathered data, pooled it, swept it, manipulated, massaged it. He layered the codes, counting on pure instinct to keep everything in order, working too fast for his mind to make sense of it all.

Before long he held a bundle of fragile sticks in his hand as if he were about to draw straws. Each one represented a life—no matter how programmed or artificial, it was a life. How could he say any different? He'd been one of them. But they were different, he told himself as the KillSims pounded his thin membrane of protection. They'd been created to do harm. Created to wreak havoc on the real world.

But hadn't he been created to do the same? In a way? He was the First, after all.

Michael!

The booming sound of Kaine's voice came from everywhere at once. Michael tore himself from his thoughts and doubts, looked down at the bundle of sticks in his hand. The artificial lives, the threads to their intelligence and being, their lifelines.

He grabbed the two ends with both fists and snapped them all into two pieces. The air lit up with the explosions behind him. He turned to face it and watched fiery clouds of red and orange erupt across the empty space beyond the Hive. Then, as if opened to another dimension, they disappeared, lightning fast, darkness settling on the world once again.

So many dead.

So many saved.

He had to remember that. Kaine said that the original inhabitants of those bodies would automatically get reinserted into the VirtNet, resume their lives. What a wake-up that would be.

There were more. He hadn't gotten all of them. But Kaine and the Tangents on his side outnumbered those who'd come to attack, and it was plain to see that the tide of the battle had turned drastically in Kaine's favor. Michael had done enough.

The KillSims kept coming. The one had opened its dark maw over a foot wide, and even as Michael looked at it, a sharp blade of darkness came swiping at his head. He ducked, letting it skim over him. Just.

The creature with the black spike hadn't stopped hammering; cracks spiderwebbed away from its point of attack, thick and white and expanding. Michael pushed himself as far away as he could, but the Code Pool resisted. It was as if it didn't want him sinking into its goop of code unless he was willing to work it. The dark blade swiped at him again, sliced some threads on his shirt.

"Kaine!" he yelled, not knowing if the Tangent would hear him. "You need to get me out of here!"

Michael saw him, just a glimpse through the white cracks and the bodies of the KillSims that had swarmed his protective Bubble. The Tangent had turned his head toward him, and their eyes met for a brief second, but then he disappeared from view. Hopefully coming to save him. Surely Kaine's friends were enough to—

Michael's vision bounced, then went blurry. It bounced again, as if he were on some amusement park ride that jolted his body. Colors smeared together, getting blurrier and distorted. Stretched, darkening, covered in mist, now brightening, everything turning white. He tried to call for Kaine again, but he couldn't get the words out. Then he was moving, picking up speed, catapulting into a brilliant light, unable to feel anything. There was a terrible rush of noise.

What . . . ? His mind couldn't form the thought, much less speak it.

The atmosphere popped, and his eardrums felt as if they'd erupted. He screamed—the sound of it was close and contained and dulled, as if he were inside . . .

A Coffin.

Something hissed loudly; then a bright line of light appeared above him. NerveWires snaked out of his skin and back to their cubbyholes. His body was soaked from head to toe, and every part of him ached.

How had he Lifted? Kaine had been coming for him. Maybe he'd—

Agent Weber's head appeared above him as the Coffin door swung open.

Her.

Again.

"How'd you find me?" he asked, though the words came out slurred and wet-sounding.

"It wasn't that hard," she said, tilting her head so that her face lined up with his. "I did program you and Kaine, after all. Might as well ask me how I find my own nose."

Michael tried to sit up, the pronouncement like a charge of electricity through his joints. He flailed his arms and slipped and smacked his head.

"Get out, get showered, get dressed," Weber said, looking away. "You have ten minutes."

CHAPTER 17

THE REAL WORLD

1

She was waiting for him at the little table in the hotel room's kitchenette, her hands folded in front of her, resting on the wooden surface. She was dressed in the same clothes she'd worn at the World Summit, or something similar. Blazer, skirt, blouse, heels—she looked like a businesswoman. She *always* did. She nodded toward a chair directly across from her. No one else was in the room.

"You should've brought some security," Michael said, trembling with anger. "I should choke you to death right now. With the hands you made me steal from Jackson Porter."

She gestured to the chair, then placed her hands on the table again. "You'd never do that to me, and we both know it. Now please sit down. I'm sure you're curious to hear what I've come to say—I flew here all the way from London, despite the million things I need to get done. I'm sure you're curious why I've used my power to Lift you out of the

VirtNet without following protocols. I'm sure you're even wondering why I didn't just come in here and end your life while you lay there, helpless in the Coffin."

"Or send that weasel Agent Scott to do it," he replied.

She only nodded, as if the idea had occurred to her.

Michael had to admit, he was curious. As he always was. He stepped over to the chair, pulled it out, then walked around the table and placed the chair close to her. He sat down, his knees almost touching hers. A small act of defiance, not sitting where she wanted him to. Pathetic, but it was all he had.

"Power?" he asked. "Your power? Sounds to me like you're enjoying this ego trip. Your head does look a little bigger, now that I think about it."

Weber turned to face him. "How many times have we met like this? How many times have you looked at me and thrown accusations like a child? It's time for you to grow up, Michael."

The laugh that burst from his chest was genuine. "And how many times have I been exactly right? It doesn't matter what you say or do or show me. I'll never trust you again."

She appeared troubled and shifted in her seat, straightening her skirt. "Fair enough," she said. His words had obviously struck a nerve, but she quickly recovered her composure. "I didn't come here to ask for your trust. Or even your cooperation. We don't . . . need you, Michael. I believe you're the one with the ego, not me. How quickly you assume that we can't accomplish a damn thing without your help."

Michael shook his head and dropped his eyes to the floor.

"Whatever, Agent Weber. Just . . . I'm not the one who made me sit at this table and listen to you."

"You're right. That was me. And as you said yourself, I didn't have to do that, did I? I could've had Agent Scott walk in here, open up your Coffin, and end it. But I didn't." She suddenly leaned toward him. Michael looked up—her face was only a few inches from his. "Despite what you may think, you mean a lot to me, Michael. I don't want you dead. That's ridiculous. A lot of trouble could've been avoided if you'd just done as you were asked and worked with me from the very beginning."

Michael's flash of anger turned his face hot. He fumbled for the right words to throw back at her and she held up a hand to stop him.

"No, don't," she said. "You don't have to respond. That was an unfair thing for me to say. We've cajoled you and manipulated you and confused you. I know that. You've had to unbury yourself from layer after layer of deceit, and go through things that no person should. I . . ."

She faltered, with a sudden tremble in her lips, then sat back in her chair, looking more flustered than Michael had ever seen her.

"*What,*" Michael said, emphasizing every word, "*is . . . wrong . . . with . . . you?* It's like you have multiple personalities or something. I think you need help." Part of him was being cruel, but he also actually believed it. Something was so . . . *off* about this woman.

Agent Weber stood up hesitantly, as if she were surprised to find herself in the hotel room with Michael. She looked at him, her face somewhere between confused and distraught, then walked away from the table, circling the kitchenette several times. The most obvious explanation seemed too . . . obvious.

"Are you a Tangent, Weber?" he asked.

She glanced sharply at him. A long moment passed. Then she shook her head.

"No." She paced back and forth. "Though I can see why you'd think that. I know that I've been . . . erratic of late. Well, really, it's when I'm around you. I just don't know how to cope sometimes. I can't believe I'm even saying this in front of you."

Was it an act? Michael observed her, tried to read something in her face. But she genuinely looked torn up inside.

"Whatever," he finally said. He considered bolting, but he figured guards were waiting outside.

Weber came back to the table and dragged her chair a little farther away from Michael. The sound of it scraping across the floor put his nerves on edge. She sat down, avoiding his gaze now.

"Michael, I . . . ," she began, appearing to struggle for the right words. "I need you to know that you're coming with me today. One way or another, I'm taking you from here. Do you understand?"

Michael was thoroughly confused. That wasn't what he'd expected at all.

Weber kept talking. "But I want to talk to you first. I'm so conflicted when it comes to you. I meant what I said earlier. I *did* program you." Her eyes finally came up to meet his once again. "Do you believe me?"

He didn't answer at first. He wanted to deny it, couldn't believe he was sitting here, listening to her, allowing her to poison his mind with an all-new batch of lies and manipulations. But . . . he *did* believe her. Maybe some deep part of him could recognize its maker.

Sickened, he nodded, just once.

"Most of your memories are real," she said. "I want you to know that. I created you over ten years ago, as part of my training with the VNS. We wanted you as lifelike as possible. More importantly, we wanted you to *believe* you were real. We did create the first few years of your life within *Lifeblood Deep* to give you a foundation, but from that moment on, from when you were about five or six, your memories— every one of them—actually happened. We fabricated nothing."

Michael tried to grasp some meaning out of all she said. "How can you say nothing was fabricated? I'm a computer program!"

"Yes, that's true. But within the world of the Deep, you actually had each and every one of those memories from the last decade of your life. With your parents. With Helga. With your friends."

"And then you took it all away from me." Michael was drained of any fight. He hated this woman, and he was so exhausted.

Weber stared at a spot on the table. "I take it he's told you the truth?"

And with that simple sentence, she proved that everything Kaine had said was true. Michael stumbled out of his chair, barely made it to the couch, collapsed onto it. He buried his head in his arms and swore he'd never get up again.

There was the sound of a chair moving and a few steps; then Weber was standing right above him. He could almost feel her shadow across his shoulders like a blanket. The door opened. Heavy footsteps. The rustle of clothing. Michael knew it was her people, but refused to give them the satisfaction of looking.

Weber crouched over him, put a hand on his back as she leaned down to whisper into his ear. "I've gone too far to turn back now. Way too far. I need to keep going for the sake of the world."

Michael flinched as if she'd hurt him.

Agent Weber of VirtNet Security stood up. "Do it."

Rough hands grabbed Michael by the arms.

He didn't fight them, the two men dressed in fatigues. He realized that Weber had gotten her wish—she now had armies at her disposal, by the looks of it. And who knew what else? Or how many people she'd taken over with Tangents to get what she wanted? Michael went with them quietly—down the hall, into the elevator, through the lobby, out the doors of the hotel, into the back of a car—but his mind was a tornado of noise, sorting out all that he knew and trying to figure out what in the world he could do about it. Before long, they were on a plane and in the air.

He refused to talk, refused to be intimidated by the guards. And they let him be, although they made it very clear he wasn't to touch his EarCuff.

Hours passed.

The plane landed and the soldiers dragged him to a car—a fancy hovercraft reserved for big government types. One of the soldiers drove; the other one sat next to Michael in the back, sure to flash the barrel of his gun as he took his seat. Weber situated herself on Michael's other side.

"I lied when I said I don't need you," Weber said. It was the first time he'd heard her voice in hours.

Michael sighed. "And what's that supposed to mean?" he asked wearily.

"There's a connection between you and the Mortality Doctrine program." She faced the window, seemingly engrossed in watching the buildings flashing by. "It's a very complex program that was created using quantum computing. Essentially, it requires so much data knowledge that the human brain can't handle it. Only artificial intelligence can manipulate it, and you're part of the ethereal connection holding it all together. Like a battery in an old gas engine. Or more like the gas itself."

Michael listened, but said nothing. He knew plenty about quantum computing and wasn't surprised at all to know that the Mortality Doctrine program used it. That was the only way to explain how they'd figured out how to utilize the human brain itself as a computer. But how it all had to stay connected through him? That he didn't get. Though he sure wasn't going to admit that to Weber.

She finally turned to look at him again. "So we do need you, Michael. We just don't need your help. Do you understand the difference?"

"I'm not an idiot," he spat out.

"No, you're not. We know that all too well."

"Where are we going?" he asked. "Why did you pull me out of the Sleep, but leave Kaine and the rest of those Tangents behind?" He wished he could pretend he didn't care, but he couldn't hold back.

"Because he's doing exactly what we need, whether he knows it or not." Weber returned her gaze to the window as the car dipped and slowed, then lowered itself to the road again. A garage was opening up in the face of a really tall skyscraper. "That group of Tangents breaking away from Kaine created yet another enemy that we didn't need. And seeing their overall numbers dwindle in all this fighting—that's just a bonus. They will all be insignificant soon enough."

The car rolled forward into the garage, drove through the dark for a bit, then pulled to a stop.

Weber reached for the door handle but paused. "There've been times when I've doubted my actions," she said, her voice solemn. "It was a plan ten years in the making, programming you and other test Tangents, creating Kaine, laying the foundation—it took a lot of work. And when it all came together, and I saw the effects . . . on you, on others, on the world . . . I wanted to stop. That's the honest truth. But like I said, we'd gone too far. If we stop now, the world will descend into chaos. I can't let things get even worse. So we move on. It's almost complete. Will be by tomorrow night, is my guess."

She opened the door and stepped out, then leaned in to continue speaking to him. "I give you my word, Michael: when our task is done and we have control over the globe and its governments, things will be better. And safer. And then the VirtNet can truly take its place as the centerpiece of life for the human race. You'll see."

She stepped away before he could respond. The soldier next to him gave him a little nudge with his elbow.

"Come on, kid," he said, his voice as rough as his weathered face. "Things aren't so bad. You get to see all of this firsthand. The biggest revolution the world has ever known. Now, are you going to cooperate or do I need to cuff you?"

Michael was too stunned to speak. He just shook his head and lowered his gaze as humbly as he could. Then he got out of the car and followed Agent Weber.

3

They led him to a giant room filled with Coffins.

The place was so massive that he found it hard to believe he was in the real world and not in the VirtNet somewhere. It was as long as a football field. Iron-railed balconies lined both walls and stretched to the ceiling hundreds of feet over their heads. Faint lights shone somewhere up there, lost in what seemed like a mist or bank of clouds. Surely his vision was just blurry from the rush of information that had dazed him.

The floor in front of him, and each balcony—as far as he could see from where he stood—was full of Coffins.

Hundreds of them, their soft lights blinking and glowing. They lined the walls, one after another, like the world's largest crypt. And most of them appeared to be in operation. The air was cool and smelled of well-oiled machinery and the metallic tinge of electricity.

"We've been building all of this to lead up to this day," Weber said, proudly throwing her arms up to indicate the giant space. "This is our command center, each NerveBox occupied by my most faithful colleagues. We've been careful. We knew that if we moved too quickly, people would lose faith in us before we could make them have faith *only* in us. You understand?"

Michael tried to keep emotion off his face. "Why are you telling me this?"

Weber shrugged. "You're the closest thing to a son I'll ever have. And you're a part of this. Great things are going to happen today. I want to share them with you."

Her comments should've sent him flying into a rage. Comparing herself to his mother—it should've been the last straw. He wanted to scream, but he knew he couldn't.

Weber smiled and continued eagerly, as if convinced he loved hearing every word she spoke. "But now we have enough support and enough Tangents in place. We've even planned for those humans who are still wild cards—we've invited them here today, to make a"—she formed quotation marks with her fingers—" 'presentation' within the VirtNet. Let's just say that when they wake up, they won't be themselves. Strategically brilliant, really. We've reached the tipping point. Any further delay and we may lose our chance.

So today, with this firepower"—she pointed toward the cavernous space above them—"we will go into the VirtNet and complete our plans."

Her smile vanished, and Michael felt his stomach twist into a knot. He couldn't stop himself from saying the next words.

"What?" he asked, hearing the tremor in his own voice. "What're you going to do?"

"It sounds worse than it is when you say it out loud," she replied in a whisper that echoed through the room, up and up until it faded into silence. "But I've always said, it's what happens in the long run that matters. And isn't it? A few sacrifices now to ensure a better future?"

Michael took a step backward, away from her. The soldiers moved with him, right at his sides.

"You're crazy," he said, half to himself. "You've gone totally insane."

She looked at him with a faint smile. "Quite the contrary. I'm saner than I've ever been. I only felt crazy when I began to doubt the plan we'd set forth. All that back-and-forth, all the doubting, all the . . . indecision. Now that I'm back on course, fully committed, I'm more alive than ever. My mind has never had such perfect clarity."

"What're you going to do!" he shouted at her.

She didn't flinch. "*We,* Michael. We. I'm not alone in this. I never have been." She turned away from him and motioned to the bottom row of Coffins. "This is my army. Those who've been by my side from the beginning. Those who trusted my vision and helped me get to this point." She then swept her arm at the remaining Coffins filling the giant room. "Soon these humans will be under Tangent control. The collateral damage will be significant, I admit. But those who aren't needed . . . Well. They aren't needed anymore."

"Just tell me!" Michael yelled. "What're you going to do to them!"

She spun around to face him again, her gaze sharp.

"I'm going to give them the true death," she said, "these Tangents that people believe Kaine poured into the world. I'm going to kill them all. For the good of our future— a future run by the VNS."

CHAPTER 18

BLACK GLASS

Michael trembled with anger. He felt powerless. He couldn't even find words to express how he felt.

"Keep him here," Weber said. "Keep him safe and watch him like a hawk. And whatever you do, do not let that boy near a NerveBox or computer of any kind. Understood?"

"I think we can handle a scrawny teenager." One of the guards grabbed Michael by the arms and the other man reached up and ripped off Michael's EarCuff.

Michael bit his lip, refusing to cry out from the pain. He glared at Weber, knowing he should be shocked at what she'd become. But hadn't he always seen it? Had there ever been a time when he truly trusted her?

"I'm Sinking now," she announced to no one in particular. "With this final sweep of Tangents, the deal will be sealed. Humanity will credit us for saving them. When I Lift out, the world will be a different place." She walked toward a Coffin along the nearest wall, one that was actually on a pedestal above the others, with three stairs leading up to it.

"Sweep?" Michael repeated. "Nice word. I think you mean murder. Mass murder."

Weber manipulated the outside controls of the Coffin and its door began to swing open. She looked over her shoulder at Michael. "Name me a war that doesn't have collateral damage, inflicted by both sides. It's part of the game. Setbacks to ensure a leap forward."

"Game?" Michael didn't even know why he was wasting his breath. There was no way he could reach her now. "How sick is it that you call this a game?"

"The Game of Lives," she said, looking almost wistful. "You of all people should appreciate the metaphor. You always were a great gamer, weren't you?" She glowed like a proud mother.

Michael tried a more reasonable approach. "Kaine knows how to reverse the Mortality Doctrine. So does Helga. Their consciousness can stay alive, here or in the Hive. You don't have to just go in there and kill them!"

The lid of the Coffin had completed its opening. Weber pulled down a privacy screen that had been installed above each device. It muffled her voice as she spoke.

"For a plan like this, we needed dramatics, Michael. If everyone returned to their bodies and there were no devastating consequences, people would forget. A year would go by, two, five, ten. They'd start saying that it wasn't so bad, merely a bump in the road. If it happened again, we'd just get our loved ones back. Why, it's all nothing but a switch of a program, they'd say. Who needs the VNS?" Something bumped the screen—an elbow, maybe—she was obviously undressing for her foray into the Coffin. "We can't have that. We need death, irreversible death, and lots of it, but stopped by their saviors before it can become another holocaust. This way, they'll never forget. Never."

"You're sick," he whispered. Talking to her felt pointless.

He heard the hiss of the Coffin coming to life, its lid swinging shut. As it did, the privacy screen rolled back up into its slot in the ceiling of the balcony above her. By the time it lifted all the way, the Coffin was closed, its lights blinking with life.

2

Michael sat in a chair, the two guards facing him. He couldn't even distinguish between the two of them. They were like caricatures, all buzz cuts and square jaws and army fatigues. No one spoke. They just sat there, staring at the floor, the hum of a thousand Coffins vibrating in the air, making Michael tired.

What was he going to do? Michael sat and thought about Weber. He wondered what she meant to do with all these people in the Sleep. Was she going to destroy the Hive in one fell swoop, mass murder at its easiest and finest?

He sat up a little straighter. Shockingly, he hadn't really thought of himself during all this. All her talk about how they needed him, how she'd programmed him . . . but he was in a human body, a Tangent himself. If she really planned to eliminate all the Tangents out there . . .

No, that couldn't be part of the plan. At least, not yet. Weber needed Tangent-controlled humans. She'd said that she had her own Tangents in place around the world and had invited those world leaders who hadn't bowed to the VNS yet to the Coffins today under some pretext—so that she could possess them as well. He wondered if she'd personally programmed all these coded demons.

He was safe for the moment. He had to be. He didn't really understand why he was so vital to the Mortality Doctrine, but it seemed clear that he was. *An ethereal connection,* Weber had said.

That didn't make him feel any better. He thought back over everything she'd said. There was no way he'd ever walk out of this building of his own free will.

Sarah.

The sudden thought of his friend gripped his heart. He thought of his other friends. Bryson. Helga. Gabby. He'd told them to go to the Mortality Doctrine factory in the Hallowed Ravine—that had to be it. When all was said and done, they had to shut it down, make sure these Tangent takeovers stopped forever. But had they made it there? Had he sent them to their deaths as well? He thought of his parents. Kaine said he'd killed them, but they were pieces of code, just like him. Maybe, just maybe . . .

He had to do something.

"Guys," he said to the soldiers. "I need to use the bathroom."

3

They let him. How could they not?

Both soldiers escorted him to a dimly lit side hallway. They passed several doors before they got to the bathrooms. One of the guards stood with him while the other checked the facility to make sure no master escape plan had been hatched. Evidently, he found nothing.

"Go on in," he said after completing his inspection. "We'll be right here."

"Thank goodness," Michael murmured. "You sure you don't want to hold my hand while I go?" They didn't so much as crack a smile, and he went through the door. When it shut behind him, he leaned against it for a second, relishing the privacy. A quick look around showed him what the guard had already established—there'd be no easy way out. It was a small bathroom, with just two stalls and one sink.

He did his business—that part hadn't been a lie—but he didn't flush the toilet right away. He wanted a little time to himself, and he didn't care what they thought. He'd stay inside until they came in after him.

Kaine. The name came to him unbidden. Kaine was on his side now. The Tangent hated the VNS as much as Michael did. Weber had created him, then turned against him, and now wanted to destroy him and everything he believed in. Michael tried not to think about the fact that he himself didn't quite believe in the same things. For now, they were working against the same enemy.

Michael paced back and forth in the small area. All he

had to do was get a message to Kaine somehow. He just needed ten seconds, with any kind of computing device linked to the VirtNet. Michael remembered an old cartoon: a lightbulb would appear over a character's head when he got an idea. That was what he needed right—

He stopped pacing. The lights. A huge building like this, with all that fancy technology . . . the tech had to be centralized and operated via a VirtNet connection. Had to be.

A guard beat on the door. "Come on, hurry it up in there!"

Michael jumped. "Yeah! Sorry!" His mind spun. "Sorry, my stomach's all messed up from the stress you guys put me through!" He winced at his lame attempt to stall.

"You've got two minutes!" the soldier yelled through the door. Michael was surprised they didn't just come barreling in, though he figured not even a guard would have the stomach for what he might walk into.

He ran to the lighting panel, a black plate of glass on the wall. It was a simple interface—the lights operated automatically based on movement, but there were also images on the glass for turning them off and on manually, and to dim them in different quadrants of the room. Michael's mind worked. He knew he could figure out how to hack into the network; he just needed time. Time he didn't have.

"One minute!" the soldier shouted, banging on the door again. Michael jumped and accidentally turned the lights off. He quickly flipped them on again, hoping they hadn't noticed out in the hallway.

He could do this. He took a deep breath and gripped the

edges of the glass screen, digging his fingers into the crevices. Then he pulled. It took three tries to slide the unit a half inch from the wall. With more leverage, he was able to yank it out all the way. Michael carefully let it dangle from the optic fiber that connected it to the main system. When he was sure it wouldn't snap, he took a look at the back of the console. There was a button to switch the interface on the glass from symbols to raw code. He quickly made the change, then shoved the console back into the wall. The black glass now displayed several lines of code that would look like absolute gibberish to most people.

Not to him.

He went to work, tapping and swiping at the code to dig down several layers, reaching past the simple lighting communications and diving into the actual systems of the building itself.

"What's wrong with you, kid!" one of the men shouted from the hallway. "I'm coming in."

Without thinking, Michael reached over and engaged the lock on the door, something he hadn't done earlier to limit suspicion. As soon as it clicked, both soldiers started pounding on the door.

"What's going on?" the other soldier shouted. "There's nothing you can do in there! Unlock it, right now! This isn't some game, kid."

Michael was busy with the code. He needed to get his message to Kaine. Let them break the door down, beat him up, lock him in a dungeon. He only needed another few seconds. Furiously, he worked at the symbols flashing on the screen, trying to find a conduit, any link to a messaging system, no matter how archaic.

The guards pounded on the door; it sounded like they were using their shoulders now. The metal slab quivered violently, but the lock held.

"Open the door!" one of them yelled.

Michael ignored them, his fingers moving faster than ever. He was almost there.

A gunshot rattled the room. Michael yelped and instinctively raised his arms to protect his face, as if that would do any good. A quick look at the handle and lock showed that it'd been damaged, but not broken yet. Even as he watched, the gun fired again, battering the lock so much it was pushed halfway out of its place.

Michael jumped back to the code. Frantically working.

There. A service line, meant to automatically alert workers when there were malfunctions in the lighting system. Michael easily expanded it to reach the outer realms of the VirtNet and tagged it to Kaine. Then he typed a quick message, even as another gunshot exploded the lock into oblivion, tiny pieces of shrapnel raining against the mirror above the sink.

PINPOINT MY LOCATION

The door slammed inward, almost breaking off of its hinges.

WEBER HAS COFFINS HERE, BRING TANGENTS

The first soldier entered, gun raised, swept the room with his eyes.

COME SAVE ME NOW

"Stop!" the guard yelled, pointing the gun at Michael. The other one ran forward, reaching for Michael with both hands.

Michael swiped the message into the VirtNet, then yanked out the connection fibers just as hands roughly grabbed him by the shirt and lifted him, then slammed his body onto the tiled floor.

An ugly face hovered just above his. "What did you do? What did you do?"

The wind had been knocked right out of Michael's chest. He gasped for air but couldn't talk. The tip of a gun touched his forehead, cold and hard.

"What," the man repeated, enunciating each word. "Did. You. Do."

Michael coughed, trying to get the words out. "Nothing . . . I . . . was just . . . I tried . . . but . . . nothing." He scrunched up his face as if he was about to cry. "Why can't . . . you just let . . . me go? Please."

"Get him out of here," the guard with the gun said. "I'll see if I can figure out what he did."

His partner dragged Michael away by the feet.

4

Soon the three of them were back in their chairs, Michael staring at the floor. But he could see all too well in his peripheral vision the barrel of the gun pointing straight at him. The men had lost any semblance of subtlety.

"Tell us what you messed with in there," the guard with the gun said. "We're not idiots. Tell us or we just might have to shoot you in the back of the head, tell the bosses that you ran for it."

Michael had tried hard to fake tears, but nothing would come. Even with no tears, though, it wasn't hard to show how much the incident had rattled him. "Look, I'm being honest. I was desperate. I tried to see if there was anything I could do. But it's just a bunch of lighting stuff. I swear. No one has to know."

"Yeah, except you ripped out the fibers connecting everything!"

Michael shrugged, keeping his eyes glued to the floor. "I can go fix that if you wa—"

"Shut up! Do you think we're morons?"

Michael kept his expression blank. Oh how badly he wanted to say "Yup."

"Let's just chill," the other man—the one without a gun—said. "No one's going to fire us because we let a kid use the bathroom. And seriously. What could he have done? Send SOS messages with the lights? He's only a child. Look at him. He can't be that smart."

Yes, I can, Michael thought. He didn't dare look up for

fear his eyes would give away just how much he was enjoying this. Kaine would come. He knew it.

Things settled after a few minutes, and the guards lapsed into silence. Michael leaned back a little in his chair and folded his arms. It didn't take long for his good mood to evaporate. With every passing second, he began to doubt a little more. How could he have been so sure, even for a moment? Even if Kaine did get the message, who was to say he'd come save him? Why would he? It wasn't like they were suddenly a magic duo committed to fighting crime and evil world takeovers.

A hiss interrupted his thoughts, loud in the stillness of the giant room. All three of them looked to the source—one of the Coffins, its lid swinging open as little trails of mist curled over the edge. It was three devices down from the platform where Weber's lay, still blinking and humming. There was another hiss, then another, then another. Four Coffins total, opening up, scattered about, but all within fifty feet or so of where Weber remained Sunk.

Neither guard seemed alarmed. They had no reason to be. These were the people they worked for. It probably seemed totally normal that some of them would come back.

"Are you gonna tell them?" one guard said to the other.

"Yeah, fine, whatever. At least it's not Weber herself. Just her little crew of wannabe bosses."

His partner shushed him. "Dude, don't play with fire," he fiercely whispered.

Privacy screens came down to hide the four people Lifting from the Sleep as they got out and dressed. Michael waited impatiently, hoping that Kaine had done exactly what he'd wanted him to do. Used the Mortality Doctrine to come save him. But had it happened too quickly?

The privacy screens rolled up, one by one, revealing three men and one woman, all of them dressed as professionally as Agent Weber herself. They smoothed out their clothing, then walked toward Michael and his two guards. No one said a word. Michael had a hard time breathing, thinking about each and every pull of air.

One of the men who'd Lifted out of a Coffin stepped up to the guard holding the gun. He glared at the weapon, his meaning obvious.

"I, uh . . . ," the guard stammered, then put the gun in its holster. "Sorry. It's just that . . . the kid wasn't very coopera-tive. He became a flight risk, Agent Stevens."

"Yes, I'm sure," the man replied, standing close enough to the soldier to tower over him. "Trust me, I know this one. Very resourceful, isn't he? Hand me your weapon."

The soldier did a double take, not expecting the com-mand. "Huh? My gun? Why?"

"Agent Weber has been observing your . . . proceedings from our place in the VirtNet. She's ordered us to come and have you stand down. I'm sorry to break the news. Hand me your weapons, and please go home. I'm sure she'll arrange a meeting with you and your superiors soon to get everything sorted out."

"This is a joke," the soldier grumbled, but he did as he was told. He pulled the gun out of his holster and handed it to Agent Stevens.

Stevens looked at it for a moment, turning it over in his hands. "Resourceful indeed." He gripped the handle of the gun and pointed it at the soldier's head, put his finger on the trigger, all in a split second. The boom of it firing rocked the air, echoing throughout the chamber. Before Michael could turn to look, Stevens spun and aimed at the other guard, fired. He missed. The guard scrambled for his own weapon, shock transforming his face, but Stevens didn't miss the second time.

Michael sat in his chair, ears ringing, stunned. He looked up at Stevens, who turned toward him, the gun held out before him, pointed at Michael.

"Why so surprised?" Stevens said. "Isn't this what you asked me to do?"

"K-Kaine?" Michael whispered. "I . . . I didn't think . . . I . . ."

"You thought I'd possess this man's body, then come and nicely ask these fine guards to let you go? Seems like a poor plan."

"Why . . . why are you pointing that at me?" He nodded at the gun.

"Oh. Sorry." Stevens—Kaine?—lowered the weapon. "It's just that I've never gotten to do that in a real person's body before. Kind of crazy, isn't it?" He looked at the gun again as if it were a precious object, eyes wide. "I'm not Kaine, by the way. He sent the four of us to save you, just like you asked. We were in the queue of the Mortality Doctrine program, ready to go. It just took a quick adjustment to send us here instead."

Michael stood, feeling the world spin around him. The events of the last couple minutes had roiled him, but he had no time to think about it. Weber was in the Sleep, wreaking her havoc. He had to stop her.

"You need to pull the plug on all these people," he said, gathering his thoughts. He started walking toward Weber's Coffin. "Don't kill them! Just . . . just initiate an emergency Lift, then pull the plugs. Maybe ask Kaine to send you some more help before you do. Whatever you think you need. Just . . . take care of it. Please. We have to stop whatever it is all these people are doing."

He reached the steps leading up to Weber, then turned back to the others. The three men and woman were looking at him, a little perplexed, probably trying to figure out why this teenage boy was barking commands at them.

"Ask Kaine first if you need to," Michael said, throwing all the authority he could into his voice. "He and I are working together now. Why do you think he sent you here?"

Stevens nodded. "We'll get some more backup, find weapons, start Lifting people. What are you going to do?"

"I'm going to take care of Weber."

He opened her Coffin without Lifting her, using the emergency release for the door. His thoughts were still leaping ahead of him, racing a million miles an hour.

She lay there—NerveWires inserted into her skin, Liqui-

Gels covering parts of her body, an IV inserted in the crook of one arm—looking for all the world as if she were taking a nap. Her chest rose and fell with steady breaths.

"What are you doing in there?" he said softly. "Where have you gone?"

He looked at her neck. Wouldn't that be the easiest way to end this problem? Kill her while she couldn't resist? Cut the head off the dragon and hope the underlings realized she'd gone too far?

But no. He couldn't risk that. He needed to find out what she was doing and where she was doing it. Who knew what kind of damage she'd already inflicted. He had to find her in the Sleep, understand what she was doing, and fix it. That was his job now. He had to fix it. Fix everything.

Michael opened up the interface to the Coffin, quickly scanned the information, memorized it. The Sleep was one screwed-up place, but he thought he could find her with the information provided. And lucky for him, three Coffins nearby had just been vacated. How fitting that his and Weber's real bodies would be lying so close together as they settled this in the place where she'd created him.

"I'm coming for you, Weber," he said to her as he input the command to close up her Coffin. He stared at her peaceful, unconscious face. "I'm coming for you right now."

CHAPTER 19

DISSOLVING PODS

1

Once in the Sleep, Michael had to fight the code a bit. He was confident in the coordinates he'd stolen from Weber's Coffin, but the deteriorating VirtNet didn't want to cooperate. He swam through clouds of purple refuse and thick black material that was the basest programming he'd ever seen. He coded a corridor through it all, visualizing his way to the place Weber had gone, and was able to create a ground to stand on. As he ran down it, things suddenly appeared in front of him.

"Buy one, get one free!" a man barked at him, holding up a VirtBox of Sims that wouldn't make too many moms of the world happy. Michael ran right through him—the man was like a ghost. "Buy none, get none, you jerk!" the salesman yelled at him from behind.

A lady dressed like an old-fashioned housewife popped up, selling cookie dough. She was blurred out by a series of fully immersive scenes from the latest 4D films, making him feel like one of the characters for a moment. He shook it off; something was now trying to mess with his mind. A kid appeared, begging for money. He was straight out of a Dickens book. Michael blasted through him, but others kept coming, selling everything from massages to antiques. The Virt-Net was so damaged, ads and spam were sinking in from everywhere. It was an utter cesspool, and he had to tunnel his way through it.

The corridor he'd built stretched out before him as he ran. He coded and coded, focused on Weber's location, pushing everything else outside the boundaries of his programmed pathway. Far ahead, based on all the input swirling around his mind, he created a door. A simple wooden door with a round brass knob. Michael leaped into the air, threw his arms forward, and flew, obliterating any other spammage that got in his way.

He landed in front of the door and sucked in an enormous breath. Light poured from its corners and it seemed to vibrate, pulsing with the power of whatever was behind it. Michael knew he'd made it. Weber was on the other side. He'd found her. He wasn't even sure he knew how he knew anymore. He was beginning to feel like the code was a part of him and he was a part of the code. Just like the old days.

He didn't bother knocking. The door was just an illusion anyway, created by him, a way of visualizing the path. It wouldn't be locked. She didn't even know he was coming, at least not this way, this quickly. He reached down, felt the cool hardness of the brass handle, turned it, and pushed the door open.

The light was blinding.

He stepped into it.

2

"Michael," she said. At first there was only her voice and white light. "I won't mince words. I'm shocked to see you here."

He shook his head, rubbed his eyes, righted himself in the world of code that he'd been so recklessly manipulating. Everything around him trembled, then snapped into focus. He took another deep breath to steady himself and looked around.

Weber was only a few feet away. She stood in front of a glowing glass case. And she wasn't alone. At least a hundred Auras stood around her. Michael knew they were there to protect her as she destroyed the world.

"You said you programmed me," Michael said, trying to hide any surprise at where he'd ended up. The room was so ordinary—what was she hoping to accomplish in such an everyday place? He'd been expecting the Hive. "Why would you be surprised that I figured out a way to come after you?"

She cocked her head, as if he'd said something profound and she wanted to consider it for a moment. "This may surprise you, but I wasn't . . . completely honest with you."

"Shocking," he replied.

"I did program you," she said, still contemplative. "You and others. Don't worry, you're still special, but we're not quite as mother-son close as you might've thought."

Michael laughed. It was maddening how skillfully this woman was able to tick him off. "Do you think I really cared? What, you thought I'd feel something for you? Think of you as my mom? Just when I think you couldn't be any farther from reality . . ." He really didn't know what to add to that.

"You were the one who went the farthest," she continued, acting as if she hadn't heard a word he just said. "Of all the ones we programmed and placed into the Deep. The Path wasn't just a test, Michael. It changed you, developed you, tied you to the Mortality Doctrine. It was all part of the programming. The complexity of it all is . . . it's beautiful. Awesome. Horrifying. It's everything."

Michael shook his head. What she said—it made sense on some level. But none of that mattered now. She obviously needed him alive. It had to be the reason he was still breathing.

"You told me you were going to kill them all," Michael said, spitting out the last three words. "I'm not sure how you plan to do it, but I can't let it happen."

Weber folded her arms. "Your body is safe and sound in a Coffin somewhere. Like I've said, I need you alive. But here, in this beautiful place that your generation calls the Sleep, we can pretty much do anything we want to you. I know you know that. Look around, Michael. Do you really think all of these good agents and soldiers standing here with the VNS today are going to let you take even one step toward me?"

"Nope," Michael said. What was taking Kaine's people so long? "I really don't think that at all. Looks like you've got them pretty brainwashed."

There was a commotion in the back of the room. What started as murmurs of conversation became a series of startled cries, then shouts and screams. Michael felt a moment of pure joy when he saw the terror that flashed across Weber's Aura. She turned away from Michael to look, and he could see it, too.

Her people were disappearing.

Nothing fancy or pyrotechnic accompanied the vanishings. Michael stood on his toes to watch as, one by one, the agents and soldiers Weber had mentioned with such pride ceased to exist within the room. There, then not there. Not even a pop of sound or wisp of smoke or blur of color to mark the instant transition. Torn from the Sleep, Lifted. The four Tangents Kaine had sent him were breaking every rule in the book back at the cavernous skyscraper.

Weber turned back to Michael, not even trying to hide her anger or shock.

"What have you . . . ," she began, then seemed to realize that she was mere seconds away from losing her army.

"Quick!" she yelled to her posse. "Before they get to you! Grab Michael, take him down, kill him! Hurry!" Her Aura couldn't hide the lunacy that blazed behind her eyes. She was breaking from the inside out.

Her cronies quickly obeyed. Michael had barely caught that fearsome look on her face before he found himself lifted into the air and thrown to the floor. The air left his lungs and he struggled to fill them again, but bodies piled on top of him, punching and kicking him, pressing him harder into the ground. Hands wrapped around his throat and squeezed. He couldn't even see who they belonged to; his vision was filled with arms and legs and hair and feet, as if they were all connected to each other, some monstrous creation from a mad scientist's lab.

"Quickly!" he heard Weber yell. "Do it!"

Michael couldn't tell what was worse, the pain of his pummeled body or the aching of his lungs, desperate for air. He coughed and sputtered, struggling against the hands that choked him. He couldn't fight all these people, no matter how good at coding he might be. He tried to flail his arms, but both of them got pinned by bony knees.

His vision blurred from the lack of oxygen, but he saw one of the figures on top of him vanish, a disorienting pop of reality. He relaxed his body, gave in to their fight against time. Another person disappeared. Then another. He could feel the lessening weight pressed against his chest. *Please,* he thought, *make the choker go next.* It felt as if his eyes were going to explode, and fire burned in his chest.

Then, finally, relief. The pressure on his neck suddenly

disappeared, and air rushed into his lungs. Colors blurred and rushed above him, but he could see enough to know. All of his attackers had disappeared.

He rolled onto his side, coughing and sucking in air. His entire body shook from the effort. He retched and spit. Then he caught Weber coming at him in the corner of his vision and he reacted, kicking out his legs and scrambling away. He flailed until his back hit a wall. But Weber had stopped. She was retreating, her face filled with horror, as if she'd come upon a rabid dog.

"You should've killed me," he said, his throat raw. The anger took over, making him petty and vengeful. "Better yet, you should never have created me in the first place." Still breathing heavily, still hurting in a hundred places, he pushed against the wall behind him and climbed to his feet. "I'm too smart for you. I've got too many people on my side. It's over, lady. I'm not going to let you hurt one more person." He took a step toward her to show the threat was real.

A hand went up to her chest protectively, and she backed away until she once again stood in front of that mysterious glass case with the glowing lights. She stared at him, not saying a word. She looked as if she was trying to figure out what she should do.

He took another step forward, not so sure himself of the plan. Getting into an all-out brawl with a grown woman wasn't exactly how he'd envisioned saving the world. But he had to get it out of her—what they'd been on the verge of doing when he'd arrived.

"Just tell me the truth," he said. "I don't want to hurt you. I could've easily just killed you back in the Wake, ended it the simple way. What were you going to do when I got here?"

"We had a plan," she said, a glazed look in her eyes. "I stuck to that plan. We had a plan!"

"Listen to yourself," Michael said. "You sound crazy. How can you be helping people by killing people? And taking over the world? It's insane."

Weber's eyes met his sharply. "We needed you. But you're really beginning to get in the way."

Michael took another step, now only three or four feet away from Weber. He could almost reach out and grab her. "Let's figure this out. What's that thing behind you, anyway?"

"Circumstances have changed," she whispered, sounding more delusional by the second. "I didn't want to . . . I don't want to kill you. Things won't run as smoothly. But we can always rebuild the Doctrine. And reprogram the ones we lose. We can always adapt, can't we?"

"What," he said, emphasizing each word. "Are. You. Talking. About."

"So be it," she said, standing up straighter. She sounded as if she were having a conversation with someone who wasn't there. "This can be on your conscience. Even though . . . even though you won't be around for it."

A fanatical look came over her face, eyes wild. "If you have even an ounce of sense left in that mind of yours, go back, Lift and leave us alone. Do not"—she held up a finger—"do not follow me. I swear if you do, I'll kill everyone. Every last one."

"What—"

She quickly turned from him and faced the glass box behind her. She put her hands on the lip of the stand it stood on and was suddenly pushing herself up, swinging her legs over the open top of the container. Michael bolted forward to grab her, but he was too late.

Then the strangest thing happened. As she descended into the container of lights, her body began to shrink. Slowly at first, then faster and faster, so that by the time she was fully in the box, she was the size of a small doll. She looked up at Michael, and for the briefest moment he'd forgotten he was inside the Sleep and was shocked by the sudden transformation. He watched as her tiny body disappeared into the lights floating in the box. Lights that Michael now realized made up a galaxy of stars.

He leaned over the edge of the box to look down. There were hundreds, maybe thousands, of tiny lights, glowing and pulsing within a murky soup of darkness. And they all swirled together, creating an enormous orb. It was the Hive—tiny compared to the real thing. He'd only seen it from its true perspective, so large that those round sides appeared as walls.

True perspective, he thought. He was in the Sleep, for crying out loud. What did that even mean? It was all a world of code, nothing but letters and numbers and symbols.

Taking a deep breath, he put all his weight onto the stand

and flipped himself into the lighted abyss. Just like Agent Weber, he shrank and fell.

4

Everything was a rush of sound and movement, spinning around him like a wild merry-go-round. Then the world righted, slamming into his consciousness like a brick onto wet mortar, and abruptly he stopped moving, his vision corrected, his mind calmed. He floated in a dark nothingness, several hundred feet from a familiar sight: the wall of the Hive, now as grand as the first time he'd seen it. The pods pulsed like heartbeats, a soft, comforting thump of sound along with each one.

There was no sign of Weber, or of Kaine and his army of Tangents. They were either done fighting or on the other side of the Hive.

But Weber. Where had she gone?

With a thought he vaulted himself through the purple air, stopping within a few feet of the glowing pods. He looked up and down, to the sides. From so close, he could barely even see the curve of the structure—which he now understood better than ever, after seeing Weber's glass case perspective. He didn't know what to do. If only that pool of code that Kaine had introduced him to would magically appear nearby. Somehow he had to dig into the information to see what Weber had planned.

Time had to be running out.

Michael flew forward, squeezing between two of the oval pods to enter the Hive's inner area. A world of orange light surrounded him now, a little fainter from the far side. Still no sign of Weber. He sent himself forward, throughout the massive chamber of the Hive, scanning its walls of pods for any sign of Agent Weber.

He didn't know how she planned to do it, but her intention had been made clear. She wanted to eliminate all the Tangents, including him when he was of no use anymore, severing the connection of the Mortality Doctrine. He'd be dead—the true death—and she could Lift back to the Wake and tell everyone that the VNS had saved the world and only they could prevent it from sinking into chaos again. As he flew, streaking up and down the curved, brightly lit walls of the Hive, he imagined the feigned look of pain on her face as she broke the news. Lives lost, but so many more saved.

He screamed in frustration, and the sound of his yell was swallowed by whatever substance surrounded him. Everything about the place was odd, different from what he was used to. It was programming on such a complex scale, it was beyond anything he'd ever dealt with before.

He flew in circles and found nothing.

Until.

There.

There.

A mere wink in his peripheral vision, like a fly buzzing by. A spark of darkness. Michael stopped his flight, turned toward whatever had captured his attention. It was far away, on the other side of the Hive from where he hovered. He threw all of his will into being there, and this time it wasn't like flight. It was teleportation. In an instant he was there.

There to witness the beginning of the end.

A pod stood empty. Surrounded on four sides by glowing, living pods of orange light. In the entire structure of the Hive, he'd never seen anything similar. He'd never seen an empty pod. And he knew it had just happened—that had been the dark blur of movement in the corner of his eye. Although he still didn't understand how she was doing it, Agent Weber had just eliminated the first victim in her grand plan.

The true death.

Michael understood what it meant, and his chest ached. The human who'd been taken, and the Tangent who'd done the possessing—they were both dead now. Gone. Forever. Even without a full grasp of the coding or the Mortality Doctrine, he knew this was so.

As he stared at the vacant slot, thinking all of these troubling thoughts, the next pod over began to dissolve. Like black specks of disease or hungry insects, darkness spread across the surface of the orange light. In a matter of seconds, the entire thing was gone, replaced by emptiness. Though he might've imagined it, Michael thought he heard a faint scream, as if from far away, right before the last bit of orange light blinked out of existence.

He floated there, watching, trembling, as another one died, eaten by darkness. The swarm of blackness consumed it like an army of ants. Not a second passed before it began on the very next one, eating away.

Never in his life had he felt so utterly helpless.

He screamed until his lungs hurt.

5

The clock kept ticking—there was nothing he could do about it. Every moment that passed without acting meant another Tangent dead, another human dead. The order of dissolved pods did have a pattern, at least. It was spreading in a straight line, from right to left. Michael made a quick timing judgment and flew to a pod about twenty slots down, trying not to think about those he'd just passed.

He reached the pod in question, drifted within a few inches. The same screen he'd seen when visiting the current resting place of Jackson Porter started to materialize with a name, but he dove into the code without looking—he didn't have a moment to spare. He dove into the code the way Kaine had shown him. The pods of the Hive blurred and shook, transforming into an array of tightly condensed symbols and letters, still glowing orange.

It was the code, dense and crowding him tightly into the small space, overwhelming him. The structure of the Hive itself had its own code, surrounding the individual pod data chunks, so that Michael was completely immersed in a blinding display of information. All of it moved at a blistering pace, up and down and sideways, in and out of his vision. Different colors and sizes and shapes. His head swam with nausea trying to take it all in.

He looked to the right, in the direction of Weber's attacks on the pods. The darkness was thicker, more menacing in code view, like a black oil that had come to life. It reached out to devour huge swaths of code at once. Weber's program had already eaten through half of the pods between him and where he'd been floating before. There was no way he had enough time to create something to stop her. At least, not there.

But he could learn something. Bringing his attention back to the data in front of him, he studied the code, the organization, the characteristics of its programming. Darkness grew in his peripheral vision. It was making a sick squelching sound as it crept toward him, like a knife sticking into flesh. He tried to ignore it. He tried to focus on the code, find a link. There had to be something in there that Weber was specifically attacking. A link between the Hive and her program.

Like tar thrown from a bucket, a splash of a strange black substance sprayed the Hive in front of him. Upon contact, half of the pod's information sizzled and died, whisking into the endless darkness of Weber's program. Another thick ribbon of inky darkness came swirling in from above, snapping at the code, then whipping toward Michael's face. He cried out as it hit his skin, latching on, burning. The pain was like acid on a wound. He screamed and the sound died in the thick blackness that had covered him. With a burst of panic he reached up and pulled at it until he ripped it off. It came back at him but launched back into visual mode and flew out to the center of the vast open chamber of the Hive.

Breathing heavily, he floated there, his skin burning as sweat trickled down his scorched face. He took in the Hive around him and saw the pod where Weber had begun her attack. At least thirty pods had now been destroyed, leaving nothing behind but empty space. And the destruction was spreading, its pace quickening.

Michael scanned the wall of consciousnesses, trying to gather his thoughts. *Focus,* he told himself. *Focus.* If ever he had to act without thinking, now was the time. Lives were dropping by the second.

A sudden, chilling thought almost froze his heart.

Jackson Porter.

In the frenzy, Michael had almost forgotten that he himself was a Tangent, that he himself had taken over a human body, that he himself could die at any second. If Weber got to Jackson's pod . . .

Still he floated there, thinking all these things, when people were dying left and right. Indecision had him in its grasp. A sickness grew in his stomach. If he went straight for Jackson Porter, Weber would know. She'd throw everything at that pod.

Do it! he almost shouted at himself. He had no choice. He could do nothing if he ceased to exist. Nothing else mattered. He had to protect himself, no matter what she brought down on him.

The Bubble.

It flashed across his mind, that membrane of protection that Kaine had programmed for him. Michael closed his eyes, tried to remember its feel, its look, its code. Complex, unusual, something he'd never done before. But it might be his only hope.

It was time to work on instinct.

As Weber's wave of dark decay swept across the Hive, Michael accessed his files, found Jackson's location, and went for it.

CHAPTER 20

LIFE

1

The pod was at least sixty or seventy rows up from the swath of destruction laid out by Weber's program. Michael zapped himself to it and dove into the code as if he were diving into the cold ocean. It was a sensory shock as it enveloped him, that beautiful, complex universe of information. He scanned the data, allowing his mind to open up and take it all in. He couldn't afford to think about it in individual pieces. He had to let it all flow past him, through him, grasping its meaning on a subconscious level.

At the same time, compartmentalizing his mind, he worked at the code for Kaine's creation, the Bubble. It had been a wonder of coding, but Michael was a wonder himself. He knew that, even if all the forces against him had made him doubt his abilities. An unexpected burst of laughter exploded from his virtual chest as he pieced his vision of Kaine's program together.

He was giddy.

He was delirious.

He was having the time of his life.

2

Near the end, things happened so fast he could barely track them all. The Bubble grew around him. He scanned the code of Jackson Porter's pod, searching for any clue that would help him rebound against Weber's program and stop it in its tracks. Then he could feel it coming—the darkness swooping. A shadow fell over him, and he turned and saw that Weber had abandoned her original course. She was now cutting across the Hive wall diagonally, heading straight for him.

Pod by pod went black as she passed.

Michael swam in the code of Jackson Porter's prison, even as he put the finishing touches on the Bubble of protection. He had no idea whether it would hold against Weber's program like it had against the KillSims. But surely it would, wouldn't it?

In his frenzied state, he remembered a line from an old flat-film.

Surely you can't be serious.

I am serious. And don't call me Shirley.

He laughed again, certain the pressure was finally starting to crack his mind wide open.

Yes, he was delirious. But he was sharper than ever.

Michael went back to the code, the Bubble around him giving him the time he needed. He hoped.

But what was he searching for? He had no idea—just had to trust that he'd know. He worked the information that pressed in from all directions, worked it like wet clay.

His entire world shook when the darkness of Weber's program hit the surface of his Bubble. Every piece of data around him shuddered and blurred for a moment, then righted itself. He looked over his shoulder and saw the visual manifestation of it all: black tendrils of some monstrous, amorphous beast attacking the invisible layer of protection between them.

From there, his instincts took over. He found things he hadn't dreamed of finding within the code. Access points to the Hive. A running history of the Mortality Doctrine program and how it did what it did to Michael's Tangent self. He even found a piece of himself in there, something he couldn't quite understand. It was almost as if he'd found his own DNA gene sequence.

He was a building block. He was beginning to see how he served as a foundation for the Doctrine and all that it had accomplished.

He took as much of the information as he could until he finally felt ready.

It was clear to Michael now that what would follow would be horrible, but it had to be done.

It was the only way.

Michael turned around and faced the Bubble. Weber's black destroyer program had now completely encased it.

With a few quick manipulations of the code, he dissolved the shield of protection and let the tarlike substance come at him and his pod.

It struck him all at once, and the stinging pain from before overwhelmed him. He resisted the urge to suck in a breath from shock, the world around him shifting between visuals and raw code, flickering like a bad WallScreen signal. Michael forced his mind to calm and made his surroundings solidify in the pool of code, the substance in which he needed to work. And work he did.

Michael floated a few feet from Jackson Porter's pod and let Weber's program devour him until it had nearly merged with his own code. He had to let it in to have access to what he wanted. The pain was excruciating, the intensity heightening. He ignored it, not caring how battered his body back in the real world might be—all he needed was to stay alive.

Darkness dimmed his vision, so he brightened the code. He dug into it like he'd done with Jackson's pod, but this time he was much more focused. He knew exactly what he was looking for: a pathway to Weber. That was the last piece of the puzzle.

Weber. He needed her.

The darkness ate at him, but it was confused by his programming because it was so different from the pods themselves. Michael knew it wouldn't take long for it to adapt, though. Like a pool of smart nanobots, it learned and changed as it worked. It was only a matter of time before it sucked the life from his Aura, leaving him as brain-dead as any KillSim would.

The true death.

Pain ignited his skin and sank into his muscles. His vision was blurry—almost black—and his own tears stung.

He pushed on.

Darkness closing in . . . Pain . . .

There.

Every program had a link to its owner, especially when it was being controlled. He'd found it. Weber was hidden somewhere, but it didn't matter. He had the link. The pain was so great he shook, barely able to reach forward and latch onto her, throw a million strings of code to lock her to him, pull her to him.

He felt her fear. Like stepping under a waterfall, it was a burst of coldness.

Through her own program, Michael had found her, and now she was his.

With his last ounce of strength, he launched an anti-program, countering every line of code encompassing the destructive darkness Weber had unleashed. In an instant it eviscerated her program, eliminating it from existence. Light poured back in, blinding and glorious, and the pain disappeared.

Michael held Weber in his grasp, the massive world of her code enclosed in his mental might. He leaped toward the wall of the Hive and found a pod that had already been half destroyed by Weber's program before he'd stopped it. Whoever it represented had no chance of survival. Gaping holes covered the orange oval so Michael could see inside to the dark purple world beyond.

It was enough. He hoped.

Michael launched himself at it, sank into its code, reached for the links to the Mortality Doctrine he'd discovered within Jackson Porter's pod, threw Weber's code into its vortex, and channeled her very being into the body connected to the pod at hand.

And Weber's essence vanished from the Sleep.

She entered a new body in the Wake, possessed its mind, linked to the pod before him. Her own link severed, the real body of Agent Weber was brain-dead.

Using his scant knowledge of the program she had created, Michael finished off the job on the half-destroyed pod that now represented everything that was left of Weber's essence. The pod disintegrated, vanished in a mist of darkness, killing anything linked to it back in the Wake. And then all was as silent and still as a windless day.

Michael had just killed Agent Weber.

CHAPTER 21

THE MORTALITY DOCTRINE

1

The sea of code vanished in a blink, replaced by the orderly world of the Hive. The scar of destroyed pods was a conspicuous gash of black in the orange light.

Michael pulled in a deep breath. He'd done it. He'd stopped Weber's program from annihilating every single life he could see, both the Tangent side and the human side. The problem was far from solved, but he'd accomplished the most immediate task. And Weber was dead. The true death. Her body now lay lifeless back in the Wake, her consciousness wiped from the earth and the VirtNet.

Exhaustion overtook him. He floated within the void of the Hive, limp. He wanted nothing more than to go back to the Wake, stay inside the Coffin, and sleep for a day or two. Let Gabby and Bryson and Helga figure out the rest. If the VNS was out of the way, things could be worked out with Kaine, right?

Michael floated in place for a while, his eyes closed, enjoying the warmth of the orange light against his virtual skin. He was too tired to even think. Too tired to Lift himself. He just wanted some time. Some sleep.

Surely he could rest now.

Don't call me Shirley, he thought with a smile.

2

Michael fell asleep at some point, waking and slipping back under several times. The Hive glowed and pulsed around him—which, combined with its soft hum, was like the world's greatest lullaby. During those short, groggy moments of half awareness, he thought of Gabby. Bryson. Helga. They were so smart. Maybe they'd already figured everything out.

Could it really be over? Michael smiled again, knowing it was too good to be true. Nothing had been okay in so long. Always, always, something was wrong.

He needed to check on them. He needed to talk to Kaine. He had to finish this.

Thoughts bounced around inside his weary mind.

He fell back asleep.

3

He didn't know how long he'd slept, but eventually Michael woke up, feeling refreshed and alive, if a little rough around the edges. Floating there in the void of the Hive, he wished a coffee cart would swing by with some wake-up juice. He briefly wondered if he could code such a thing, steal a cup of grow-joe from one of the many virtual restaurants he'd plundered throughout the years. The thought seemed ridiculous now. Silly. Gloriously silly. He missed it so much.

He rubbed his eyes, looked around. He winced when he saw the dark gash in the Hive wall again, its emptiness so stark a reminder of the lives lost. And he'd just begun to feel a little upbeat. People were dead. Tangents were eliminated, gone forever. If only he could've been a little faster.

He sighed, looked at the other side of the Hive, where everything was whole and brightly lit. Pod after pod after pod. That made him feel a little better.

With another sigh, he realized just how sick of that place he was. Time to move on. He wondered about going back to the VNS building to see how Kaine's Tangents had done cleaning the place up, but decided against it. He'd gotten the rest he needed, and he missed his friends. It was time to find them. And if they hadn't already infiltrated the Doctrine and figured out a way to kill it, he'd help them. They'd do it together. With the VNS no longer breathing down their necks, it shouldn't be too hard.

For the third time that day, Michael accessed his history files to search for a previously visited location. This one was a little tougher. It had more firewalls than even the Hive. But he'd gotten there once, so he knew he could do it again. Once, the Path had taken him there, the place where he'd first met Kaine, the place where he'd been born into a human body for the first time. The Hallowed Ravine.

He jumped into the code and made his way.

4

He saw Gabby first, and even though he barely knew her, her face brightened his day. Not until she stood before him, her Aura looking so much like her actual body, did he realize how lonely he'd been. For so long he'd gone at this all by himself.

"Hi," she said, obviously startled at his sudden appearance. They stood on a rolling hill of wind-flattened grass, a thick forest at the bottom. "I . . . We . . . Where'd you come from?"

Michael shrugged. "Oh, I've been out and about. Saving people, killing bad guys—that sort of stuff."

She stepped forward and threw her arms around him, hugging him as fiercely as if they'd known each other forever. He hugged back, thankful for the human touch. The light went on in his mind: no matter what happened, she saw Jackson Porter in him, and Jackson Porter was her boyfriend.

She pulled away and looked up at him. "It's good to see you. Any word on . . . I don't even know what to ask, actually. Did you do it? Whatever it was?"

He nodded, feeling more confident by the second. He'd half expected to be greeted by KillSims when he'd arrived, something that had happened in this very place not that long ago. But there were trees, and there was grass and a bright blue sky. Kaine must have really worked hard to protect the place from the ruination of the VirtNet.

"Yeah," he said, "I think so. I think the VNS is done, and Weber's days of making our lives miserable are over for sure. What about here? Any luck?"

She gestured for him to look around. "We've been looking and looking, but there's nothing. There's an old cabin in those woods, and an abandoned castle on the other side of the forest that's barely standing. Not much else. Bryson's checking out the castle, and Helga's in the woods somewhere. I feel like I'm wearing a path up and down this hill."

Michael let out an exaggerated sigh. "Do I have to do everything myself?" He quickly laughed it off, hoping she didn't think he was a jerk. "Just kidding. That's really good, actually. I'm glad you weren't attacked by KillSims or Rodents of Unusual Size."

"Huh?"

"Nothing. Let's go find the others. I need more hugs."

Michael remembered everything about the Hallowed Ravine. The castle, overrun by VNS agents and Tangents loyal to Kaine and KillSims charging out of the ruins to attack him. He remembered confronting Kaine in the cabin, being dragged through the woods by that giant of a man. He remembered the world spinning into chaos and dissolving around him.

But strangely, it looked like none of that had ever happened. The castle was still standing—old, yes, but in one piece. It was confusing, and Michael wondered yet again what had truly happened that day he'd been sucked through the Mortality Doctrine program and placed into the body of Jackson Porter.

Michael and Gabby walked into the wide clearing between the forest and the castle, and before he could let his thoughts get too dark, they slipped from his mind. Bryson came charging out of the entrance of the castle and bounded down the stairs with a ridiculous smile on his face, and Michael couldn't stop his own smile from forming.

"Michael!" Bryson yelled, just as he tripped on a loose stone in the bottom step. He tumbled, flipped, jumped right back up onto his feet, and kept running. "I'd kill you if I wasn't so happy to see your ugly mug!" He reached Michael and grabbed him, pulling him off his feet into the biggest hug he'd ever received.

Through a grunt, Michael barely managed to say "Good to see you, too."

Bryson put him down and took a step back. "You look seven minutes from death, dude. Especially in the eyes. Let me guess—rough couple of days?"

"You could say that." Michael glanced at Gabby, who had a genuine look of happiness on her face. He was liking her more and more, and the whole fiasco at the farmhouse felt like a distant memory or a half-forgotten dream. "But I think we're doing okay. Kaine helped me, you know. I never could've done it without him."

"Done what?" Bryson asked.

"The VNS . . . we don't have to worry about them anymore. Or their mass murder program. Or Agent Weber. I . . . stopped her."

Bryson and Gabby exchanged a look, both of them knowing that last phrase communicated a million different things. Luckily, they didn't push him to explain because right then Helga came running out of the woods, having already spotted him, her face lit up. Tears streamed down her cheeks, and she pulled Michael into a hug even more viselike than Bryson's. She even swung him around a couple of times for good measure.

Once the world had stopped spinning and he was on his own two feet again, Michael laughed, as genuinely as he ever had.

"Man," he said, "I don't even know what to say. You guys are all right, I'm all right, we're back together again. If only Sarah . . ." He faltered there, grief plucking at his heart. The pain was still heavy and hot, but it didn't overwhelm him like it had at times before.

"I know, sweetie," Helga said, hugging him one more time, holding on for a beat longer than normal. "I need to . . . well, uh . . ." She stepped back, and the look on her face was strange, mysterious.

"What?" Michael asked.

She looked away. "For now, it's nothing."

"What?" Michael pressed, his curiosity close to uncontrollable now.

"Later," she replied emphatically. "I promise."

Michael threw his hands up. "Okay. I guess we don't need to spoil the party any more than we already have."

Gabby stepped closer to him and lightly touched his arm. "What're we doing here, Michael? Back at the tree house you were going nuts—all those KillSims, Kaine . . . we were scared to death. Then you sent us off, and ever since, we've been tramping around trying to find this factory you're talking about. There's nothing here."

"She's right," Bryson added. "Not a thing, not a person. So what are we doing here?"

With a sinking feeling, Michael realized he didn't know. Not fully, anyway. "I assumed this was where the Mortality Doctrine . . . factory was. Whatever you want to call it. This is where I came—this was the end of the Path." He pointed to the center of the field in which they stood. "I was standing right there when the world spun around me and I was sucked into the Doctrine program's vortex. Next thing I knew, I was a different dude in a real body. This has to be it."

Bryson, Helga, and Gabby all turned in a circle to take in their surroundings, as if his pronouncement would make them see things differently. But everything in sight was programmed with superior code—it felt almost as real as *Lifeblood Deep*. Nothing stood out as unusual or menacing. Grass, hills, forest, the ruins of an ancient castle, and a cabin—all of which had been searched thoroughly by Michael's friends.

They faced him again.

"What is it?" Gabby asked. "What is the factory? Where are we?"

Michael shrugged, eager to dive into the code of the place—something he was now ten times better at than he'd been two days earlier. "This has to be the heart of the Mortality Doctrine," he said, almost to himself, then addressed his friends. "It has to be. The Hive is the storage; the Ravine, the actual program. We need to destroy it, make sure no Tangent ever takes over a human again. *Ever.* Wipe it out, along with every last remaining trace of its source code. Then we go back to the Hive, reinsert people into their own minds and bodies, and release the Tangents back into the Sleep. Simple as that."

"Simple as that," Helga repeated.

Michael just nodded. "One step at a time. I seriously think the hardest part is over. The VNS were behind all of this—they were the real enemy. And we don't have to worry about them anymore. We can finish this thing, with or without Kaine's help."

"Have you really thought this through?" Helga asked him, a motherly tone in her voice. "Like, say, for example, what happens to me and you?"

Michael looked at the ground. He'd never allowed himself to follow that line of thought, though it had hovered on the edges of his mind since the first day he'd awakened in Jackson Porter's body. He supposed it was time to address it.

"Whatever has to happen will happen," he said coldly. He pictured the face of Jackson Porter, so strongly that for a second he thought it was real, a glitch in the code. But then it was gone. And it had made him jealous, even though he'd lived the vast majority of his life with a different face.

"What is that supposed to mean?" Helga asked. "The Tangents I partnered with to use the Mortality Doctrine—"

"I know," he said, cutting her off. "I . . . I just can't talk about it right now. I can't."

Silence fell on the group, and finally, Bryson broke it.

"So," he said with a single clap of his hands. "Let's get this show on the road, shall we?"

Michael nodded, trying to clear the image of his face— Jackson's face—from his thoughts. "Okay, yeah, you're right. Let's get started."

"Get started with what, exactly?" Gabby asked. "I still don't understand what you want us to do with a bunch of grass and trees and an old junk pile of brick and stone."

Michael focused on Helga. "You know the Doctrine program to an extent, right? I mean, you guys figured it out, used it. Right?"

Her nod didn't show a lot of confidence. "I wasn't what you'd call an expert in that field. Others did more than I did. But yeah, I got a good taste of how it worked."

"So did I," Michael responded. "When I was in the Hive, fighting it out against Weber and her own version of a Kill-Sim, I saw it, saw the connections, saw how it worked. I mean, I understood it enough to send her into another person's mind and terminate the connection." He paused. "It killed her."

If he'd expected rebukes, they didn't come. Bryson actually started to pump a fist before he stopped himself.

Michael continued. "I think if we hook up, we can dig into the code of this place. But we need to dig deep. Deeper than ever. I know this is the heart of Kaine's program. With all of us working together, we can find it, dissect it, and blow the thing apart. You guys in?"

Helga gave a firm nod. Gabby said yes with her eyes, not a hint of doubt there. Bryson gave two thumbs up.

"Let's do this the old-fashioned way," Michael said, stepping closer to Gabby and motioning for the others to move in. "We'll hold hands, keep a solid connection between us. Let's stay in constant communication. I wanna do this fast, and I don't want anyone to be alone in case trouble comes."

"Trouble?" Bryson repeated. "You expecting trouble from you-know-who?"

"He'll understand" was all Michael said. He knew he should explain his plan to Kaine first. Things would go much better if they really did stay on the same side, but Michael didn't want to burn any more time. "We can only do what we can do, right? He's not here."

"You're just bursting with confidence," Bryson said. "Look, man, if you think this is the thing to do, then I'm in. Let's get it over with."

"Come on, then," Michael responded, holding out his hand. Bryson took it. Gabby took the other. Then Helga joined in to complete the circle.

"Seek and destroy," Michael whispered as they closed their eyes.

6

Down, down, down they went, sinking into the code. It felt to Michael like slipping into a warm bath, a comfort after the awkward conversations with his friends. Blades of grass became lines of symbols, trees became towering blocks of data, the castle a jumbled mess of letters and numbers, the sky awash in that purple haze that so often represented the most basic formative programming of the VirtNet. Michael felt the reassuring pressure of Bryson's and Gabby's hands, felt the links between them all. They combined their skills and knowledge and began to dissect the massive amount of information in which they found themselves.

An hour passed. Two. Three. Michael kept a timer within his files, knowing how prone he was to losing track of minutes and hours when he was in the zone. He didn't want to go too long without a break or they might make errors.

At four hours, no one wanted to stop. They'd discovered so much, come to understand so much. Michael was swept up to the point that he'd practically forgotten the dire circumstances that had made the task necessary in the first place.

He had been right. The Mortality Doctrine lived and breathed within the Hallowed Ravine program, like the basic building blocks of genetic code. Michael had never seen anything like it. If the Ravine had veins, the Doctrine was the blood that pumped through it. You couldn't look at the code for one without seeing the other. All of it was linked together, like some beautiful man-made biological creation.

And Michael planned to destroy it.

"Let's go out," he messaged to the others. Sensing their reluctance, he let go of Gabby's and Bryson's hands and opened himself back to the visual side of things. The universe of code disappeared, replaced by greenery and blue sky.

Helga blinked against the brightness of the sun. "Well, that was . . . fascinating."

"Weird," Bryson said. "And cool."

Gabby nodded her agreement. "I wonder if my dad knows about this place."

Michael's heart skipped a beat. He'd totally forgotten that her dad worked for the VNS. Had he been in one of those Coffins back in that enormous building?

Gabby obviously sensed his concern. "Don't worry, Jax. I mean, Michael. I know my own dad. There's no way he's one of the bad guys. I've been messaging him—he's safe and nowhere near the office. I guess you could say he called in sick."

She gave him a weak smile, and it made Michael think of the last time he'd seen Sarah do that. She'd always tried to deflect his worries with a grin, too—even if it was a weak one.

"That's good to hear," he said.

"So what're we going to do?" Bryson asked. "You really want to destroy this place?"

Michael nodded. "We don't have a choice."

"We need rest," Helga said.

Michael couldn't have agreed more. "And food, but we can't afford to Lift right now. Bryson, you were always the best at it. Code us in some grub from Dan the Man Deli."

Back in the Coffin, they'd be fed with an IV—nothing to write home about—but here in the Sleep it'd all taste divine.

"You got it, maestro."

7

They ate. They took naps. They spent two or three hours strategizing and planning. It was going to take a monumental effort—they all knew that. But not one of them doubted it could work. Linked together, with a lot of hard work and brilliant coding, they could destroy the Mortality Doctrine program. Michael knew it. They were hours from victory.

"When we're done," he told the others as they prepared to join hands again, "the Hive is the last step. But I think at that point we can ask for help. Lots of help. The world can't expect us to do everything." He was mostly joking, but he felt a stab of pride all the same. As absurd as it sounded, he *had* saved the world. With a lot of help from his friends. He smiled, and it felt good.

"Let's do us some deconstructing!" Bryson yelled, followed by obnoxious hoots and hollers. Surprisingly, Helga joined in. Gabby just glanced at Michael, exaggerating a mortified look.

"Kids these days," Michael said to her.

He held out his hands. Gabby and Bryson took them, then linked with Helga.

Michael's eyes were halfway closed when a man's voice spoke behind him, snapping them open again.

"Enough of that."

Michael let go of his friends' hands and spun around, but he already knew who it was. Kaine. The Tangent stood there in his youngest Aura yet, sharply dressed, tie loosened, sleeves rolled up a couple of times. He looked like some movie star on the cover of a StyleBop.

"Hey," Michael said, hurrying to stand. "I was going to talk to you about all this—"

"Stop." Kaine held up a hand, bowing his head slightly. His expression was unreadable. "Don't say another word. This is the point when, for once in your life, you are going to listen."

"Kai—"

"I said be quiet!" the Tangent screamed, his eyes flashing. "Act like a child, be treated like a child. Do not say another word, any of you! How could you do this to me, Michael?"

Michael realized at that moment how terribly he'd misjudged Kaine. Despite what he'd been telling himself, this end had been inevitable. Kaine wanted immortality, at any cost. Michael had to kill him or die trying.

Kaine folded his arms over his chest. "After all I've done for you. I saved your life. I helped you bring down the VNS. And now this." He held his hands up to the sky, looking around at the world he created. "This is how you repay me. You want to destroy my very reason for existing!"

Michael wanted to explain, but he didn't dare speak.

Kaine shook his head in disgust. "What a stupid, stupid thing you've done, Michael. It was your idea to send *my* people to the very place where your body rests in a Coffin, right now, right this second."

Fear—fear like he'd never known before—exploded in an icy burst within Michael.

Kaine gave him the coldest glare he'd ever seen.

"And I'm sure at least one of them doesn't care if you live or die."

CHAPTER 22

GODS AND MONSTERS

1

Helga marched past Michael before he could stop her. He thought for one terrible moment that she was going to attack Kaine, but instead she dropped to her knees in front of him. The Tangent never flinched.

"Please," she said. "Spare this boy. I'm begging you, Kaine."

"What is this?" He stepped away from her in disgust. "Some kind of tri—"

Before he could finish, Helga lashed out with a wire-thin rope hidden in her sleeve. Kaine had barely reacted before it wrapped around his neck, cinching tight. She gave it a hard pull and he crumpled to his knees. In an instant Helga had him facedown and she was tying his wrists behind him.

Michael watched in disbelief, not sure what to do. He took a step forward, but stopped when he saw Kaine's face.

Instead of the look of anger Michael expected to see, Kaine was perfectly calm, almost smiling.

"Really?" he asked, his speech muffled with his face pressed to the grass. "You really think some whip conjured from a cheap game is going to stop me? Here? In the place I built?"

Helga rapped a knuckle against his ear, just hard enough to garner a wince from the Tangent. "Nope," she said. "But it distracted you enough for me to throw up a firewall to your communications. Go ahead and order your goons to slash my boy's throat. Try it."

To Michael's shock, panic flashed across Kaine's face.

"It won't last very long, now, will it?" Kaine said. He puffed out his cheeks and everything around him suddenly blurred with motion. He flew off the ground and landed on his feet, while Helga was sent windmilling backward through the air until she slammed into a crumbling castle wall. She fell with a crash among the rocks and lay still on the grass.

She's okay, Michael thought. *It's the Sleep. She's okay.*

He was still looking at her when she disappeared, fading from existence. It was a good sign. It meant she'd been Lifted out. This place was like a game, after all.

Michael turned his attention back to Kaine, who still looked troubled. Maybe Helga had pulled off a miracle that would last just long enough to give them the time they needed to fix this mess.

"Listen," Michael said. Gabby and Bryson had moved closer, standing on either side of him. "I know you're angry. But can we talk this through?"

Kaine's eyes narrowed. "No. We can't. I saw what you did to Weber. I heard the things you said here. Your intentions are clear, and they're not acceptable. There's no room for negotiation, Michael. I've given you chance after chance to join me in a noble cause. And it always comes back to this. You, standing before me, thinking you have the right of it. Thinking that you can . . . win this game of yours. Well, as they say in your gaming halls, game over."

"Man, I hate this guy," Bryson said loud enough for Kaine to hear.

Kaine ignored him. "I had *such* a plan. For the benefit of everyone. And all I've been met with is betrayal. Weber, the VNS, now you. You're tied to all this, Michael. You're a part of it. You should be able to recognize its potential more than anyone. And yet you came here to destroy it? Do you have any idea how much that hurts me?"

Michael didn't want to fight. He didn't know *how* to fight Kaine even if he wanted to. It had been an uneven match from the start. His only hope was to reason with him.

"It's not an answer," Michael said. "You're right—I totally get the Mortality Doctrine now—better than most. I've seen what it does to people. To the world. And I'm telling you—nobody can be trusted with this much power. Nobody. It has to end, Kaine. It has to."

Kaine stood there, taking one deep breath after another, as if he were about to dive underwater for a long swim. "If that's what you think, then you don't understand, son." He looked at Gabby, then at Bryson, then back at Michael. "I'll give you one last chance. Help me make this dream a reality.

Immortality, Michael. No more physical death for humans, and no more Decay for Tangents. We'll all live forever. If you don't see how . . . glorious that is, then something's wrong with you."

Gabby started to say something, but a sharp glare from Kaine made her stop.

"Just give me an answer," Kaine snapped. "Yes or no. With me or against me. Those are your options. I can tell you right now, you've caused me enough trouble that I can't afford to . . . Let's just say that choosing to go against me wouldn't be the wisest thing right now. Choose eternal life or misery. What'll it be?"

Gabby squeezed Michael's arm. "Let's finish what we came here to do," she said, not a trace of fear in her voice. And Michael knew why. The Mortality Doctrine had stolen her best friend from her.

"Yeah," Bryson added. "There's one of him, three of us. He already knows our answer."

Michael looked gravely at Kaine. "It doesn't have to be this way."

"What's your answer!" the Tangent screamed. Michael swore he saw a flash of red behind his eyes, like a demon coming to the surface. Fear chilled him to the bone.

"We have to destroy your program," Michael said. "I'm sorry."

The manic anger vanished from Kaine's face, and he actually smiled. "Then by all means, give it your very best shot. At least you'll finally be out of my hair. I'll just have to establish another connection to replace yours."

He brought his arms up and blinding lights flashed from the palms of his hands. The ground beneath their feet suddenly lost all solidity, turning into a mist of green and brown.

And then they were falling.

2

Chaos took over Michael's world.

His feet landed in a mysterious substance. It was purple and looked slick, like it could be wet, but it was firm, like hard rubber. It rippled out from where he stood, as if a giant rock had landed in a pool right before it froze solid. Bryson was above him, Gabby below, but they were still together.

"What's happening?" Bryson yelled.

"And where's Kaine?" Gabby added.

A shadow passed over them, answering her question. A massive winged creature descended from a misty green sky, each flap of its wings sending a fierce wind blowing over Michael and his friends. It sailed downward and landed in front of them, huge claws digging into the rubbery surface beneath their feet. Its scaly golden skin glimmered like oil on water. Kaine sat on the back of the beast, in a saddle, holding tight to reins. Michael had never seen a creature more terrifying. It had enormous horns protruding from its head and eyes like black marbles. It opened its huge mouth to reveal impossibly large teeth, and then it screamed, a sound so piercing that bright stars burst in his vision.

"I should never have offered you one last chance." Kaine

spoke from the monster's back. "I was wrong, but I've learned my lesson. Now here we stand, the very core of the Mortality Doctrine at your feet, Michael. How fitting that you and your friends will die right atop its skin."

Figures began to step out from behind Kaine's beast, as if a trapdoor had opened and released his minions. There were KillSims, mostly—enormous wolves and black-cloaked ghosts, an unseen wind blowing around them. And there were other creatures. Demons, similar to those from the place Gunner Skale had gone to hide along the Path, big and bloody and angry. Monsters from storybooks—trolls and goblins and wights. Two dozen, three dozen, four dozen creatures, amassed in a line behind Kaine and his winged beast.

"Maybe you should've brought a bigger army," Kaine announced from his perch. "For the good of both man and Tangent, I can't show mercy today. For that, I'm sorry."

He raised a hand, then slowly lowered it to point directly at Michael.

"Kill them," he commanded, his voice booming. "Starting with him. But first, remove their Cores. Let's give them this true death they keep harping about."

The Core. The link that kept a mind tethered to reality. Part of the NerveBox programming. Almost impossible—not to mention illegal—to code.

Michael snapped into action as Kaine's army charged. He ran over the slick surface, slipping twice, to reach Bryson and Gabby. "Use the fly program from *Invisible Wings*!" he yelled, transferring the code to them in case they didn't have it. "We'll survive a lot longer if we're in the air. Pull in every weapon you can think of, fight them off! I'll take Kaine—I need his link to deconstruct the Doctrine."

They had to be in the air for this or they'd never last. The first KillSims were almost on them, loping across the ground, growling those awful electronic growls.

"Got it!" Gabby shouted, even as she rose twenty feet off the ground. Bryson and Michael used the same program and leaped up to join her, just missing the first wave of attack right below them.

"What if we can't do this?" Bryson yelled at Michael, his eyes wild with fear.

Michael understood. He smiled at his friend. "Give it your best shot, man," he said. "But kill your Aura and Lift before you let them get to your Core. Deal?" Bryson nodded and they both looked at Gabby, who nodded as well. They were in it together.

A gust of wind blew over them, and the three friends turned to see Kaine's creature flapping its giant wings, rising into the air. Kaine stared straight at Michael. The demons and KillSims had followed Kaine's lead and had begun igniting their own flying programs. It looked like it would be an aerial battle.

As it all unfolded before him, Michael felt a sudden and complete loss of hope. It was just the three of them against so many. He knew they didn't have to win the fight, they only needed to hold them off long enough to destroy the Mortality Doctrine code. But how could they even do that? He turned to face his friends, to tell them they should all just give up and get out of there. It'd be much smarter to regroup with more backup.

But Bryson and Gabby were gone. Michael looked up and saw them flying through the odd-colored sky, fighting, twisting, and turning in battle. His heart sank.

Something crashed into the side of his head.

Crying out, he lost control and plummeted; he hit the rubbery ground hard and bounced twice. The winged beast landed next to him, its enormous claws piercing the purple substance. Michael looked up at its hideous face—its black eyes, its sharp teeth. The creature screamed again, and Michael threw up his hands to cover his ears.

He stood. Fear trickled down his back, and he shuddered. He'd never been so terrified. Never. But he brought his hands up, curled them into fists, and searched his mind for the right weapon to pull from his files. And then he froze. Everything was blocked. He'd hoped the whole time that in the weakened state of the Sleep, they'd have more power to manipulate and swing in code from other sources.

He'd been wrong.

He had nothing. His fists. That was it. Well, his fists and Bryson and Gabby. And now they were all about to be pummeled.

Kaine's beast lashed out with a wing, hitting Michael hard in the face. It knocked him off his feet and sent him flying.

He landed ten yards away, on his back, pain consuming his whole body. The creature leaped into the air, flapped its wings twice, then dove at Michael, landing with a terrible thump on his chest. Every molecule of breath left his lungs. He choked out a muffled cry.

Kaine jumped down from the monster's back, and after another piercing scream, the creature flapped its wings and rose into the air, leaving Michael for his true nemesis.

"You could've had it all," the Tangent said. Then he kicked Michael in the ribs. "Immortality." Another kick, even more vicious. Blinding pain filled Michael's world. "A place by my side." Another kick.

Kaine leaned over him. "You should've known." This time, a punch to the face. An eruption of more pain. "You should've known from the beginning that I couldn't be defeated. Not by someone lesser than me.

"I will have my way." Kaine's voice was suddenly calm, almost soothing. He spoke slowly. "And you will die. I don't need your connection anymore. It's been—how did they used to say it?—corrected with troubleshooting. That's the beauty of the code, Michael. In time, anything can be programmed. Anything."

He reached down and touched Michael's temple with his finger, and a sharp claw suddenly snapped out of its tip, aimed at the very spot where Michael's Core resided. Michael pulled his head away, but the pain from his beating was unbearable. He leaned over, threw up. He had no strength left to fight.

"Sarah," he whispered. "Sarah." He'd sworn to die with her in his mind.

Kaine brought up his newly clawed finger, making sure Michael saw it.

"I do this for the future of intelligence," he pronounced. "For the next step in evolution." He reached for Michael, who had no power to resist.

And then, as had so often happened in Michael's life, things changed in an instant.

There was an eruption of noise and a searing wind of heat, and Kaine's body catapulted into the air, disappearing in the distance.

Michael lay on the ground, so exhausted and weak from pain, he thought he'd never move again. It took everything he had left in his body to turn and look up, only to see his salvation.

4

Portals were opening all around him, dark spaces through which countless figures poured. They swarmed Kaine's massive winged beast and his KillSim army, falling on them with every weapon imaginable. Some of the newcomers were familiar—warriors and robots and superheroes and aliens from dozens of games Michael had played with his friends over the years. Others were new to him. A thing that looked like a giant tree with a face, swinging its many branches with ruthless force. A rock creature, sharp angles of stone erupting from its chest. There was even a six-legged steel horse with a humanoid on its back made from a hundred sharp blades.

Michael breathed out in relief and disbelief. An army of Tangents had come to save them. They'd been so close to true death. And Bryson and Gabby were still out there, fighting. He had to go—

Someone put a hand on his shoulder when he tried to get up, gently pushed him back down. Michael turned to see Helga, dressed in armor, kneeling beside him. She leaned against a massive sword of fiery light that she'd driven point-first into the ground.

"What's going—" he started to say, but she stopped him.

"Stop talking. We don't have time. I pressed Kaine into killing me so I could Lift and get help. But I wasn't fast enough. Someone's coming for you in your Coffin—Kaine's broken through my firewall. You have to go back, *now*."

Michael scrambled to his feet, fighting the pain. "What . . . no! Bryson and Gabby are out there! I have to help!"

Helga grabbed him by the shirt with both hands and pulled him close. "We've got this, Michael. Sometimes you have to let go. Sometimes you have to let others share your burden. You understand me?"

He nodded weakly, but felt helpless.

"I've left a pathway for you." Helga squeezed his shoulders. "Now go. Save yourself. And have faith in us—we can win, and I know how to destroy the Doctrine. Remember my little trick to get us to the Hive undetected? The build-and-destroy?" She didn't wait for a response. She pulled her sword from the ground and leaped into the air, cutting in half two KillSims that had been diving toward them. *"Go!"* she yelled.

Michael focused on the Portal path provided by Helga, closed his eyes, coded, and Lifted himself to the Wake.

5

The hiss of the Coffin door opening. The wet tug of NerveWires retreating from his skin to their cubbyholes. The glowing blue lights, the hum of the machine, the real world expanding to life above him. The pain was there, in every part of him, but not nearly as bad as it had been in the Sleep.

A face stared down at him. Then there was a flash, a glint of light on steel.

Michael was up in a rush. He battered the arm to the side just as it came at him with the knife, then kicked out with his leg, catching the man in the face. Michael scrambled out of the Coffin, following the man's descent, jumping on top of him, his blood pumping with adrenaline. He punched him, then saw an arm coming again, still brandishing the weapon. Michael brought his elbow up, felt the cold blade, the bright sear of pain. He swung his fist around and knocked the knife out of the man's grip.

Run, he thought. He was done fighting. All he wanted to do was run.

Michael pushed himself to the side, tripped as the man grabbed his foot, kicked him off, scrambled to his feet, started running. He was inside that massive room, surrounded by the balconies of Coffins. He could see the doors through which he'd entered. Michael fixed on the exit and ran for it.

Then, in a blur of pain, his face cracked against hard tile. He was on the ground; his attacker had jumped on him from behind. Michael flipped onto his stomach, arching his elbow around as he did, connecting with the man's jaw. He cried out and fell off, clutching his face, but landed a kick to Michael's stomach as he did. Michael curled up, clutching himself, coughing. His entire body still ached from the ordeal inside the Sleep, and now a new wave of nausea broke over him. He crawled to his feet and struggled against a spinning world.

His attacker was on his feet, breathing heavily, and Michael got a good look at him for the first time. He was familiar, but before he could place him, the man charged, rage painting his face dark. Michael planted his feet. He had no time to flee, and the man slammed into him, sending them both flying to the ground again. Michael kneed him in the groin, scrambled out from under him. He stood up, stumbled away, looked back. This had to end.

Michael noticed what he hadn't before: one of the guards who'd died earlier was slumped in a chair, blood covering his face and chest. At his feet, there was a gun. He sprinted for it. He could hear his attacker yelling like a lunatic. Michael slid toward the chair like a ballplayer for the win and grabbed the weapon, twisted around to aim.

The man pulled to a stop, eyes big, hands raised. And in an instant, a transformation came over him. His rage vanished, replaced by fear. His lips trembled and he fell to his knees.

"Don't," he whimpered, the most pathetic of sounds. "Don't shoot me. I'm . . . This is my only hope. I'm out of options. I need this body." He lowered his head.

Michael slowly got to his feet, keeping the gun trained on the man. And then that sense of familiarity solidified, turning into recognition.

"You visited me at the jail," Michael said, stunned by the revelation. He couldn't believe it hadn't come to him sooner. "You came in there, talking about what's real and what's not, how we can never know. That we could Lift a thousand times—"

"And still be in the Sleep," the man interrupted. "Yes, yes. How can we ever know? We can't. We can only live, boy. And I want to live, more than anything else in this godforsaken universe. Please don't take that away from me."

"Who are you?" Michael asked, not so much a question as a demand.

The man still acted timid. "I'm the friend you've always had—something I guess you've never realized. And I'm your sworn enemy."

"What the hell are you talking about?"

"It's me, Michael. It's Kaine."

The world shifted at Michael's feet. He had to steady himself. "You think I'm stupid?" he asked. But the threat was empty. He wanted to pretend that he didn't believe him, but he did. Kaine the Tangent had stolen a body and was kneeling before him. He knew it was true.

"Don't go judging me like you always do," Kaine said. "This man I took wanted to end his life, had even written a suicide note! I didn't do anything to him he didn't want already."

"Nothing surprises me anymore," Michael said quietly, half to himself. He stared at the floor. "I was just . . ."

"It's how my plan works. Every two weeks, I downloaded the latest version of myself into this man. Just in case things didn't quite work out in the Sleep over the last year or so. It's my own . . . insurance policy. And by the looks of it, I'm thinking it was the wisest thing I've ever done."

"What do you mean?" Michael asked, looking Kaine in the eye.

The man—the Tangent—shrugged, then finally lowered his hands. "I just lost all contact. With myself, my partners, my army. So I can only assume that you've won. I don't know how or where or when, but it's over. I guess that's two weeks of memories I'll never get back. Not that I'd want to. All my people are gone or dead, as far I can tell—you have way more supporters than I thought. The only reason I knew you were here is because I intercepted a message from . . . myself to . . . myself."

Michael just stared at him, completely lost. He did understand, actually, but his mind felt like a big ball of hardened twine, like one length might snap and the whole thing explode in a pile of dust at any second. He kept the gun pointed at his enemy, wanting so badly to pull the trigger.

"Look, I'm nothing anymore," Kaine said. "Without the Mortality Doctrine, without my resources, without the support of the VNS infrastructure . . . I even created my own little Hive, tucked away in oblivion, and I don't think I could find the thing if I had a hundred years to search for it. Everything in the virtual world is lost to me now. I can feel its absence." And then, right there, at Michael's feet, the most terrifying figure the world had ever known wept like a frightened child.

"Please," Kaine whimpered. "Just let me live in this world. I'll never access the Sleep. Never again. You have my word. You took away immortality. Let me have mortality. I'm begging you."

Michael took a step forward, pointing the tip of the gun right at Kaine's forehead. But he couldn't do it. There was just no way he could pull that trigger. Sorrow engulfed him.

"You," Michael whispered, trembling. "You and . . . Weber. I hate you. You took everything from me. My parents. My life. Sarah."

"I'm sorry," Kaine said. "I swear I did what I thought was—"

"Shut up," Michael snapped. "Get up and walk out of here. Now. If I ever see your face again, you're dead. You hear me? There won't be a second chance. I swear it on every last person's life that you took."

Kaine nodded. He was a miserable, pathetic creature. As Michael turned away, he heard him run across the room and through the doors, out into the street.

Michael let him go, hoping that he didn't come to regret it someday.

6

Several minutes later Michael was still standing in the same place, staring at the floor. He didn't have the energy to move, not even to sit down. He wished his mind would turn off and give him peace.

The Coffin he'd used earlier chirped loudly across the room. He'd been sent a Bulletin message. He walked over and flipped on its NetScreen to see a simple message clearly displayed across its glowing blue surface.

A message from Helga.

It's done.

CHAPTER 23

ONE MONTH LATER

1

Michael stood among friends.

Including Sarah's parents.

"I'm sorry if I blamed you for her death," Gerard said. He was standing with his arm wrapped tightly around his wife's shoulders. "It was hard at first, seeing you come back safe and sound. Seeing you all over the NewsBops, being praised as a hero. I was selfish, I know. It just—" His voice hitched and tears filled his eyes. "It just hurts so much. I miss my baby girl."

Michael's heart ached as Sarah's mom and dad embraced him, both of them shaking as they cried. They pulled away and took a step back.

"It's not your fault," her dad continued. "I know that. You're a hero, and so was Sarah. If she had it all to do over again, I know she'd make the same choice. Every time."

Michael could only nod, the grief too much. It probably

wasn't possible, but he sure felt like he missed her just as much as Gerard.

"We love you," Nancy said with a sad smile. "You'll always be like a son to us." She paused, an uncertain look in her eyes. "Can we keep in touch?"

Michael did his best to smile. "Absolutely. You can visit me or message me. . . . I'd like that."

Gerard reached out and squeezed his shoulder, gave that manly nod only a dad can give to a boy in love with his daughter.

"Take care, son," he said. "We'll let you finish your goodbyes."

They walked over to the side of the room, and Gabby stepped up to greet Michael.

"Hi," she said, tears streaming down her face. It touched him. They'd grown a lot closer since the madness ended a month earlier, and he had no doubt they'd be friends for a very long time. "I can't believe you're leaving. It always seemed so far away."

"Yeah." He wrapped his arms around her and squeezed. "You better come hang out with me sometimes. Feel free to bring the boyfriend around, if you have to."

She laughed, a short burst that came through her nose. "That's gonna be weird, huh? It doesn't even seem possible that you two haven't met. So weird."

"Oh, we've met," Michael said, releasing her from the hug. It had felt so good. "In more ways than one. And hey, I know you. He can't be too much of a dirtbag if he's your special guy."

"Ha. Yeah." She paused, looking him straight in the eye. "We'll definitely come visit you. A lot. You two will like each other. And . . . what you're doing for him . . . it's . . ."

"Please," Michael said, swatting the air with his hand. "Don't even mention it, ever again. It's not even a choice."

She nodded, fresh tears springing forth. "Okay. Well, we'll come see you really soon. Let us know where, okay?"

"For sure."

Last but not least was Bryson. They hugged, doing the requisite pounding of the backs to make it macho.

"I love you, man," Bryson whispered in his ear.

Michael barked out a laugh, but then Bryson squeezed him tighter. "No, I'm serious. I love you. You're the best friend any person could ever ask for. The bravest, the craziest, the funniest, the best. You're my best friend, always have been, always will be. And I'm going to visit your butt every single day."

He pulled away and turned, went toward the door.

"Bryson!" Michael called.

Bryson just waved without looking, then walked through the door. It'd been abrupt, but Michael understood. It had been the perfect goodbye.

And so that was that.

Tears stinging his eyes, he went over to the open Coffin and lay down. He was fully clothed, figuring he'd spare anyone having to see him naked. The body wouldn't be inside that long anyway.

He closed his eyes and let the NerveBox work its magic.

When those eyes opened up in an hour or so, Jackson

Porter would see the real world once again. And Gabby would be right there waiting for him.

2

The process hurt.

It was like Squeezing through firewalls and having your brain sucked on by a KillSim at the same time. There was darkness, there was blinding light. Quiet mixed with ungodly sounds of metal screeching and nails scratching concrete. And through it all, the pain.

But like so many other things in Michael's strange life, it finally ended.

He blinked his eyes as they focused. The pain faded so there was just an echo of it floating through his bones and joints and head. He hadn't known what to expect. He'd wondered about it, thought about it every night for a month. Would he wake up in a pod at the Hive? Outside the Hive, floating in that darkness like he'd done several times before? At a Portal? In some kind of factory? He had no clue.

Worst of all, he hadn't known with any certainty that he'd wake up at all. So in that sense, everything was hunky-dory. But to his surprise, he came to inside a Coffin not much different from the one in which he'd just left behind the body of Jackson Porter. A guy he'd been close to in ways most people would never experience.

There was a hiss; then the lid of the Coffin swung open and NerveWires receded from his body. Everything seemed so real. Spectacularly real. And even as his old bedroom materialized in the space opening above him, he understood. Sure enough, there was Helga, smiling down at him, just as Gabby was probably doing that very second to Jackson back in the Wake.

"Welcome home," Helga said.

3

He sat with Helga in the kitchen, having just stuffed his belly with her famous waffles and eggs and bacon. Michael enjoyed every bite, but he could never think about food the same way again. For the second time in his weird existence, he wasn't a human. Everything about him was programmed. He had no real stomach or organs to digest food.

He was code. Complicated code, but code all the same.

Honestly, he didn't really mind so much. Life had been great before Kaine, Weber, and that stupid Path ruined his sweet bliss. He'd get back to that. Memories of the real world would dull and fade, and *Lifeblood Deep* would again become his true home.

"I'm not sure which version of you I like better," he said after one last gulp of OJ. "The one who makes this sweet breakfast or the one who goes around killing bad guys."

Helga rolled her eyes. "I'm one and the same, Mikey boy. One and the same. And don't think life's going to be a peachy road. Don't do your homework, don't behave . . . well, you may see Helga the Warrior come back."

Michael pictured her in an old barbarian's getup with that fiery sword and snickered until his chest hurt. Yeah, he felt good, all right. Life was going to be just fine.

"Thanks for doing all this," he finally said. Taking a cue from Bryson's brave display in the real world, he decided to share his deepest, most sincere feelings with this miraculous woman. "I know you worked hard to program this place—to make it look like our old home. It's amazing." He paused, choking back a sudden wave of emotion. "Thanks for coming after me and saving me. And for figuring out a way we could keep on living in the Deep."

Helga walked around the counter and gave him a hug, her eyes moist, then went back to her own seat.

"I have something to tell you," she said in a quiet voice.

His curiosity was piqued. "You do?"

She nodded, and he felt a sudden dread blossom in his chest.

"No, no," she quickly countered, "it's not bad. I promise. I wanted to wait until . . . until I was certain everything worked out and we could both continue existing in the Virt-Net. And . . . here we are."

After a long, awkward pause, his pulse pounding in anticipation, he said, "Okay. What is it?"

"Do you remember . . ." She faltered. "Never mind, of course you remember. The day Sarah died."

Michael could only nod, a roar of blood in his ears.

"That day, I sent you out of the room so I could work with our programmers back in the Sleep to download her information. Her consciousness. I needed to do it before she took her last breath in that world."

He couldn't swallow; he couldn't breathe.

"I think," she continued, "I *know,* that we got it all. We had plenty of experience working with the Mortality Doctrine by that point. The only thing is, we weren't able to capture her on the other side. At the Hive. We weren't able to insert her into a pod."

Michael stood up, then sat back down again. "What . . . what does that mean?"

"It means that she's out there." Helga looked up and around at the ceiling, as if looking for a ghost. "Scattered. Maybe across billions of data points. I don't know. She might be like a bucket of sand tossed in the ocean. But . . . but at least you know she's out there. Somewhere. That's a little something to hope on, right?"

Michael had his hands on the counter in front of him. He stared at the backs of his knuckles, shell-shocked. There were so many emotions swirling inside him, he couldn't focus on one.

"What about . . . my parents?" he managed to ask.

Helga gave him the sincerest of understanding smiles. "I miss them, too. So much. I think they're different, I'm sorry to say. It's like . . . it's like this. Imagine a chalkboard—you know, from the old stories? A chalkboard with names written across its surface. With your parents, I think it's like they've been erased, never to come back. But with Sarah . . . well, with her, I think it's like her name is still written there. The chalkboard itself has just been lost in a warehouse as big as a universe. The odds of finding it are small, but she's out there, somewhere."

Michael nodded sadly.

"Maybe not the greatest analogy," she said. "But I do think there's at least something to hold on to with Sarah." She fell silent, letting everything sink in.

"Thanks for telling me all this," Michael finally whispered, then got up. He needed to be alone. He turned and walked away, but stopped at the door to the hallway and turned back toward his nanny. "I love you, Helga."

Then he went to his room, the one he grew up in.

4

"Just like old times," Bryson said, raising his drink. The other three people around the table clinked their glasses with his and took a big swig. They were at Dan the Man Deli, and it was indeed just like the good old days. A big plate of bleu chips had already been half devoured.

"This place is even starting to look like it used to," Michael said as he grabbed another chip. "Looks like the new VirtNet Commission is doing a pretty good job. I just can't believe they haven't asked me to work for them yet."

Bryson glared. "Not. Funny."

"VNC just sounds so stupid." That came from Gabby, who'd brought along her boyfriend, one Jackson Porter. He'd taken on a completely new Aura to lessen the awkwardness of it all, but it still weirded Michael out. It was like he had an evil twin or something. "Reminds me of a hideous disease. They should've just called it the Commission."

"How're things back in the big bad world, anyway?" Michael asked. "I do my best to avoid all NewsBops these days. They give me the runs."

Gabby groaned, something Sarah definitely would've done back in the day.

Jackson answered; he was getting more and more comfortable with his new friends. "They're not too bad. Most of the special elections are done, markets are rebounding, people are brave enough to Sink into the Sleep again. Another few months and it'll all be back to normal."

Bryson tapped the table absently, a faraway look in his eyes. "Good thing we stopped them when we did. Seriously. I think if a week or two more had gone by, the world would have been toast. Good on ya, mate." He raised his glass again, and the sound of glass clinking filled the air. It was a happy sound.

"What about you?" Gabby asked. That kind smile on her face was something Michael had started to get used to, virtual or not. "How're you holding up?"

Michael thought about it for a second, then nodded with confidence. They didn't have to know about the emptiness that still felt like an abscess in his heart.

"Things are really good," he said. "Obviously I miss my parents. I miss you guys. I miss . . . Sarah. But it's great to be with Helga and to have started school again in *Lifeblood Deep*. The great thing about that place is no one knows who's real and who's not, which suits me just fine. I'm lovin' it, actually. I mean, hey, if I can beat back the Decay—and they're saying being sentient does the trick—I'll live a lot longer than you guys."

"That's the most beautiful thing you've ever said to me," Bryson replied, the beam of joy on his face exaggerated.

"Who's to say what's real and what's not, anyway?" Gabby asked. "For all we know, the Wake is just an even more complicated program, run by a bunch of aliens. Or God. Or both. Maybe there's an infinite number of levels. Maybe it gets rebooted every million years."

That was some major food for thought. Everyone sat in silence for a good long minute, pondering the universe.

"Well," Jackson said, standing up from his chair. "I gotta go. Project due tomorrow."

"Yeah, me too," Gabby agreed. She stood as well. "See you guys here on Friday. Same time?"

Bryson pushed his chair back, looking genuinely sad that the party was over for now. "Same time. And I know this is blasphemy, but next go-round, let's get something that isn't bleu chips? Please? For the love of God?"

Gabby laughed an evil laugh as she and Jackson walked away. Michael watched them go, wondering if people would believe their story once a few years went by. It was nuts.

Bryson smacked him on the shoulder, then gave him a rough handshake. "Games are opening back up in two weeks," he said. His voice was solemn, as if he'd announced a peace treaty. "I say we skip school—sniffle, sniffle—and go twenty-four hours straight. Hit 'em all." He slapped Michael on the shoulder again, then turned to go. He flashed two thumbs-up. "What say you?" he shouted.

"Sounds good!" Michael yelled back, flashing the same sign.

Man, did it ever sound good.

EPILOGUE

Michael sat in the completely repaired tree house on the outskirts of *Lifeblood,* exhausted. Darkness had fallen hours before, and it was well past his bedtime. Helga didn't mind, though. She knew exactly what he'd been working on the last few weeks. And she knew he was close. She'd probably gone to bed by now anyway.

Even though he was skilled enough to access the code of his surrounding world within the Deep, he'd made a promise to himself—and Helga—that he wouldn't do it while in that world. They both needed to adopt some semblance of a real life, to keep things steady and stable—and *Lifeblood Deep* had become that place for him. He could dink around on a NetScreen or WallScreen anytime he wanted, but to truly immerse himself, he had to Lift up a level, to the Sleep that the vast majority of citizens experienced when they Sank.

What an odd life he lived.

He settled himself in Bryson's beanbag chair, its worn and cracked surface feeling like an old friend. He leaned his head back and took a deep breath. His eyes hurt from working so much. Working and searching and analyzing. It'd taken every last ounce of his skill and strength, but he'd done an excellent job. *If I do say so myself,* he thought.

Sitting there in the quiet, which was broken every now and then by a branch scraping against the outside wall, he thought about it all. About the insane turn his life had taken. Finding out he was a string of code. Traveling the world, both real and virtual. Fighting enemies that the biggest and baddest armies in the world couldn't stop. Watching Sarah die. Horribly. Twice. If that didn't scar a kid for life, what would?

But it had all turned out okay, hadn't it?

Here he was, alive and well. Because of the Mortality Doctrine, he had an understanding of a person's intelligence— their consciousness—far beyond that of the average person. He was real, and that was that. No one could take that away from him.

With a big stretch, he sat up straighter. For weeks he'd been working his tail off. Late nights, bloodshot eyes at school, walking around like a Flare-infested Crank, falling asleep at the dinner table. He'd done that once and he still couldn't believe it. His face had almost fallen right into a bowl of tomato soup. Helga had just shaken her head.

But it had all been worth it. So worth it. He had it now. He was almost one hundred percent positive. After scouring the Sleep from one end to the other, searching high and low, gathering data, and breaking into so many high-security places it was a wonder he hadn't been thrown in jail.

Gathering, gathering.

Collecting.

Piece by piece, string of code by string of code, and now he had it all in one place. In a mixed-up, confusing, jumbled mess, sure, but it was all there.

Tomorrow was a Saturday, and he had one last, long day of work.

He almost twitched with excitement, eager to get on with it. But he'd wait. Make sure he was well rested and up to the task. Make sure he got a nice, filling breakfast from Helga before he came back to the tree house. Yes, he'd wait one more day.

Tomorrow, he'd start coding Sarah back together again.

ACKNOWLEDGMENTS

As we come to the conclusion of this trilogy, I'm so thankful for the people who made it happen. My agent, Michael Bourret. My editor, Krista Marino. My international agent, Lauren Abramo. All the awesome people at Random House, far too many to try naming without getting in trouble. My publishers abroad, who've taken my stories and given them to countless cultures and languages. The many bookstore workers, librarians, and teachers who've connected me with readers. The retail outlets, in all their shapes and forms, making the books so widely available (often on sale!).

Thank you, all of you.

And, as always, never changing, most importantly, I thank you, the one who decided to read this book. Thank you. With all that I have, thank you.

ABOUT THE AUTHOR

James Dashner was born and raised in Georgia but now lives and writes in the Rocky Mountains. He is the author of the #1 *New York Times* bestselling Maze Runner series: *The Maze Runner, The Scorch Trials, The Death Cure,* and *The Kill Order.* *The Game of Lives* is the final book in the Mortality Doctrine series. Look for the first two books in the series, *The Eye of Minds* and *The Rule of Thoughts,* also available from Delacorte Press. To learn more about James and his books, visit jamesdashner.com, follow @jamesdashner on Twitter, and find dashnerjames on Instagram.

If you loved *The Game of Lives,* turn the page
for a sneak peek at the first book in
James Dashner's Maze Runner series:

BOOK 1 IN THE #1 *NEW YORK TIMES* BESTSELLING SERIES BY

JAMES DASHNER

NOW A MAJOR MOTION PICTURE
FROM TWENTIETH CENTURY FOX

THE MAZE RUNNER

Excerpt copyright © 2009 by James Dashner.
Published by Delacorte Press, an imprint of Random House Children's Books,
a division of Penguin Random House LLC, New York.

CHAPTER 1

He began his new life standing up, surrounded by cold darkness and stale, dusty air.

Metal ground against metal; a lurching shudder shook the floor beneath him. He fell down at the sudden movement and shuffled backward on his hands and feet, drops of sweat beading on his forehead despite the cool air. His back struck a hard metal wall; he slid along it until he hit the corner of the room. Sinking to the floor, he pulled his legs up tight against his body, hoping his eyes would soon adjust to the darkness.

With another jolt, the room jerked upward like an old lift in a mine shaft.

Harsh sounds of chains and pulleys, like the workings of an ancient steel factory, echoed through the room, bouncing off the walls with a hollow, tinny whine. The lightless elevator swayed back and forth as it ascended, turning the boy's stomach sour with nausea; a smell like burnt oil invaded his senses, making him feel worse. He wanted to cry, but no tears came; he could only sit there, alone, waiting.

My name is Thomas, he thought.

That . . . that was the only thing he could remember about his life.

He didn't understand how this could be possible. His mind functioned without flaw, trying to calculate his surroundings and predicament. Knowledge flooded his thoughts, facts and images, memories and details of the world and how it works. He pictured snow on trees, running down a leaf-strewn road, eating a hamburger, the moon casting a pale glow on a grassy meadow, swimming in a lake, a busy city square with hundreds of people bustling about their business.

And yet he didn't know where he came from, or how he'd gotten inside the dark lift, or who his parents were. He didn't even know his last name. Images of people flashed across his mind, but there was no recognition, their faces replaced with haunted smears of color. He couldn't think of one person he knew, or recall a single conversation.

The room continued its ascent, swaying; Thomas grew immune to the ceaseless rattling of the chains that pulled him upward. A long time passed. Minutes stretched into hours, although it was impossible to know for sure because every second seemed an eternity. No. He was smarter than that. Trusting his instincts, he knew he'd been moving for roughly *half* an hour.

Strangely enough, he felt his fear whisked away like a swarm of gnats caught in the wind, replaced by an intense curiosity. He wanted to know where he was and what was happening.

With a groan and then a clonk, the rising room halted; the sudden change jolted Thomas from his huddled position and threw him across the hard floor. As he scrambled to his feet, he felt the room sway less and less until it finally stilled. Everything fell silent.

A minute passed. Two. He looked in every direction but saw only darkness; he felt along the walls again, searching for a way out. But there was nothing, only the cool metal. He groaned in frustration; his echo amplified through the air, like the haunted moan of death. It faded, and silence returned. He screamed, called for help, pounded on the walls with his fists.

Nothing.

Thomas backed into the corner once again, folded his arms and shivered, and the fear returned. He felt a worrying shudder in his chest, as if his heart wanted to escape, to flee his body.

"Someone . . . help . . . me!" he screamed; each word ripped his throat raw.

A loud clank rang out above him and he sucked in a startled breath as he looked up. A straight line of light appeared across the ceiling of the room, and Thomas watched as it expanded. A heavy grating sound revealed double sliding doors being forced open. After so long in darkness, the light stabbed his eyes; he looked away, covering his face with both hands.

He heard noises above—voices—and fear squeezed his chest.

"Look at that shank."

"How old is he?"

"Looks like a klunk in a T-shirt."

"You're the klunk, shuck-face."

"Dude, it smells like *feet* down there!"

"Hope you enjoyed the one-way trip, Greenie."

"Ain't no ticket back, bro."

Thomas was hit with a wave of confusion, blistered with panic. The voices were odd, tinged with echo; some of the words were completely foreign—others felt familiar. He willed his eyes to adjust as he squinted toward the light and those speaking. At first he could see only shifting shadows, but they soon turned into the shapes of bodies—people bending over the hole in the ceiling, looking down at him, pointing.

And then, as if the lens of a camera had sharpened its focus, the faces cleared. They were boys, all of them—some young, some older. Thomas didn't know what he'd expected, but seeing those faces puzzled him. They were just teenagers. Kids. Some of his fear melted away, but not enough to calm his racing heart.

Someone lowered a rope from above, the end of it tied into a big loop. Thomas hesitated, then stepped into it with his right foot and clutched the rope as he was yanked toward the sky. Hands reached down, lots of hands, grabbing him by his clothes, pulling him up. The world seemed to spin, a swirling mist of faces and color and light. A storm of emotions wrenched his gut, twisted and pulled; he wanted to scream, cry, throw up. The chorus of voices had grown silent, but someone spoke as they yanked him over the sharp edge of the dark box. And Thomas knew he'd never forget the words.

"Nice to meet ya, shank," the boy said. "Welcome to the Glade."